Time Out
SHORTLIST

Paris
2013

WHAT'S NEW | WHAT'S ON | WHAT'S BEST

www.timeout.com/paris

D0812842

Contents

Published by Time Out Guides Ltd
Universal House
251 Tottenham Court Road
London W1T 7AB
Tel: + 44 (0)20 7813 3000
Fax: + 44 (0)20 7813 6001
Email: guides@timeout.com
www.timeout.com

Editorial Director Sarah Guy
Management Accountants Margaret Wright, Clare Turner

Time Out Guides is a wholly owned subsidiary of Time Out Group Ltd.

© **Time Out Group Ltd**
Chairman & Founder Tony Elliott
Chief Executive Officer David King
Chief Operating Officer Aksel Van der Wal
Editor-in-Chief Tim Arthur
Group Financial Director Paul Rakkar
Chief Commercial Officer David Pepper
Time Out International Ltd MD Cathy Runciman
Group IT Director Simon Chappell

Time Out and the Time Out logo are trademarks of Time Out Group Ltd.

This edition first published in Great Britain in 2012 by Ebury Publishing
A Random House Group Company
Company information can be found on www.randomhouse.co.uk
Random House UK Limited Reg. No. 954009
10 9 8 7 6 5 4 3 2 1

Distributed in the US and Latin America by Publishers Group West (1-510-809-3700)
Distributed in Canada by Publishers Group Canada (1-800-747-8147)

For further distribution details, see www.timeout.com

ISBN: 978-1-84670-273-0

A CIP catalogue record for this book is available from the British Library.

Printed and bound in Germany by Appl.

The Random House Group Limited supports The Forest Stewardship Council (FSC®), the leading international forest certification organisation. Our books carrying the FSC label are printed on FSC® certified paper. FSC is the only forest certification scheme endorsed by the leading environmental organisations, including Greenpeace. Our paper procurement policy can be found at www.randomhouse.co.uk/environment .

Time Out carbon-offsets all its flights with Trees for Cities (www.treesforcities.org).

Paris Shortlist

The **Time Out Paris Shortlist 2013** is one of a series of annual guides that draws on Time Out's background as a magazine publisher to keep you current with everything that's going on in town. As well as Paris's key sights and the best of its eating, drinking and leisure options, it picks out the most exciting venues to have opened in the last year and gives a full calendar of annual events from September 2012 to December 2013. It also includes features on the important news, trends and openings, all compiled by locally based editors and writers. Whether you're visiting for the first time in your life or the first time this year, you'll find the *Time Out Paris Shortlist* contains all you need to know, in a portable and easy-to-use format.

The guide divides central Paris into ten areas, each containing listings for Sights & Museums, Eating & Drinking, Shopping, Nightlife and Arts & Leisure, and maps pinpointing their locations. At the front of the book are chapters rounding up these scenes city-wide, and giving a shortlist of our overall picks. We also include itineraries for days out, plus essentials such as transport information and hotels.

Our listings give phone numbers as dialled within France. From abroad, use your country's exit code followed by 33 (the country code for France) and the number given, dropping the initial '0'.

We have noted price categories by using one to four euro signs (€-€€€€), representing budget, moderate, expensive and luxury. Major credit cards are accepted unless otherwise stated. We also give Event highlights.

All our listings are double-checked, but places do sometimes close or change their hours or prices, so it's a good idea to call a venue before visiting. While every effort has been made to ensure accuracy, the publishers cannot accept responsibility for any errors that this guide may contain.

Venues are marked on the maps using symbols numbered according to their order within the chapter and colour-coded as follows:

❶ Sights & Museums
❶ Eating & Drinking
❶ Shopping
❶ Nightlife
❶ Arts & Leisure

Map Key	
Major sight or landmark	
Hospital or college	
Railway station	
Park	
River	
Autoroute	
Main road	
Main road tunnel	
Pedestrian road	
Arrondissement boundary	
Airport	✈
Church	✚
Métro station	Ⓜ
RER station	Ⓡ
Area name	LES HALLES

Time Out **Paris** Shortlist 2013

EDITORIAL
Editor Anna Norman
Proofreader Ros Sales

DESIGN
Senior Designer Kei Ishimaru
Picture Editor Jael Marschner
Picture Researcher Ben Rowe

ADVERTISING
Sales Director St John Betteridge
Head of French Advertising Sales
Charlie Sokol

MARKETING
Senior Publishing Brand Manager
Luthfa Begum
Group Commercial Art Director
Anthony Huggins
Circulation & Distribution Manager
Dan Collins

PRODUCTION
Group Production Manager
Brendan McKeown
Production Controller
Katie Mulhern-Bhudia

CONTRIBUTORS
This guide was researched and written by the writers of *Time Out Paris*.

PHOTOGRAPHY
Pages 7, 29, 39, 47, 49, 116, 129, 141 Heloise Bergman; 8, 21, 22, 40, 41, 42, 43, 45, 50, 51, 53, 55, 63, 75, 82, 90, 100, 119, 132 (top left), 148, 156, 163, 176 Oliver Knight; 11 Sophie Boegly; 14, 56, 87, 93, 95, 110, 126, 132, 137, 153, 158, 173 Olivia Rutherford; 26 Ben Rowe; 30 www.flickr.com/yorgda; 44, 104, 122 Karl Blackwell; 34 We Love Green 2011, Parc de Bagatelle - Paris ć Vincent Sannier; 36 Zdenek Krchak/Shutterstock.com; 48, 70, 145 Jean-Christophe Godet; 78 Patrick Berger et Jacques Anziutti architectes/L'autre Image; 114 ć MANUELLE GAUTRAND ARCHITECTURE- Photo/Vincent Fillon; 125 Elan Fleisher.

The following images were supplied by the featured establishments/artist: pages 64, 98, 161, 164, 169.

Cover photograph: Arc de Triomphe by Olivia Rutherford.

MAPS
JS Graphics (john@jsgraphics.co.uk).

About **Time Out**

Founded in 1968, Time Out has expanded from humble London beginnings into the leading resource for those wanting to know what's happening in the world's greatest cities. As well as our influential what's-on weeklies in London, New York and Chicago, we publish nearly 30 other listings magazines in cities as varied as Beijing and Mumbai. The magazines established Time Out's trademark style: sharp writing, informed reviewing and bang up-to-date inside knowledge of every scene.

Time Out made the natural leap into travel guides in the 1980s with the City Guide series, which now extends to over 50 destinations around the world. Written and researched by expert local writers and generously illustrated with original photography, the full-size guides cover a larger area than our Shortlist guides and include many more venue reviews, along with additional background features and a full set of maps.

Throughout this rapid growth, the company has remained proudly independent, still owned by Tony Elliott four decades after he started Time Out London as a single fold-out sheet of A5 paper. This independence extends to the editorial content of all our publications, this Shortlist included. No establishment has been featured because it has advertised, and no payment has influenced any of our reviews. And, for our critics, there's definitely no such thing as a free lunch: all restaurants and bars are visited and reviewed anonymously, and Time Out always picks up the bill.
For more about the company, see www.timeout.com.

Don't Miss 2013

Sacré-Coeur

Sights & Museums

The French capital has been busy rejigging and renovating itself over the past few years, to create a contemporary city of culture par excellence. After a ten-year renovation project, the belle époque Gaîté Lyrique theatre (see p115) has been turned into Paris's first digital cultural centre; the expanded Institut du Monde Arabe (see p144) has reopened after a three-year, €5 million extension; and the Musée d'Orsay revamp is also now complete – the museum reopened its gleaming doors in autumn 2011 to gasps of admiration. Even the Arc de Triomphe (see p56) has had a polish, and is now sparkling at the top of the Champs-Elysées. And come 2013, there will be more new or good-as-new cultural treats awaiting arts lovers, including a renovated Musée Picasso, the new Fondation Jérôme Seydoux-Pathé showcase of film memorabilia; and the high-profile Louvre-Lens museum.

Paris, of course, already reigned supreme when it comes to sights and museums, with three of the world's top ten most visited art museums within its clutch – the Louvre (see p74) holds an unassailable lead with 8.5 million visitors per year, some three million ahead of its closest rival the British Museum, while the Pompidou and newly revamped Musée d'Orsay (see p133) squeeze in at no.7 and no.8 respectively. Across the rest of the city, the list of sights worth your time is almost endless – from iconic treasures like the Eiffel Tower (see p122) to lesser-known gems like the Musée

Jean-Jacques Henner (see p61). All this, and much more that we haven't yet mentioned, in a city that's a manageable size and boasts one of the best transport networks anywhere in the world.

Neighbourhood culture

As well as these exciting revamps in central Paris, culture is also migrating around the capital. Western Paris is now home to the Musée Belmondo (see p161) – not an *homage* to the Nouvelle Vague heartthrob, but rather to Jean-Paul's father, Paul, one of France's most important 20th-century sculptors. Out east, meanwhile, the Biennale de Belleville is now in its third year. Taking place in the autumn, it features contemporary art exhibitions and street performances in the neighbourhood, and has raised the area's hip factor even further. Also worth a mention is the Maison de Jean Cocteau (see p159) to the south, a fitting tribute to one of France's finest artists.

The lie of the land

Parisians identify parts of their city by two systems: there are the named districts, whose frontiers aren't always clear – the Marais, the Latin Quarter, Montparnasse and so on – and the 20 numbered arrondissements that spiral out, clockwise and in ascending order, from the Louvre. Together they comprise an urban jigsaw. Each piece has a particular connotation or function: the fifth is academic; the sixth is arty and chic; the 16th is wealthy and dull; while the 18th, 19th and 20th arrondissements are riotously multicultural. Residents are frequently assessed, on first meeting at least, by their postcode, and as a consequence often develop a fierce sense of

SHORTLIST

Best new/revamped
- Arc de Triomphe (see p56)
- Gaîté Lyrique (see p115)
- Institut du Monde Arabe (see p144)
- Musée Belmondo (see p161)
- Maison de Jean Cocteau (see p159)
- Musée d'Orsay (see p133)

Best secret
- La Collection 1900 (see p70)
- Musée Fragonard (see p160)

Best art
- Centre Pompidou (see p100)
- Musée du Louvre (see p74)
- Musée d'Orsay (see p133)
- Musée de l'Orangerie (see p74)

Best dead
- Cimetière du Montparnasse (see p154)
- Cimetière du Père-Lachaise (see p101)

Best outdoors
- Jardin du Luxembourg (see p130)
- Bois de Boulogne (see p160)
- Parc des Buttes-Chaumont (see p96)

Best views
- Arc de Triomphe (see p56)
- Cathédrale Notre-Dame de Paris (see p118)
- Eiffel Tower (see p122)
- Institut du Monde Arabe (see p144)
- Sacré-Coeur (see p91)
- Tour Montparnasse (see p155)

Best tours
- Bateaux-Mouches (see p57)
- Vedettes du Pont-Neuf (see p116)

The most comfortable and modern boats in Paris

vedettes de paris

The sightseeing cruise of Paris
Get the best in 1 hour
www.vedettesdeparis.com

Location:
At the foot of the Eiffel Tower
Port de Suffren, 7th district + 00 33 (0)1 44 18 19 50
M° Bir-Hakeim & Trocadero; RER C Champ de Mars

This Parisian sightseeing cruise has to be at the top of your list of things to do when you are in the French capital.

Ideally located at the foot of the Eiffel Tower, its charming boats enhance the pleasure of a guided cruise on the Seine.

Listed by UNESCO as World Heritage, the river banks offer you some of the most well-known monuments such as the Eiffel Tower, the Louvre, the Orsay Museum and Notre Dame Cathedral amongst others.

Recorded multilingual commentary and a bar service on board.

Sparkling cruise

The magic of Paris by Night

Departures :
Everyday every 30/45min from 11am to 10pm. Times vary depending on the season. Check out our website for exact times.

Sightseeing or «by Night» cruise:
€12: Adult; €5: Children 5-12s; free under 4s

Exclusive :
Sparkling cruise, Sugar cruise or Snacking cruise
from €18 to €22

Snacking cruise

Get a sample of the best monuments

Exclusive: a bar on board

local pride. Indeed, many of them will tell you that Paris isn't so much a city as a jumble of villages.

We've divided this book into areas, though not necessarily into shapes that residents would recognise; we've imagined the city as a series of visitor-friendly concentrations of shops, sights, restaurants and bars. The Champs-Elysées & Western Paris section has the famous avenue as its spine, lined with high-end shops. It also contains fashion's most glamorous thoroughfare, avenue Montaigne, which is almost matched in terms of lustre and allure by rue du Fbg-Saint-Honoré.

Montmartre & Pigalle has, at its northern end, picturesque Montmartre with its vertiginous flights of steps, narrow winding streets and the massive bulk of Sacré-Coeur (see p91). To the south lies Pigalle, famous for the Moulin Rouge and its strip clubs and scuzzy bars (though it's far more salubrious today than it once was).

Opéra to Les Halles used to be the centre of royal power in Paris, and you can get a sense of this by taking a stroll around the Palais-Royal (see p74). Today, however, it's the city's commercial and cultural powerhouse: it's home to the Les Halles shopping complex, the jewellers and fashion houses of place Vendôme, and to the Louvre, Palais Garnier (see p86) and Monet showcase Musée de l'Orangerie (see p74).

North-eastern Paris is the area visitors from the UK are likely to see first: Eurostar trains terminate at the Gare du Nord (see p95) in the tenth arrondissement. The area is on the up, with its main artery, the charming Canal St-Martin, lined with boutiques and cafés. Further north and east of here is the magnificently odd Parc des Buttes-Chaumont (see p96), a warren of cliffs and grottoes carved out of a former quarry. Marais, Bastille & Eastern Paris is barfly territory, especially along rue Oberkampf, rue Jean-Pierre Timbaud and rue

Musée d'Orsay p8

St-Maur. The ever-trendy Marais is chock-full of independent galleries and quirky shops, and is also the centre of gay life in Paris.

The Islands – the Ile de la Cité, the oldest part of the city and home to Notre-Dame cathedral (see p118), and the more elegant Ile St-Louis – are highly distinctive and essential ports of call.

Undeniably, the main attraction of the affluent 7th & Western Paris area is the Eiffel Tower, universal emblem of the French capital. Its ironwork is most alluring at night, when it is lit up by thousands of shimmering lightbulbs. This is also the best time to climb it, because the queues are at their shortest.

For many years, St-Germain-des-Prés was the intellectual heartland of the city. But these days it's more about fashion than philosophy, and the expensive cafés are no place for starving writers. The city's most beautiful park, the Jardin du Luxembourg (see p130), won't cost you a *sou*, however; and the Musée d'Orsay is still excellent value, and positively gleaming after its recent revamp. Due east, the Latin Quarter is home to several of Paris's most august academic institutions, including the Sorbonne. And to the south, Montparnasse, although no longer the artistic stronghold it was in the 1920s, still boasts excellent cafés and restaurants, and the resting place of some of France's most illustrious dead, the Cimetière du Montparnasse (see p154).

The missing piece in Paris's cultural jigsaw at the moment is the Musée Picasso, which has been closed since 2009 for extensive renovation work, to upgrade facilities and increase exhibition space for a reopening in 2013. But Paris still provides opportunities aplenty to view the works of its famed former resident, from the Pompidou to the Musée de l'Orangerie.

Getting around

Vélib', the municipal bike hire scheme that puts some 20,000 bicycles at the disposal of residents and visitors, continues to flourish. Emboldened by the bikes' runaway success, Mayor Bertrand Delanoë launched another green transport innovation: an eco-friendly car hire system, which began operating in December 2011. Dubbed 'Autolib' (www.autolib-paris.fr), the new project allows subscribers to pick up and drop off a car at any one of 1,000 designated stations, 700 of which are located in central Paris, and the rest in the suburbs. The scheme has a fleet of 3,000 green (100 per cent electric) cars, and subscription fees range from €12 per month for an annual pass to €10 per day for a one-off daily pass. The half-hourly rate, meanwhile, ranges from €5 to €8. Each vehicle is tracked in real time, and when drivers have finished their hire period, they are guided to the nearest available parking spot.

If you don't feel confident about your chances in Paris traffic, the métro is extensive and reliable, and buses are clean, frequent and cheap. Some of the bus routes are worth riding just for the sightseeing opportunities they offer: no.24 takes you through St-Germain-des-Prés and the Latin Quarter; no.69 runs all the way from Gambetta in the east, via the Louvre, to the Champ de Mars in the west; and no.73 connects the Champs-Elysées to the futuristic concrete jungle of La Défense.

But when all is said and done, you really can't beat walking for getting around. Paris is compact enough to be navigated fairly easily on foot, and this is the best way to hear the heartbeat of the city.

Le Dauphin

Eating & Drinking

A surprising number of new restaurants are thriving in the difficult economic climate, showing that Parisians will always appreciate good food at fair prices. Wander through the streets of St-Germain, the Marais, Canal St-Martin or Pigalle any night of the week and you'll be hard-pressed to find a table, while the most popular restaurants fill up weeks or months ahead. Except for the simplest restaurants, it's wise to book ahead. This can usually be done on the same day as your visit, although really top-notch establishments require bookings weeks or even months in advance and confirmation the day before.

Bistro chic

Thankfully, the French continue to love classic bistro style. Many are old favourites, but the last few years have also seen the rise of the neo-bistro scene, updated for a new generation. At the very centre is Le Chateaubriand (see p108), the *coeur d'artichaut* of this dining trend, which the compulsive categorisers call 'bistronomy' (not a word necessarily embraced by the chefs themselves – marketing speak is truly not their thing).

So, what are the magic ingredients of the bistronomy boom? First, take the same flair long associated with Parisian gastronomy but use a little less finesse and significantly more innovation; next, add world-beating raw ingredients of thoroughly researched provenance and chefs who are generally young autodidacts enjoying success with their first business (Inaki Aizpitarte, Le Chateaubriand's Basque chef-owner, was previously a *paysagiste*, his sommelier an actor, his olive oil supplier a tight-rope walker). Finally, sprinkle liberally with reasonable prices and an atmosphere that is informal, relaxed and intentionally unbourgeois.

The Chateaubriand's kitchen buys many of its delectable treats locally. The olive oil comes from La Tête dans les Olives (2 rue Ste-Marthe, 10th, 09.51.31.334, www.latetedanslesolives.com), a tiny shop in pretty rue Ste-Marthe. Owner Cedric Casanova goes to Sicily every six weeks, where he organises and advises 26 farmers on how to make the fruit of their 20,000 olive trees attractive to the Paris market. Should you wish to sample more of his Sicilian products, including pasta made by his fishing buddy, Cedric has opened a restaurant with one table next door. It seats five, but if you're only a party of two it costs the same – €150. Booking is by email and there's a three-month waiting list to enjoy his tomatoes, figs and extraordinarily heady oregano.

Aizpitarte's other big opening in 2011 was the Rem Koolhaus-designed Le Dauphin (see p108), a tapas-style restaurant/bar a few doors down at 131 avenue Parmentier, where sub-€10 dishes include *magret séché, tempura de gambas* and *tarte au citron meringuée*. As at Le Chateaubriand, sourcing is all-important. Bread comes from Du Pain et des Idées (see p112), voted best baker in Paris in 2008 by Gault Millau.

Such is the hoopla that Aizpitarte has created, there is inevitably talk of a new scene in the 11th. Property prices are rising and the proprietors of the *branché* Chez Jeanette and Chez Justine have chosen a site opposite Le Chateaubriand and Le Dauphin for their new catering venture, Le Floréal (see p109) – an

American-style diner serving up hamburgers and cupcakes.

Another Chateaubriand success story of the past couple of years has been former sommelier David Loyola's hugely successful Aux Deux Amis (45 rue Oberkampf, 11th, 01.58.30.38.13). This tiny bar is permanently packed with a hipster crowd, but it's a different vibe from the student hangouts around the Oberkampf metro nearby. Vodka caramel is *interdit* – instead, customers enjoy organic wines and deliciously simple dishes such as *tortilla de Jeannine* for just €3.50.

Brasserie classics

Paris brasseries still have their appeal, even if most now belong to chains such as the Flo group, the Frères Blanc or the Costes. The spectacle of sitting amid art nouveau extravagance, as waiters in black and white rush between tables serving platters of oysters and choucroute, comes at a price, but is cheaper at lunchtime or late at night. Bofinger (see p107) and La Coupole (see p155), both part of the Flo chain, pull in a crowd of locals and tourists. The Costes brothers set the standard for the modern brasserie experience with stylish restaurants like Georges (6th floor, Centre Pompidou, 19 rue Beaubourg, 4th, 01.44.78.47.99); they have also taken over a few old bistros, such as Chez Julien (1 rue du Pont Louis-Philippe, 4th, 01.42.78.31.64).

Top tables

To crank it up a notch, you could opt for a spot of all-out luxury in one of the city's haute cuisine restaurants. And it doesn't come much more haute than Jules Verne (see p128), Alain Ducasse's classy venue perched in its eyrie on the second floor of the Eiffel Tower. For once, the food is as good as the views, with dishes such as turbot with champagne zabaglione. Other sumptuous dining experiences are to be had at Le Meurice (see p79), Stella Maris (see p65) and Alain Passard's L'Arpège (see p127).

Restaurants where you can easily spend €200 or more a head often have lunch menus for €75-€80 – still a lot of money, but for this you are treated to a full-blown experience from *amuse-bouches* to *mignardises*. Ordering the lunch menu often means having a more limited choice of dishes, but staff are likely to draw on the freshest ingredients from the market. A notch down from haute cuisine, restaurants such as Le Restaurant (see p135) and Pétrelle (see p91) offer sumptuous dining experiences for less than €100 per person.

Café culture

Since the smoking ban came into effect, Parisians have gradually been growing more health-conscious. This shows in the popularity of cafés such as Rose Bakery (see p92) and Cantine Merci see p108), where a plate of crunchy salads topped with sprouts and served with carrot juice might replace the traditional steak-frites washed down with red wine.

A growing trend is the Anglo-style snack shop. Cojean (17 bd Haussmann, 9th, 01.47.70.22.65), La Ferme (55 rue St-Roch, 1st, 01.40.20.12.12) and Bob's Juice Bar (15 rue Lucien Sampaix, 10th, 09.50.06.36.18) all serve healthy sandwiches, soups, salads and juices to eat in or take out. The Anglo theme continues at Bread & Roses (see p134), a mostly organic bakery run by a French couple that is passionate about British food, especially cakes.

The ubiquitous Parisian café, where wine is cheaper than water, is still present, although the iconic, scruffy neighbourhood haunt with its peeling paintwork is fortunately becoming a thing of the past. Many cafés have upgraded their interiors and prices accordingly, but you can still find affordable snacks such as omelettes and croques monsieur.

Just a handful of venues cling to their shabby-chic image – generally in the artsy north-east. A perfect example is Chez Jeanette (see p96), which despite the new owner's decision to preserve the 1970s decor, grease 'n' all, has never been busier. If grime gets you down, you still can't beat a chic café experience in the famous Left Bank institutions Les Deux Magots (see p134) and Café de Flore (see p134), or at Café de la Paix (see p76), whose millefeuilles are unrivalled.

If you're after something stronger, the tenth and 11th, especially around rue Oberkampf, continue to be the most happening areas for bars. Café Charbon (see p107), both a restaurant and pre-club cocktail bar, and L'Alimentation Générale (see p106), whose excellent concerts give stage space to up-and-coming musicians, are places to be seen. Also worth a trip is the area of St-Blaise, in the 20th, where a handful of buzzing venues have turned the area into a hub of urban subculture.

For those with money to burn, the city's other party central is the area around Champs-Elysées. Abandoned by all but a 'wannabe' crowd a few years ago, the area has regained favour with the smart set and now boasts some very posh addresses.

Snacks and foreign food

If you are looking for a snack, bear in mind that the hundreds of Chinese *'traiteurs'* in Paris are almost uniformly mediocre. You are much better off finding a bakery or packing a picnic. There are a number of decent crêperies around Montparnasse, where the Bretons originally settled, or you could try gourmet crêperie Breizh Café (109 rue Vieille-du-Temple, 3rd, 01.42.72.13.77) in the Marais.

Apart from fast-food outlets, non-French food is increasingly popular. The streets around Belleville (20th) and the southern end of the 13th are crammed with decent Chinese, Vietnamese and Laotian restaurants; the second, around rue Ste-Anne, is flourishing with Japanese eateries, including the excellent Kaï (see p77). Rue des Rosiers in the Marais is a centre for Jewish cooking, and Italian, Indian, Moroccan and Lebanese cuisine can be found across the city. Even North American food has been getting a look in, with gourmet burger van Le Camion qui Fume (www.lecamion quifume.com) one of the great success stories of 2012, and burger joints Blend (44 rue d'Argout, 2nd, www.blendhamburger.com) and Big Fernand (55 rue du Faubourg Poissonnière, 01.47.70.54.72, www. bigfernand.com) fuelling the trend.

In the know

Many venues close for their annual break in August, and some also close at Christmas. All bills include a service charge, but an additional tip of a few euros (for the whole table) is polite unless you're unhappy with the service.

As a general rule, the closer the tourist site and the better the view, the worse the food – although there are exceptions, such as bistro Au Bon Accueil (see p127), which serves sophisticated fare with a view of the Eiffel Tower from its terrace.

Finally, try to avoid anywhere with a menu labelled 'menu touristique' or 'we speak English'.

EXPLORE FROM THE INSIDE OUT

Time Out Guides written by local experts

Our city guides are written from a unique insider's
perspective by teams of local writers.

Covering 50 destinations, the range includes the
official London 2012 guide.

visit timeout.com/shop

'UNSURPASSABLE'
The Times

Lanvin p23

Shopping

Paris shopping has never been in better shape. Where else in the world can you find so many independent boutiques and specialist shops, in the middle of some of the most picturesque areas of the city? Whether it's tasting cheeses for a dinner party, getting measured up for a bra or selecting handmade gloves or a one-off piece of vintage clothing, shopping in Paris is a sensual pleasure based around quality, not quantity. Although chain stores have made their mark, Paris is a long way removed from the uniformity of so many provincial high streets.

Different areas of the city have different specialities. There are clusters of antiques shops in the seventh arrondissement, and second-hand and rare book outlets in the fifth; crystal and porcelain

manufacturers still dot rue de Paradis in the tenth; furniture craftsmen as well as children's clothes shops inhabit rue du Fbg-St-Antoine; bikes and cameras are clustered on boulevard Beaumarchais; and the world's top jewellers can be found on place Vendôme. The historic covered passages in the second and ninth are also fun places in which to shop, with chic stores mixed in with philatelists and booksellers.

Family-run food shops have thankfully not been eroded by supermarket culture, and tend to cluster in 'market streets' such as rue des Martyrs and rue Mouffetard, as well as around the many covered and open-air food markets. Here, everything from a vintage bottle of armagnac to a single praline chocolate is lovingly presented, served and wrapped. Informed discussion is still very much part of the purchasing process, and beautiful, old-style shops, unchanged for decades, add to the pleasure.

Green, organic and ethical have also become sexy concepts to the French. Even luxury brands have embraced them, seen at the first sustainable luxury trade fair, called 1.618. The not-for-profit concept store Merci (see p113) offers guilt-free clothes shopping, and Designpack Gallery (see p80) recycles packaging into funky and ingenious objects for the home.

Cool concept

The concept shop trend is a central feature of the shopping scene, crossing the boundaries between clothes, music and product design. The capital's concept kings have very different personalities. There's cosmopolitan, metropolitan, glamorous but down-with-the-kids Colette (see p80); bobo I-probably-care-more-about-my-home-than-my-wardrobe Merci; sophisticated, avant-garde L'Eclaireur (see p112).

And then the smaller ones: tomboyish Spree (16 rue de La Vieuville, 18th, 01.42.23.41.40, www.spree.fr), full of music and film industry cool; and new girl on the block Hotel Particulier (15 rue Léopold Bellan, 2nd, 01.40.39.90.00, www.hotelparticulier-paris.com). But what they all have in common is a product range that is both entertainingly diverse and seductively scarce.

At Colette, you can find Zippo lighters a few feet away from Smythson diaries, a few feet away from Ladurée macaroons, all one flight of stairs away from Alexander Wang and Valentino. At Merci, perfume and porcelain sit happily alongside each other on the main floor. And in Spree, antique furniture at the entrance gives way to a corridor with Dr Hauschka cleansers and toners, which in turn opens on to a room with racks of cute designer clothes. On the high-tech front, Sony has opened its first European concept store, Sony Style, on avenue George V (see p67), and Apple has opened a gloriously indulgent store next to the Opéra Garnier (see p80).

Colette

Boutique chic

The stretch of rue St-Honoré and rue du Fbg-St-Honoré from the Hôtel Costes to the Hôtel Bristol is wall-to-wall fashion boutiques, with Givenchy (see p66), Lanvin (see p83) and Jimmy Choo (376 rue St-Honoré, 8th, 01.58.62.50.40) the three major highlights.

Nearby rue Boissy d'Anglas has a branch of L'Eclaireur with its Fornassetti café (10 rue Boissy d'Anglas, 8th, 01.53.43.03.70, www.leclaireur.com).

Avenue Montaigne's headliners include Fendi at no.22, the Roberto Cavalli flagship at no.50 and, next door at no.52, Ralph Lauren's three-floor womenswear store. The small streets criss-crossing the Golden Triangle also have a few surprises, such as Lola.J (15 rue Clément Marot, 8th, 01.47.23.87.40), a boutique that brings together luxury clothes with attitude for men and women, including Ni-Search Swarovski-studded jeans.

Palais-Royal & around

If you're visiting Colette, don't miss a detour to the Marché St-Honoré. This former food market, rebuilt in glass by Ricardo Bofill, combines bistros and boutiques, with Marc by Marc Jacobs (see p83) the big attraction.

Easily reached on foot from here, the Palais-Royal gets better and better. On the eastern side, galerie du Valois has Stella McCartney (see p84), cult Swedish brand Acne Jeans at no.124, the covetable and racy gloves of Maison Fabre at no.128. Opposite, with the idyllic gardens in between, is galerie de Montpensier, containing Marc Jacobs (see p84) and vintage wear from Didier Ludot (see p81), as well as Martin Margiela in the road behind (see p84). Also in the area

SHORTLIST

Best recent openings
- Apple Store (see p80)
- Hermès (see p138)
- Storie (see p157)

Best concept stores
- Colette (see p80)
- L'Eclaireur (see p112)
- LE66 (see p66)
- Merci (see p113)

Best hand-picked fashion
- L'Eclaireur (see p112)
- Kokon To Zai (see p83)

Best for accessories
- Colette (see p80)
- Marc by Marc Jacobs (see p83)

Best for eveningwear
- Lanvin (see p83)
- Yves Saint Laurent (see p140)

Best souvenirs
- Arty Dandy (see p138)
- Diptyque (see p149)

Best food and wine
- Alléosse (see p65)
- Christian Constant (see p138)
- Lavinia (see p83)
- Du Pain et des Idées (see p112)
- Pierre Hermé (see p139)
- Première Pression Provence (see p113)

Literary life
- La Hune (see p139)
- I Love My Blender (see p112)
- Shakespeare & Company (see p149)

The classics
- Le Bon Marché (see p138)
- Galeries Lafayette (see p81)
- Printemps (see p84)

Bags packed, milk cancelled, house raised on stilts.

You've packed the suntan lotion, the snorkel set, the stay-pressed shirts. Just one more thing left to do – your bit for climate change. In some of the world's poorest countries, changing weather patterns are destroying lives.

You can help people to deal with the extreme effects of climate change. Raising houses in flood-prone regions is just one life-saving solution.

**Climate change costs lives.
Give £5 and let's sort it *Here & Now***

www.oxfam.org.uk/climate-change

Be Humankind Oxfam

is Kitsuné (52 rue de Richelieu, 1st, 01.42.60.34.28), the record label now selling its own-brand clothing.

Further east, the Etienne-Marcel area is the centre for club and streetwear, with boutiques and chains such as All Saints (49 rue Etienne-Marcel, 1st, 01.44.88.91.30) and Kiliwatch (see p83).

Marais mode

The northern part of the Marais, dubbed NoMa, has sealed its identity as the essential district for hot and hip fashion. Here, you'll find multi-label boutique Shine (see p113), and young French label Swildens (22 rue de Poitou, 3rd, 01.42.71.19.12), which boasts Carla Sarkozy as a client. Stylish menswear is also strong here, with Frenchtrotters Homme (116 rue Vieille-du-Temple, 3rd, 01.44.61.00.14. www.frenchtrotters. fr), and Christophe Lemaire's lounge lizard separates (28 rue de Poitou, 3rd, 01.44.78.00.09).

Going Gauche

St-Germain tends to be more conservative, but is increasingly offering a mirror image of the Right Bank, with brands insisting on a presence on both sides of the Seine. These include Paul & Joe (see p139) and Vanessa Bruno (see p140), plus a stunning Hermès store (see p138) set in an old swimming pool. Shoe heaven is found along rue de Grenelle with all the top brands. Other highlights include bobo bags in colourful fabrics and denim from the former prêt-à-porter designer Jérome Dreyfuss (1 rue Jacob, 6th, 01.43.54.70.93), Hélène Lamey's French-made nightwear and childrenswear at Bluet (18 rue du Pré-aux-Clercs, 7th, 01.45.44.00.26), and multi-brand shop Kyrie Eleison (15 carrefour de l'Odéon, 6th, 01.46.34.26.91) with lush creations

by Orla Kiely, Eros-Erotokritos, Velvet and La Fée Parisienne.

On the luxury scene, opium-coloured walls and lacquered ceilings provide a showcase for Stephane Pilati's creations at Yves Saint Laurent (see p140), while at Sonia Rykiel's St-Germain flagship (see p140) black mosaics, smoked glass and multiple mirrors evoke a '70s nightclub. And if you're in the market for some jewellery, don't miss out on a trip to Marie-Hélène de Taillac's Left Bank store (see p139), a Tom Dixon-designed space.

Further south, new Montparnasse shop Storie (see p157) is drawing curious, creatively bent shoppers to the area, offering an eclectic mix of homewares from around the world.

Foodie heaven

The layout of Fauchon (28 & 30 pl de la Madeleine, 8th, 01.70.39.38.00), with different areas (pâtisserie, bakery, fruit and vegetables, etc) and chefs on hand at each to offer advice and recipes, provides an excuse to indulge at this luxury store. Food markets are found in all arrondissements – two of the most popular are the historic Marché d'Aligre in the 12th, and the Marché des Enfants Rouges in the 3rd, which focuses on organic produce. Near the Marché d'Aligre, pop into Première Pression Provence (see p113), an olive oil paradise.

Practicalities

Shops are generally open from 10am to 7pm Monday to Saturday. Some are closed on Monday mornings. Sunday opening is found in the Marais, on the Champs-Elysées, at Bercy Village and in the Carrousel du Louvre. Many shops on the Champs-Elysées stay open until midnight, and Thursday is late closing at department stores.

L'Arc

Nightlife

When it comes to hardcore clubbing, the French capital is no longer a global challenger – serious nighthawks migrated long ago to more happening cities such as London, New York and Berlin, and the best Paris experiences tend to be reserved for those connected enough to be in the know or on the guestlist. In addition, the ban on all-you-can-drink events in 'open bars', which was introduced in 2009 in an effort to prevent binge drinking, dealt a further blow to the city's late-night revellers. However, all is not lost: the city is fighting back with a string of great new venues aimed at a more laid-back crowd.

Music-wise, jazz is enjoying a mini revival, new rock bands are emerging, as are venues to host them, and *chanson* is reinventing itself for a 21st-century audience.

Nightclubs

The big name on Paris's nightlife scene in the past couple of years has been André Sareiva. Having gone from underground street artist to head of a multi-national brand, he has single-handedly redefined the meaning of cool in under a decade. Much hype surrounded L'Appartement, an ephemeral project launched by Sareiva and Lionel Bensemoun, aka La Clique. The duo are at the helm of a string of venues, each one more exclusive than the last, with Sareiva decorating the place and Bensemoun taking care of finance. Hidden away in a Left Bank *hôtel particulier*, invite-only L'Appartement allowed the chosen few to party in a 3,000 sq ft flat, with everything arranged to make them feel at home: you could pour your own drink, tuck into a gourmet buffet and rifle through the collection of old vinyl. The only rule was to keep the address a secret and let the rumour spread.

Other Sareiva successes include Le Baron (see p67), an old escort bar taken over in 2003, and Le Montana (28 rue St-Benoît, 6th, 01.44.39.71.00), an even smaller venue near Café de Flore, revamped by La Clique in 2009 and preferred by those who now deem the Baron too passé. In 2011, Sareiva opened bar-restaurant, Phantom, in the Gare de l'Est area.

If it's more mainstream, big-room clubbing you're after, Queen (see p69) is a gay-friendly club known for its wild disco nights, while Rex (see p85) offers up mainstream and experimental electro on one of the best sound systems in Europe.

For standard house try Le Folie's Pigalle (see p94), but don't ignore the city's smaller venues, which frequently feature leading DJs. It is not unusual to find Jarvis Cocker at the Nouveau Casino (see p115) or Birdy Nam Nam at the Social Club (142 rue Montmartre, 2nd, 01.40.28.05.55). These intimate gigs are also where you'll discover most of Paris's 'after' parties too, with almost as many early Sunday morning events as there are Saturday nighters. Worth checking out are the floating Batofar (see p152) and, in summer, the Bateau Concorde Atlantique (23 quai Anatole-France, 7th, 01.47.05.71.03).

If you like your clubbing cosy, plenty of bars around Bastille, Oberkampf and the Grands Boulevards are willing to oblige. Panic Room (see p115) is one of the hippest, with a stream of French electro nights. Traditionalists can choose their poison too; a host of school disco-type nights where the DJ is no superstar take place at the

SHORTLIST

Best new/revamped
- La Machine du Moulin Rouge (see p94)
- Silencio (see p85)

Best bands
- Le Bataclan (see p113)
- La Cigale (see p94)
- Point Ephémère (see p99)

Best sound systems
- Panic Room (see p115)
- Rex (see p85)

All night long
- Batofar (see p152)
- Red Light (see p157)

Sunday sessions
- La Bellevilloise (see p29)

Perfect for posing
- L'Arc (see p67)
- Le Baron (see p67)

Best for star DJs
- Rex (see p85)

Best for party snacks
- Chacha Club (see p85)
- Le Showcase (see p69)

Best gay club
- Queen (see p69)

Best for jazz
- Caveau de la Huchette (see p149)
- Au Duc des Lombards (see p85)
- Le Sunset/Le Sunside (see p85)

Killer cocktails
- L'Arc (see p67)

Life is a cabaret
- Le Lido (see p67)
- Moulin Rouge (see p94)

twice-monthly Bal at Elysée Montmartre (72 bd de Rochechouart, 18th, 01.44.92.45.36) and salsa and world music get a good hammering at Le Divan du Monde (see p94).

Another new nightlife twist is the recent wave of designer-led hotel cocktail bars, which are attracting some big-name DJs. Mama Shelter (see p173) may be famous for its great design by Philippe Starck, but it's also picking up style points for its music selection; the Hôtel Ritz (see p171) boasts some of the finest resident DJs in the bar at weekends; the Murano Urban Resort (see p176) hosts Lucky Star on Thursday nights, when a famous French actor and/or singer takes over the decks; and the Kube Hotel (see p172) has daily DJ sets. In the same vein as the slick hotel bars is private members' club/bar Silencio (see p85), director David Lynch's new Paris joint, named after the cult setting in his 2001 movie *Mulholland Drive*.

August is traditionally the time when most Paris clubs shut down. But one beacon of summer light is Ed Banger Records, which has been throwing amazing parties instead.

Because Paris clubs don't really get going until 2am, people usually hit a DJ bar before, and diehards finish their evening at an 'after' on Sunday morning. Free passes can be found on various flyers; flyer information is available at www.flyersweb.com. Other good sites are www.radiofg.com, www.novaplanet.com and www.lemonsound.com. Also look out for big, one-off events in venues such as Rex and Point Ephémère (see p99).

The last métro leaves at around 12.45am (1.45am on Friday and Saturday), and the first gets rolling at 5.45am; in between you'll have to use a night bus, Vélib or taxi.

Rock, roots & jazz

Paris's music scene is bubbling with talent, and the recent emergence of some great new bands speaks volumes about the creativity of today's up-and-coming artists. The capital is overflowing with authentic concert venues, from monster stadiums to intimate bars and jazz clubs, and venues like Nouveau Casino and L'International (5-7 rue Moret, 11th, 01.49.29.76.45) give precious stage space to those on the way up the ladder. Much-loved indie and electro venue La Flèche d'Or (102bis rue de Bagnolet, 20th, 01.44.64.01.02), which closed its doors in April 2009, has now reopened under new management.

Chanson française is still going strong, helped by the revival of Les Trois Baudets (see p94), a government-subsidised *chanson* hall in the heart of Pigalle – French law dictates that 40 per cent of music broadcast in France must be in the French language.

Jazz is having a mini revival too: after the disappearance of old flames like Le Slow Club (once one of the most famous jazz joints in Europe), Le Bilboquet and Les 7 Lézards, a handful of new joints have opened up, while flagship clubs Au Duc des Lombards (see p85), New Morning (see p99) and Le Sunset/Le Sunside (see p85) continue to book top-notch acts from around the globe.

Paris is also a European leader for world music, particularly African and Arab acts. And don't forget that every 21 June, the city turns into one giant music venue for the Fête de la Musique, when a party in the street is guaranteed.

Website www.gogoparis.com selects regular concert highlights and also features a decent gig list for the coming months;

www.infoconcert.com is also well worth a look. The weekly magazine *Les Inrockuptibles* is a valuable resource. Alternatively, try reliable, bi-monthly gig bible *Lylo*, free in bars and branches of Fnac. The Fnac (see p66) and Virgin Megastore ticket offices (see p67) also display details of up-and-coming concerts. For reduced-price tickets try www.billetreduc.com.

Prices for gigs vary according to a group or artist's pulling power, but several excellent venues, like La Bellevilloise (19-21 rue Boyer, 20th, 01.46.36. 07.07), host regular free nights – ideal if you're feeling adventurous and/or are on a budget. For concerts, it's best to turn up at the time stated on the ticket: noise curfews mean that times are adhered to pretty closely.

Cabaret & comedy

The promise of busty babes slinking across stage in frilly knickers has turned glamour cabarets into some of the hottest spots around. The Moulin Rouge (see p94) popularised the skirt-raising concept during the 19th century, and since then venues such as Le Lido (see p67) have institutionalised garter-pinging.

These days, a cabaret is an all-evening, smart-dress affair, with a pre-show meal and champers. The Moulin Rouge is the most traditional revue and the only place with cancan. Toulouse-Lautrec posters, glittery lamp-posts and fake trees lend tacky charm, while 60 Doriss dancers cover the stage with faultless synchronisation. Sadly, elbow room is nil, with tables packed in like sardines.

For space go to Le Lido. With 1,000 seats, this classy venue is the largest, priciest cabaret of the lot: high-tech touches optimise visibility and star chef Paul Bocuse has revolutionised the menu. The slightly tame show, with 60 Bluebell Girls, has boob-shaking, wacky costumes and numerous oddities. For a more risqué performance, try the Crazy Horse (12 av George V, 8th, 01.47.23.32.32).

Le stand-up hit town in a big way a few years ago thanks to comedian Jamel Debbouze, who opened Le Comedy Club (42 bd de la Bonne Nouvelle, 10th, 08.11.94.09.40).

Le Lido

Palais de Tokyo

Arts & Leisure

A number of major cultural developments and innovations, and several new sites, have given a significant lift to Paris's cultural scene in the last couple of years. Biggest news comes in the form of the revamped Théâtre de la Gaîté Lyrique (see p115), which reopened in 2011, after a ten-year renovation, as the capital's first digital cultural centre, and the completion of the extension of the Palais de Tokyo (see p61), Paris's most happening art space, in early 2012. The latter is now also the home of La Triennale.

Construction is also well under way on the Cité Européenne du Cinéma in the northern suburb of St-Denis. Backed by maverick French film director Luc Besson, the massive complex will house nine studios and promises to give the national film industry a massive boost when it opens in late summer 2012. Even so, the French film industry remains in good health, with more tickets per head bought here than anywhere else in Europe.

Another major building project is the much-vaunted Philharmonie, which is rising near the Cité de la Musique. Architect Jean Nouvel's 2,400-seat concert hall is now due to open in 2014 and will give the city a major venue for the classical repertoire, as well as hosting jazz and world music.

What's especially good about the arts here is the accessibility: there are any number of festivals and discount promotions on offer throughout the year, many organised by the city council, that bring what the Brits often consider to be 'elitist' art forms within reach of the public.

Film

Cinema-going is a serious pastime in Paris. In any given week there's a choice of some 350 movies – not including the numerous festivals (see p34), many of which offer free or discounted entry. The city houses some 90 cinemas and around 400 screens, almost a quarter of which show nothing but arthouse. Even the multiplexes regularly screen documentaries and films from Eastern Europe, Asia and South America. This vibrant scene is constantly evolving, with new multi-screen complexes under construction and classic picture houses constantly under renovation.

Visiting one of the city's many picture palaces is an experience in itself – from the glorious faux-oriental Pagode (see p128) to the innovative surroundings of the Forum des Images (see p86). New releases hit the screens on Wednesdays .

Opera & classical

The Opéra National de Paris (see p86) continues to thrive under director Nicolas Joel, who came to the capital after 18 years at Toulouse Opera. With a reputation for traditional values, Joel favours a classical repertoire, while music director Philippe Jordan offers some youthful energy. Major productions for 2013 include *Kaguyahimé* and *La Sylphide*. The Théâtre National de l'Opéra Comique (see p86), meanwhile, continues to capitalise on new financial security following its promotion to National Theatre status by offering a crowd-pleasing season of revivals and classics, including Charpentier's *David and Jonathan*.

Elsewhere, at the Châtelet (see p86) director Jean-Luc Choplin's populist programming has included a string of retro musicals recently,

S H O R T L I S T

Wonderful settings
- La Pagode (see p128)
- Palais Garnier (see p86)
- Théâtre Marigny (see p69)

Most innovative
- International opera at Festival d'Automne (see p35)

Most romantic
- Candlelit recitals for the Festival Chopin (see p38)
- Lovers' seats at MK2 Bilbliothèque (see p152)

Best bargains
- €3.50 film tickets, Printemps du Cinéma (see p36)
- Free concerts at Paris Jazz Festival (see p38)

Best alfresco
- Cinéma en Plein Air (see p39)
- Festival Classique au Vert (see p40)
- Fête de la Musique (see p38)

Best film venues
- Forum des Images (see p86)
- La Pagode (see p128)

Best opera venues
- Palais Garnier (see p86)
- Théâtre National de l'Opéra Comique (see p86)

Original creations
- 104 (see p159)
- Maison des Métallos (see p115)
- Théâtre de la Gaîté Lyrique (see p115)

Culture after dark
- Palais de Tokyo (see p61)
- Nuit Blanche (see p35)
- Nuit des Musées (see p38)

MOULIN ROUGE ®

PARIS

COLOR 2012
in ROUGE

DISCOVER "*FÉERIE*",
THE SHOW OF THE MOST FAMOUS CABARET IN THE WORLD !

DINNER & SHOW AT 7PM FROM 175€ • SHOW AT 9PM AND AT 11PM : 105€
Montmartre - 82, Boulevard de Clichy - 75018 Paris
Reservations : 33(0)1 53 09 82 82 - www.moulin-rouge.com
www.facebook.com/lemoulinrougeofficiel

including big-hitters *Show Boat* and *Sweeney Todd*.

The main musical provider in summer is the Paris Quartier d'Eté festival (01.44.94.98.00, www.quartierdete.com), with concerts in gardens across the city. The Festival de Saint-Denis (01.48.13.06.07, www.festival-saint-denis.com) also offers top names in a spectacular setting.

Many venues offer cut-rate tickets to students (under 26) an hour before curtain-up. During the Fête de la Musique (21 June) all events are free, and year-round freebies crop up at the Maison de Radio France and the Conservatoire de Paris.

Dance

Paris is home to a thriving dance scene, with sumptuous ballet productions at the Palais Garnier and international companies at Châtelet. In May 2012, guest company the Tokyo Ballet took over the Palais Garnier to perform *Kabuki*, which was followed in June by Frederick Ashton's version of *La Fille Mal Gardée*.

In the sphere of contemporary dance, the prestigious Centre National de la Danse (1 rue Victor-Hugo, 93507 Pantin, 01.41.83.27.27), just outside the city centre, is an impressive headquarters for France's 600-plus regional dance companies. Every season sees some kind of contemporary dance festival in or near Paris; the Festival d'Automne (see p35) has been a star fixture on the circuit for more than 40 years.

Theatre

French-speaking theatre buffs can choose from some 450 productions every week: from offbeat shows in small, independent venues to high-brow classics in grandiose auditoriums like the Comédie Française (2 rue Richelieu, 1st, 08.25.10.16.80), whose staple shows feature the giants of French drama: Molière, Corneille and Racine

Fortunately for Anglophones, the Paris theatre scene is becoming ever more international, with translations of English and American plays firmly in vogue. The restored and re-baptised Odéon Théâtre de l'Europe (pl de l'Odéon, 6th, 01.44.85.44.00) offers plays in a number of languages, including at least one per season in English. Anglophone performances are occasionally programmed at the Théâtre des Bouffes du Nord (37bis bd de la Chapelle, 10th, 01.46.07.34.50), while the cutting-edge MC93 Bobigny (1 bd Lénine, 93000 Bobigny, 01.41.60.72.72) regularly hosts international companies performing in their mother tongue.

Meanwhile, the Improfessionals (www.improfessionals.com) stage regular improvised performances in English, and Shakespeare in English is performed every summer at the Bois de Boulogne's Théâtre de Verdure du Jardin Shakespeare by London's Tower Theatre Company (www.towertheatre.org.uk).

What's on

For listings, the best sources are the weekly magazines *L'Officiel des Spectacles* or *Pariscope*. When it comes to films, take note of the two letters printed near the title: VO (*version originale*) means a screening in the original language with French subtitles; VF (*version française*) means that it's been dubbed into French. Cinema seats can be reserved at www.allocine.fr. For new blockbuster releases, it pays to buy tickets at least one screening in advance.

Calendar

We Love Green Festival

This is the pick of events that had been announced as we went to press. On public holidays, or *jours feriés*, banks, many museums, most businesses and a number of restaurants close. New Year's Day, May Day, Bastille Day and Christmas Day are the most piously observed holidays. Dates highlighted in **bold** indicate public holidays.

September 2012

Early Sept **Jazz à la Villette**
Parc de la Villette
www.jazzalavillette.com
One of the capital's best jazz festivals, including Jazz for Kids concerts.

Until 25 Sept **Festival Classique au Vert**
Parc Floral de Paris
www.classiqueauvert.fr
Free classical recitals held in a park.

Early Sept-mid Oct **Festival Paris Ile-de-France**
Various venues
www.festival-ile-de-france.com
Classical, contemporary and world music festival set in various venues.

Early Sept **We Love Green Festival**
Parc de Bagatelle
www.welovegreen.fr
This brand new two-day eco festival had its first outing in 2011, with Pete Doherty topping the bill.

Mid Sept-end Dec **Festival d'Automne**
Various venues
www.festival-automne.com
This major annual arts festival focuses on bringing challenging theatre, dance and modern opera to Paris.

Mid Sept **Journées du Patrimoine**
Various venues
www.journeesdupatrimoine.culture.fr
Embassies, ministries, scientific establishments and corporate headquarters open their doors to the public.

Mid Sept **Techno Parade**
www.technoparade.fr
This parade (finishing up at Bastille)
marks the start of the electronic music
festival Rendez-vous Electroniques.

Late Sept **Fête de la Gastronomie**
Various venues
www.fete-gastronomie.fr.
This nationwide festival launched in
2011, aimed at celebrating the wonders
of French cuisine. The inaugural theme
was 'terroir', with more than 3,000
events across the country.

October 2012

Ongoing Festival d'Automne (see
Sept); Festival Paris Ile-de-France
(see Sept)

Early Oct **Nuit Blanche**
Various venues
www.nuitblanche.paris.fr
Galleries, museums, swimming pools,
bars and clubs stay open till very late
for one night only.

Early Oct **Prix de l'Arc de
Triomphe**
Hippodrome de Longchamp
www.prixarcdetriomphe.com
France's richest flat race attracts the
elite of horse racing.

Early Oct **Fête des Vendanges de
Montmartre**
Various venues
www.fetedesvendanges
demontmartre.com
The modest 1,000-bottle harvest of the
Clos Montmartre vineyard is the pre-
text for a weekend of street parties.

Mid Oct **FIAC**
Various venues
www.fiac.com
The Louvre and Grand Palais are the
two venues for this week-long contemporary art fair.

November 2012

Ongoing Festival d'Automne
(see Sept)

1 **Toussaint (All Saints' Day)**

Early Nov **Festival des
Inrockuptibles**
Various venues
www.lesinrocks.com
This rock, pop and trance festival
attracts top indie, rock, techno and trip
hop acts. Bill-toppers in 2011 included
Laura Marling and Friendly Fires.

11 **L'Armistice (Armistice Day)**
Arc de Triomphe
The President lays wreaths to honour
the French combatants who died during the World Wars.

Mid Nov **Fête du Beaujolais
Nouveau**
Various venues
www.beaujolaisgourmand.com
The new vintage is launched to packed
cafés and wine bars.

Nov-Dec **Africolor**
Various venues in St-Denis
www.africolor.com
African music festival with a spirited
wrap party.

December 2012

Ongoing Africolor (see Nov); Festival
d'Automne (see Sept)

Dec-Mar **Paris sur Glace**
Various venues
www.paris.fr
Paris opens up its outdoor ice rinks for
the season.

24-25 **Noël (Christmas)**

31 **New Year's Eve**
Jubilant crowds swarm along the
Champs-Elysées, and restaurants hold
expensive soirées.

January 2013

Ongoing Paris sur Glace (see Dec)

1 **Jour de l'An (New Year's Day)**
The Grande Parade de Paris brings
floats, bands and dancers.

6 Fête des Rois (Epiphany)
Pâtisseries all sell *galettes des rois*, frangipane-filled cakes in which a *fève*, or tiny charm, is hidden.

Mid Jan **Mass for Louis XVI**
Chapelle Expiatoire
On the Sunday closest to 21 January, royalists and right-wing crackpots mourn the end of the monarchy.

February 2013

Ongoing **Paris sur Glace** (see Dec)

Feb 13 **Nouvel An Chinois**
Various venues
Lion and dragon dances, and lively martial arts demonstrations to celebrate the Chinese new year.

Early Feb-mid Mar **Six Nations**
Stade de France
www.rbs6nations.com
Paris is invaded by Brits and Celts for big weekends of rugby.

March 2013

Ongoing **Paris sur Glace** (see Dec); Six Nations (see Feb)

Early Mar-Apr **Banlieues Bleues**
Various venues in Seine St-Denis
www.banlieuesbleues.org
Featuring five weeks of top-quality jazz, blues, R&B and soul.

End Mar **Printemps du Cinéma**
Various venues
www.printempsducinema.com
Film tickets across the city are cut to a bargain €3.50 for this popular three-day film bonanza.

29 Le Chemin de la Croix (Way of the Cross)
Square Willette
Good Friday pilgrimage as crowds follow the Archbishop of Paris from the bottom of Montmartre to Sacré-Coeur.

31 Pâques (Easter Sunday)

April 2013

Ongoing **Banlieues Bleues** (see Mar)

Early Apr-end May **Foire du Trône**
Pelouse de Reuilly
www.foiredutrone.com
France's biggest funfair runs for nearly nine weeks, noon to midnight daily.

Early Apr **Marathon de Paris**
Av des Champs-Elysées to av Foch
www.parismarathon.com
More than 35,000 runners take part, cheered on by 200,000 spectators.

End Apr-mid May **Foire de Paris**
Paris-Expo
www.foiredeparis.fr
Enormous lifestyle fair, full of craft and food stores, plus health exhibits.

Marathon de Paris

End Apr-early May Grand Marché d'Art Contemporain
Place de la Bastille
www.joel-garcia-organisation.fr
Contemporary artists display and sell their work at this annual arts fair.

May 2013

Ongoing Foire du Trône (see Apr); Foire de Paris (see Apr); Grand Marché d'Art Contemporain (see Apr)

Early May **Le Printemps des Rues**
Various venues
www.leprintempsdesrues.com
Annual street-theatre festival.

1 Fête du Travail (May Day)
Key sights close; unions march in eastern Paris via Bastille.

8 Victoire 1945 (VE Day)

Mid May **La Nuit des Musées**
Various venues
www.nuitdesmusees.culture.fr
For one night, landmark museums across Paris stay open late and put on special events.

Mid May **Art St-Germain-des-Prés**
Various venues
www.artsaintgermaindespres.com
See box p37.

Mid May **Festival Jazz à Saint-Germain-des-Prés**
Various venues
www.espritjazz.com
A ten-day celebration of jazz and blues on the Left Bank.

Mid May-early June **Quinzaine des Réalisateurs**
Forum des Images
www.quinzaine-realisateurs.com
The Cannes Directors' Fortnight programme comes to Paris.

9 Jour de l'Ascension

20 Lundi de Pentecôte (Whit Monday)

Arty parties

Get in the picture during Art St-Germain-des-Prés.

Timing your trip to the French capital to coincide with a night of *vernissages* (private views) gives a taste not only of the art on offer but also of the personalities who frequent the art scene, a real entrée into Paris life. Providing you look the part – obvious freeloading is ill-advised – you can turn up to most private views without an invitation.

The journal *L'Officiel Galeries & Musées*, which you can pick up free in most galleries, has a diary of *vernissages*. The second and last Thursdays of the month are the most popular dates, with ten to 15 galleries opening a new exhibition. But the big rendezvous of the year – unmissable if you are serious about this sort of thing – is the **Art St-Germain-des-Prés** (see left) in May. Nicknamed the 'block party', it gets more than 50 local galleries get together to showcase their top artists, with red carpets spread outside each gallery.

The galleries involved are mostly concentrated on rue de Seine, rue des Beaux-Arts, rue Visconti, rue Guénégaud, rue Bonaparte and rue Mazarine, and a whole cross-section of boho locals turn out for a drop of wine and conversation: artists, art dealers, ageing musicians, film directors, eccentrics, fur-clad ladies, rich kids and celebrities – this is most definitely one weekend of the year when *flânerie* will get you everywhere.

End May-mid July **Foire St-Germain**
Various venues
www.foiresaintgermain.org
St-Germain lets its hair down with concerts, theatre and workshops.

End May-early June **French Tennis Open**
Stade Roland Garros
www.rolandgarros.com
Glitzy Grand Slam tennis tournament, and second home to Rafael Nadal.

June 2013

Ongoing Quinzaine des Réalisateurs (see May); French Tennis Open (see May); Foire St-Germain (see May)

Early June **Fête du Vélo**
Across Paris
www.tousavelo.com
Cycling tours and activities as Paris's two-wheelers take to the streets.

Early June-July **Paris Jazz Festival**
Parc Floral de Paris
www.parisjazzfestival.fr
Two months of free jazz weekends at the lovely Parc Floral.

Early June-early July **Festival de St-Denis**
Various venues in St-Denis
www.festival-saint-denis.com
Four weeks of concerts showcasing top-quality classical music.

June-July Festival **Chopin à Paris**
Orangerie de Bagatelle
www.frederic-chopin.com
Romantic candlelit piano recitals in the Bois de Boulogne.

21 **Fête de la Musique**
Various venues
www.fetedelamusique.fr
Free gigs take place across the city.

Late June **Gay Pride March**
www.inter-lgbt.org
Outrageous floats and costumes parade towards Bastille, followed by an official party and various club events.

July 2013

Ongoing Foire St-Germain (see May); Paris Jazz Festival (see June); Festival de St-Denis (see June); Festival Chopin à Paris (see June)

Early July **Paris Cinéma**
Various venues
www.pariscinema.org
Premieres and restored films at the city's summer film-going initiative.

Early July **Solidays**
Hippodrome de Longchamp
www.solidays.com
A music bash for AIDS charities, featuring French, world and new talent.

Early-late July **Etés de la Danse**
Théâtre du Châtelet
www.lesetesdeladanse.com
International classical and contemporary dance festival.

July-Aug **Cinéma en Plein Air**
Parc de la Villette
www.villette.com
A summer fixture on the city calendar: a themed season of free films screened under the stars.

14 **Quatorze Juillet (Bastille Day)**
Various venues
France's national holiday commemorates 1789. On the 13th, Parisians dance at place de la Bastille. At 10am on the 14th, crowds line the Champs-Elysées as the President reviews a military parade. By night, the Champ de Mars fills for a huge firework display.

Mid July-mid Aug **Paris, Quartier d'Eté**
Various venues
www.quartierdete.com
Classical and jazz concerts, plus dance and theatre, in outdoor venues.

Mid July-mid Aug **Paris-Plages**
Various venues
www.paris.fr
Palm trees, huts, hammocks and around 2,000 tonnes of sand on both banks of the Seine bring a seaside

Tour de France

vibe to the city. As well as sunbathing, there's a floating pool, concerts, boules, art classes and a lending library too.

Late July **Tour de France**
Av des Champs-Elysées
www.letour.fr
The ultimate cycle endurance test climaxes on the Champs-Elysées.

August 2013

Ongoing Cinéma en Plein Air (see July); Paris, Quartier d'Eté (see July); Paris-Plages (see July)

15 Fête de l'Assomption (Assumption Day)
Cathédrale Notre-Dame de Paris
Notre-Dame again becomes a place of religious pilgrimage.

Late Aug **Rock en Seine**
Domaine National de St-Cloud
www.rockenseine.com
Three days, one world-class line-up of rock and indie groups. Green Day, The Black Keys and Placebo were the headling acts in 2012.

September 2013

Early Sept **Jazz à la Villette**
Parc de la Villette
www.jazzalavillette.com

This is one of the best jazz festivals in a city that loves jazz music.

Sept **Festival Classique au Vert**
Parc Floral du Paris
www.classiqueauvert.fr
Free classical recitals in a park setting.

Early Sept-mid Oct **Festival Paris Ile-de-France**
Various venues
www.festival-ile-de-france.com
Classical, contemporary and world music festival in venues around Paris.

Mid Sept **Techno Parade**
Various venues
www.technoparade.fr
This parade (finishing up at Bastille) marks the start of electronic music festival Rendez-vous Electroniques.

Mid Sept-late Dec **Festival d'Automne**
Various venues
www.festival-automne.com
Major annual festival for theatre, dance and modern opera performances.

Mid Sept **Journées du Patrimoine**
Various venues
www.journeesdupatrimoine.culture.fr
Embassies, ministries, scientific establishments and corporate headquarters open their doors to the public.

October 2013

Ongoing **Festival d'Automne** (see Sept); **Festival Paris Ile-de-France** (see Sept)

Early Oct **Nuit Blanche**
Various venues
www.nuitblanche.paris.fr
One of Paris's best and most interesting festivals. Galleries, museums, swimming pools, bars and clubs stay open till very late for one night only.

Early Oct **Prix de l'Arc de Triomphe**
Hippodrome de Longchamp
www.prixarcdetriomphe.com
France's richest flat race attracts the elite of horse racing.

Early Oct **Fête des Vendanges de Montmartre**
Various venues
www.fetedesvendanges
demontmartre.com
The modest 1,000-bottle harvest of the Clos Montmartre vineyard is the not entirely flimsy pretext for a weekend of street parties.

Mid Oct **FIAC**
Various venues
www.fiac.com

Paris sur Glace

The Louvre and Grand Palais are the two venues for this week-long contemporary art fair.

November 2013

Ongoing **Festival d'Automne** (see Sept)

1 **Toussaint (All Saints' Day)**

Early Nov **Festival des Inrockuptibles**
Various venues
www.lesinrocks.com
This rock, pop and trance festival attracts top indie, rock, techno and trip hop acts. Bill-toppers have included Laura Marling and Friendly Fires.

11 **L'Armistice (Armistice Day)**
Arc de Triomphe
The President lays wreaths to honour French combatants who died in the World Wars.

Mid Nov **Fête du Beaujolais Nouveau**
Various venues
www.beaujolaisgourmand.com
The new vintage is launched to packed cafés and wine bars.

Nov-Dec **Africolor**
Various venues in St-Denis
www.africolor.com
African music festival.

December 2013

Ongoing **Africolor** (see Nov); **Festival d'Automne** (see Sept)

Dec-Mar **Paris sur Glace**
Various venues
www.paris.fr
Paris opens up its outdoor ice rinks for the season.

24-25 **Noël (Christmas)**

31 **New Year's Eve**
Jubilant crowds swarm along the Champs-Elysées, and restaurants hold expensive soirées.

Itineraries

Comédie Française

Dead Famous

The French capital has some of history's most influential characters buried on its soil; the Montparnasse cemetery alone shelters hundreds of writers and artists within its confines, including the likes of Baudelaire, Beckett and Man Ray. But these are the lucky ones. Other historical figures did not always get to their final resting place in one piece – their bones, hair or innards led to great traffic back in the day. This trip around central Paris gives you the chance to get up close and personal with some of the city's more macabre relics.

Start on place du Palais-Royal, 1st (M° Palais Royal Musée du Louvre). Turn your back on the Louvre and walk into the **Comédie Française** (2 rue de Richelieu, 1st). Founded in 1640 by Louis XIV with Molière as its lead playwright, 'La Comédie' is still the only state theatre with a permanent troupe of actors. In the foyer, look out for an old armchair inside a glass cage. It is believed to be the one from which Molière delivered his last lines at a performance of *Le Malade Imaginaire* in 1673. He died shortly after the curtain fell. As a tribute to the playwright, the seat is put back on stage every 15 January, the anniversary of his birth.

In the same room, the statue of an old man regards theatregoers with a sarcastic smile. You may have recognised Voltaire, the French Enlightenment philosopher, immortalised here by sculptor Jean-Antoine Houdon. But it is a lesser-known fact that the statue serves as reliquary for the philosopher's brain, sealed inside its pedestal.

After Voltaire's death in 1778, the apothecary who performed the autopsy removed his brain and heart and put them in boiling alcohol to solidify them. Voltaire's brain then passed through many hands before finally ending up at the Comédie in 1924.

Bibliothèque Nationale –
Richelieu

As for his heart, it remained on display for a long time at the Château de Ferney, where Voltaire died. It was only when the philosopher's body was declared 'property of the state' in 1791 that the heart was given to Napoléon III, who decided to keep it at the Imperial Library, now the **Bibliothèque Nationale – Richelieu**. Walk to the entrance – currently at 5 rue de Vivienne, as the site is under renovation until 2017 – and ask to see the *salon d'honneur*, a stunning oak-veneered room presided over by a statue of Voltaire identical to the one at the Comédie. The heart is enclosed in its wooden pedestal.

The next destination is on the Left Bank, a perfect opportunity to test out Vélib, Paris's hugely popular municipal bike scheme. There is a *borne* opposite the library, at 71 rue de Richelieu.

Head south and turn left into rue des Petits Champs. Cycle across place des Victoires and turn right into rue du Louvre. Follow the traffic all the way down to the river, and turn left on to quai du Louvre, a section of riverbank lined with *bouquinistes*. Carry on to Pont au Change, where you can use the bus lane to cycle across the bridge. Once on the island, keep going

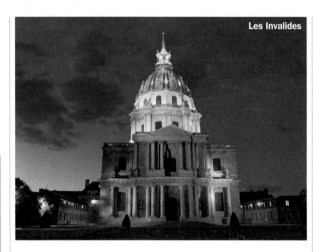

Les Invalides

south, passing the impressive gates of the Palais de Justice, and turn left on to quai du Marché Neuf. Go straight ahead until you're facing Notre-Dame cathedral. You can drop your bike at the *borne* on the side of the square, on rue d'Arcole.

Head south across Pont au Double. On quai de Montebello, walk around the small park in front of you and take rue de la Bûcherie. If you're feeling peckish after all that cultural dissection, you can indulge yourself with a dish of gently sautéed brains at offal specialist **Ribouldingue** (see p147) around the corner.

With rested feet and a full stomach, you're ready for more relic-hunting. Find rue St-Jacques at the end of rue de la Bûcherie and walk down to rue Soufflot. The columns of the **Panthéon** (see p146) should be clear to see on your left. As the last home of many French *grands hommes*, the Panthéon could be seen as the ultimate reliquary, even though there's not much to peep at in terms of old bones. The crypt gathers the shrines of over 70

illustrious Frenchmen, including Victor Hugo, Alexandre Dumas and our old friend Voltaire, whose carcass – or what remains of it – can finally rest in peace here.

A somewhat more sensational relic can be found in the **Eglise St-Etienne-du-Mont** (see p142), just around the corner from the Panthéon. The church, a masterpiece of Flamboyant Gothic architecture, displays a finger bone belonging to Sainte Geneviève, the patron saint of Paris, in a glass reliquary next to her sarcophagus.

Next, retrace your steps towards boulevard St-Michel and brace yourself for a creepy rendezvous. You can pick up a Vélib from the *borne* at 174 rue St-Jacques or cross through the Jardin du Luxembourg for some much-needed greenery.

From boulevard St-Michel, take rue de Médicis, followed by rue de Vaugirard which hugs the north side of the Jardin du Luxembourg. After passing the Sénat, turn right into rue Garancière, then left into rue St-Sulpice. Carry on along rue du Vieux Colombier until you reach

Musée de l'Homme

rue de Sèvres. Look out for Vaneau métro station and the Vélib *borne* around the corner.

Find the **Chapelle des Lazaristes**, identifiable by its tall green doors next to no.95 rue de Sèvres, and climb up the stairs to the side of the altar. Here lies the surprisingly fresh-looking corpse of Saint Vincent de Paul, patron saint of the poor. While his skeleton was preserved in its entirety, his face and hands were covered in wax and moulded to resemble the deceased, giving the disturbing impression that he passed away only minutes ago. The people of Paris, very attached to Saint Vincent de Paul, clubbed together to pay for the sumptuous silver and gold coffin in which the body lies.

Pick up a Vélib on rue Vaneau and head north. Turn left into rue de Babylone and then right into boulevard des Invalides. Keep cycling towards the Seine, with the golden dome of **Les Invalides** (see p124) on your left, the last resting place of Napoléon. The emperor could easily win the title of most scattered cadaver in history. While his heart and innards are in Austria, you will need to travel to New York to get near his penis.

After such intense reflections, you should arrive on quai d'Orsay, by the Seine. Cross the Pont Alexandre III and turn left on to cours Albert I. At place de l'Alma, where other pilgrims are gathered by the Princess Diana memorial, take avenue du Président Wilson on your right. Carry on until you reach place du Trocadéro. A Vélib *borne* on avenue d'Eylau will allow you to dispose of your bike.

The **Musée de l'Homme** (17 place du Trocadéro, 16th, closed for refurbishment until 2014) is home to philosopher René Descartes' skull. The rest of his body is buried on the Left Bank, which makes the perfect start to another trek. But by now you will probably have had your share of gravestones for the day. Take a pew on the steps and enjoy one of the best views there is of the city. Chances are you've never felt more alive.

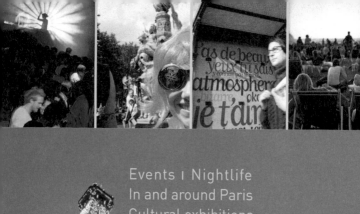

Events ı Nightlife
In and around Paris
Cultural exhibitions
Must See ı Gourmet

The very best of Paris and its region
is here for you to discover and to share:

ı new-paris-idf.com
ı facebook / Paris Tourisme

Come and join us

le nouveau
Par!s
Île-de-France

Exploring the Louvre

The world's largest museum is a city within the city, a vast multi-level maze of galleries, staircases and escalators. It's famous for the artistic glories it contains within, but the very fabric of the museum is a masterpiece in itself. You can be systematic and do a trail through the greatest hits, by department, by wing or by theme, or you can follow the route mapped out here and let yourself be sidetracked and beguiled by Flemish landscapes, Byzantine icons, Ancient Egyptian funerary chapels, and France's earliest portrait.

Part of the fascination of the Louvre is that it is not just a museum, but was a royal and later imperial palace and seat of government. The building's history is entwined with that of Paris and France. Behind the 35,000 works of art and 8.5 million annual visitors, you'll also find the giant staircases, sumptuous ceilings and carved panelling of the original palace.

Start on rue du Louvre, with its pedimented classical façade, and go through the central doorway into the Cour Carrée. Although the main entrance is now via the glass pyramid, this courtyard, with its richly sculpted western façade by Pierre Lescot and Jean Goujon, marked the introduction of Renaissance taste to Paris by François 1er as he established his court in the capital. Head through the arch to the Cour Napoléon, where the two wings added under Napoléon III are set off by I M Pei's glass pyramid in the centre – main entrance since 1993, exactly 200 years after part of the Louvre first became a museum. Pick up a plan of the museum at the welcome desk: the eight collections are colour-coded on it, and signs point to the most popular exhibits.

Start by the Richelieu wing, going up to the Cours Puget glazed sculpture court, on the lower ground floor. Here four vast green

bronze captives by Martin van den Bogaert, which originally stood at the foot of a statue in place des Victoires, represent Spain, Brandenburg, Empire and Holland, territories conquered by France. Next go through to the Cours Marly with its pairs of equestrian sculptures by Guillaume Coustou and Antoine Coysevox, and other statues commissioned by Louis XIV for the park of his favourite château at Marly-le-Roi.

Up the stairs to the side, the French Renaissance sculpture galleries are full of caryatids, monuments and fireplaces. Here, you'll find treasures such as the Fontaine de Diane from Anet, a whimsical confection of stag and nude huntress sitting on an urn, plus nymphs, sea beasts and swirling waves by Jean Goujon from the Fontaine des Innocents.

Next, take the Escalier Lefuel to the first floor decorative arts department. Sidetrack through the OTT apartments of Napoléon III, a feast of 19th-century bad taste, to admire the sheer excess of the dining room with its sculpted and gilded ceiling, and the *grande salle* where the circular sofa evokes palmy days of official functions.

Head to the medieval gallery (rooms 1-4) for Byzantine icons and ivories, the medieval treasure of St-Denis (golden eagle wings around an antique porphyry vase) and Limoges enamel reliquaries and caskets, before taking the escalators up to the second floor, which is home to the departments of French and northern European painting.

Here, your first stop should be the Galerie Médicis (room 18), one of the places where the history of France and the museum coincide in 24 virtuoso canvases by Rubens depicting episodes in the life of Marie de Médici – including Henri IV receiving her portrait, her arrival by boat in Marseille accompanied by thrashing sea monsters, her accession as regent and the marriage of Louis XIII.

There's more Rubens just around the corner (room 21) with his two sensitive portraits of his second wife Hélène Fourment. Continue

through Flemish landscapes and Dutch paintings, with Rembrandt in all his registers, from the tenderness of *Bathsheba at her Bath* to the raw meat and thick brushstrokes of *The Flayed Ox* (room 31), Vermeer's *Lacemaker* and Franz Post's Brazilian landscapes (room 38).

Back out on the landing, follow signs for French painting, said to start (room 1) with the 14th-century *Portrait of Jean II the Good*, deemed to be France's earliest independent portrait. There's a much more Gothic verve to Enguerrand Quarton's extraordinary *Pietà*, while Jean Clouet's *François 1er* is a stripy-sleeved incarnation of the dashing Renaissance monarch, a precursor to the wispy figures of the Ecole de Fontainebleau and Antoine Caron's paintings of court festivities.

Against the colour and bravura of 17th-century official Baroque painting for church and state, there is a more ascetic edge in Lubin Baugin's pared-back *Still Life with Wafers* (room 27), while Georges de la Tour's paintings (room 28) still

inspire awe with their incredible stillness and calm, simplification of forms, moulding by candlelight and shadow in *Mary Magdelene* or the more worldy moral theme of *The Card Cheat*.

Cross the Salle Alexandre (room 32), a vision of grandiose official history painting in Charles Le Brun's massive battle scenes full of thrashing horses and muscled bodies. This is followed by the 18th-century lightness and frivolity of Watteau's *Gilles*, the dreamy portraits and still lifes of Chardon, and paintings by Fragonard, at his best in his wonderfully free 'fantasy portraits' (room 48).

Exit by the spiral staircase down to Ancient Egypt on the ground floor. Pop into the Mastaba of Akhethetep (room 4), a circa 2400 BC funerary chapel of a royal dignitary from Saqqara with an interior chamber covered in painted reliefs. End your walk where it all began – the underground remains of the sturdy defensive walls, moats and conical towers of the medieval Louvre.

Didier Ludot p52

Vintage on a Vespa

Vintage shops in London and New York have been adding retro flair to wardrobes for years, but it has taken Paris – the city of 'serious' haute couture – a little longer to jump on the bandwagon. Today, though, the city is dripping in everything your vintage heart could desire, from rare 1920s Chanel accessories and art deco lighting to '60s rock LPs and 1980s kitten boots. And the good news is that many of the best vintage boutiques are condensed on the Right Bank between Palais-Royal and Faidherbe Chaligny (east of Bastille) – an easy distance to cover in one well-planned afternoon.

To really look the part, and for whizzing between the shops for maximum rifling time, hire a vintage-style Vespa from **Left Bank Scooters** (06.78.12.04.24, www.leftbankscooters.com; over-20s only). There are two models to choose from, each with a handy compartment for stashing your shopping: the metallic green, 1955-style Vespa LXV 125cc with chrome trimmings and leather seats (€80 a day) or the red Vespa S 50cc (€70 a day), which is based on the 1962 Primavera model. Both can be delivered to and picked up from your hotel at no extra cost.

French law now stipulates that you need a motorcycle licence to drive a 125cc scooter, but your standard driving licence will do for the 50cc. And don't worry too much about parking. Where possible, look out for parking bays for motorbikes (*parking moto*). But if you can't find room under the official parking sign, the traffic police are generally pretty lenient, as long as you don't block the road or pavement.

START: Park your Vespa at the *parking moto* area on the corner of rue Paul Bert and rue Faidherbe, 11th (M° Faidherbe Chaligny). Most vintage boutiques on this tour only open in the afternoon, so start with a retro lunch on rue Paul Bert. If you're looking for old school Paris, **Bistrot Paul Bert** (see p107) never fails to deliver, with its zinc bar, 1930s tiles, and lip-smacking dishes such as suckling pig with potato gratin. Alternatively, for a mix of hippy chic and slabs of Argentinean steak, try **Unico** (15 rue Paul Bert, 11th, 01.43.67.68.08, www.resto-unico.com), a former 1970s butcher's shop that has kept its original orange and white tiles.

After lunch, leave your Vespa and walk down rue Faidherbe, stopping briefly to admire **Les Années Scooter** (23 rue Faidherbe, 01.46.59.47.90, www.lesanneesscooter.com), a tiny den of mid 20th-century scooters, table lights, clocks, jukeboxes and street signs. Philippe, the passionate owner, can tell you the story behind every piece on display. A few doors further down, **Restaur'Bronze** (41 rue Faidherbe, 01.43.71.44.25, www.restaurbronze.com) is one of the last places in Paris to specialise

in metal objects from the 1930s and '40s, including some show-stopping art deco lights, all perfectly restored by owner Marc Arguence, who learned the trade from his father.

One thing's for sure: you can't scoot around town with a 1932 crystal candelabra in tow, so head back to your Vespa. Drive back down rue Faidherbe and turn left down rue de Charonne. Park up opposite the Bistrot du Peintre café (where you'll be coming back for coffee in a while) – there are usually a few free *moto* spots available. Take a right down bohemian rue Keller, lined with galleries, bars and emerging clothes designers, to **Born Bad** (17 rue Keller, 01.43.38.41.78, www.bornbad.fr), an Aladdin's cave of second-hand new wave, soul, 1950s rock and '60s surf LPs and CDs that attracts music-savvy Parisians from across town.

Turn left on to rue de la Roquette and walk to **Adöm** (35 & 56 rue de la Roquette, 01.48.07.15.94), which

Didier Ludot p52

is split into two small boutiques. Girls head to no.56 for 1970s and '80s jeans and '60s shift dresses, while boys drop into no.35 for 1950s baseball jackets, cowboy boots and a selection of sneakers.

Now retrace your steps to the art nouveau surroundings of **Le Bistro du Peintre** (116 av Ledru-Rollin, 11th, 01.47.00.34.39, www.bistrotdupeintre.com), where you can peruse your purchases over a fortifying *café au lait*.

Sustenance over, the boutique-filled Haut Marais beckons. Return to your Vespa and head south down av Ledru-Rollin, then right on to car-clogged rue du Faubourg-St-Antoine. At place de la Bastille, take a right up bd Beaumarchais and park near St-Sébastien Froissart métro station.

During the last six years, this previously forgotten northern stretch of the Marais has been transformed into one of Paris's hottest shopping areas, with numerous one-off boutiques coveted by fashionistas – including two wonderful vintage finds. The first is **Studio W** (6 rue du Pont-aux-Choux, 3rd, 01.44.78.05.02), a sparsely stocked vintage shop where quality is king. There are clothes – mostly rare designer vintage dresses by YSL and Chanel – but it's the accessories that shine: 1970s boots, '80s stilettos and enough dinky '60s leather clutch bags to make your heart swoon. The second shop, **Matières à Reflexion** (19 rue de Poitou, 3rd, 01.42.72.16.31, www.matieresareflexion.com), is the ultimate vintage bag-maker – a place where old leather jackets and clothes are crafted into one-off bags and satchels fastened with aged brass hardware.

From here, hop back on the bike and whizz down rue du Pont-au-Choux, turn left on to rue de

Turenne and then right on to rue St-Antoine. Park near St-Paul métro station. Walk up rue Pavée and turn left on to rue du Roi de Sicile, and you'll find two vintage hotspots. For punky London retro style, try **Noir Kennedy** (12 & 22 rue du Roi de Sicile, 4th, 01.42.71. 15.50, www.noirkennedy.fr), which is chock full of leather coats, lumberjack shirts, ripped jeans and funky 1980s T-shirts. If '40s fashion is more your forte, try **Mam'Zelle Swing** (35bis rue du Roi de Sicile, 4th, 01.48.87.04.06), where Bérénice stocks well-selected pieces, many under €100.

Back on your Vespa, drive all the way down rue de Rivoli, turn right up rue de l'Echelle and right down rue St-Honoré, then park wherever you can at Palais-Royal. There are usually spots on place André Malraux next to the Comédie Française. From here, take a stroll under the arcades of the Palais-Royal gardens to Paris's ultimate temple of luxury vintage, **Didier Ludot** (see p81). You just have to glimpse the window displays to see that there is something special about Ludot's pieces, many of which look like they could have been cast-offs from Audrey Hepburn or Marilyn Monroe. If you're daring enough to go in, you'll discover modern outfits by today's up-and-coming designers too – or the vintage pieces of tomorrow, as the owner likes to call them.

Shopping over for the afternoon, head back east for a fittingly retro-style dinner at red- and white-checked **Astier** (44 rue Jean-Pierre Timbaud, 11th, 01.43.57.16.35, www.restaurant-astier.com), where chef Christophe Kestler revives vintage French dishes such as smoked herring, braised Charolais beef, and vanilla cream with sophisticated flair.

Noir Kennedy

LE MARCEAU BASTILLE ★★★★

Hôtel-Gallery
13 rue Jules César
75012 Paris
Tél: 00.33(0)1 43 43 11 65
Fax: 00.33(0)1 43 41 67 70
infos@hotelmarceaubastille.com
Géneral Manager: Christophe Diallo

Le Marceau Bastille – Hotel gallery is a charming and contemporary 4 stars hotel, located nearly a few steps away from the Bastille square, as well "Gare de Lyon" train station and the historic Marais neighbourhood. The hotel interiors denote a characteristically contemporary style.

Le Marceau Bastille Hotel offers 55 rooms of two kinds: First, the "urban" option guarantees a cozy and resolutely avant-garde type atmosphere swathed in vibrant color, still seeped in elegance. The "ecological" option provides calm and sunny rooms set off by bright yet soft tones, natural materials, organic forms and sleek lines. The furnishings are contemporary and combine delicacy with modern technology. The living room and the breakfast room walls are dedicated to the Art with the permanent collections of contemporary artists.

Hotel Facilities
General
Bar, 24-Hour Front Desk, Newspapers, Non-Smoking Rooms, Rooms/Facilities for Disabled Guests, Elevator, free Safety Deposit Box, Heating, Design Hotel, Luggage Storage, Air-conditioning, Fitness room.

Services
Massage, Room Service, Laundry, Dry Cleaning, Breakfast in the Room, Fax/Photocopying.
Free! All children under 2 years stay free of charge for cots.
Free! Wi-Fi is available in the entire hotel and is free of charge.
Free! Pets are allowed on request. No extra charges.
Extra beds are available on request only. Any type of extra bed or baby cot is upon request and needs to be confirmed by the hotel. Public parking is possible at a location nearby.

Hotel Policies
Check-in 13:00 & Check-out 12:00
Accepted credit cards
American Express, Visa, Euro/MasterCard, Carte Bleue, Diners Club, JCB
Area Information
Architect, Historic and Art Area.
Place de la Bastille - L'Opéra Bastille - L'Hôtel Sully - L'Hôtel Carnavalet - L'Institut du Monde Arabe et la Mosquée de Paris - Le Pavillon de l'Arsenal. Le Quartier du Marais. La Place des Vosges - Cour Saint - Emilion
Stroll and Walk Area
La Promenade Plantée - Le Port de Plaisance de Paris Arsenal - Le Jardin des Plantes and Muséum National d'Histoire Naturelle - L'Ile Saint Louis.

Paris by Area

Arc de Triomphe

Champs-Elysées & Western Paris

In truth, *'la plus belle avenue du monde'* is not especially beautiful and it heaves with cars and crowds at pretty much any time of the day. The hordes aren't here for beauty, though. They're here for the shops, which the avenue, after years in the retail doldrums, now supplies in upmarket abundance. Fortunately, in the midst of all this rampant consumerism and airy affluence are a good number of museums covering such cerebral topics as architecture, human evolution and life on the ocean waves.

The western end of the Champs-Elysées is dominated by the renovated arch of the **Arc de Triomphe** towering above place Charles-de-Gaulle, also known as L'Etoile. Built by Napoleon, the arch was modified to celebrate the Revolutionary armies. From the top, visitors can gaze over the square (commissioned later by Haussmann), with 12 avenues radiating out in all directions. South of the arch, avenue Kléber leads to the monumental buildings of the panoramic Trocadéro.

Sights & museums

Arc de Triomphe

Pl Charles-de-Gaulle, 8th (01.55. 37.73.77). M° Charles de Gaulle Etoile. **Open** *Oct-Mar* 10am-10.30pm daily. *Apr-Sept* 10am-11pm daily. **Admission** €9.50; free-€6 reductions. **Map** p58 B2 ❶
The Arc de Triomphe has long been one of the capital's quintessential landmarks, drawing in 1.5 million visitors a year. But until recently, the interior was unimpressive, having changed little since the 1930s. After a revamp by architect Christophe Girault and artist Maurice Benayouna, a new museum opened with interactive screens and multimedia displays allowing visitors

to look at other arches around Europe and the world, as well as screens exploring the Arc's tumultuous 200-year history. In June 2010, the finishing touches were once again revealed to the public in all their splendour.

Bateaux-Mouches

Pont de l'Alma, 8th (01.42.25.96.10, www.bateaux-mouches.fr). M° Alma-Marceau. **Tickets** €11; free-€5.50 reductions. **Map** p58 C4 ❷

If you're after a whirlwind tour of the sights and don't mind tourists and schoolchildren, this, the oldest cruise operation on the Seine, is a good option.

Cinéaqua

2 av des Nations Unies, 16th (01.40. 69.23.23, www.cineaqua.com). M° Trocadéro. **Open** 10am-7pm daily. **Admission** €19.50; free-€15.50 reductions. **Map** p58 B5 ❸

This aquarium and three-screen cinema is a wonderful attraction and a key element in the renaissance of the once moribund Trocadéro.

Cité de l'Architecture et du Patrimoine

Palais de Chaillot, 1 pl du Trocadéro, 16th (01.58.51.52.00, www.cite chaillot.fr). M° Trocadéro. **Open** 11am-7pm Mon, Wed, Fri-Sun; 11am-9pm Thur. **Admission** €8; free-€5 reductions. **Map** p58 A4 ❹

Opened in 2007 in the east wing of the Palais de Chaillot, this architecture and heritage museum impresses by its scale. The ground floor is filled with mock-ups of cathedral façades and heritage buildings, and interactive screens place the models in context. Upstairs, darkened rooms house full-scale copies of medieval and Renaissance murals and stained-glass windows. The highlight of the modern architecture section is the walk-in replica of an apartment from Le Corbusier's Cité Radieuse in Marseille. Temporary exhibitions are housed in the basement.

Galerie-Musée Baccarat

11 pl des Etats-Unis, 16th (01.40.22. 11.00, www.baccarat.fr). M° Boissière or Iéna. **Open** 10am-6.30pm Mon, Wed-Sat. **Admission** €5; free-€3.50 reductions. **Map** p58 B3 ❺

Philippe Starck has created a neo-rococo wonderland in the former mansion of the Vicomtesse de Noailles. See items by Georges Chevalier and Ettore Sottsass, services made for princes and maharajahs, and show-off items made for the great exhibitions of the 1800s.

Galeries Nationales du Grand Palais

3 av du Général-Eisenhower, 8th (01.44.13.17.17, www.grandpalais. fr). M° Champs-Elysées Clemenceau. **Open** times vary. **Admission** €11-€12; free-€8 reductions. **Map** p59 E4 ❻

The Grand Palais was built for the 1900 Exposition Universelle and the design was the work of three different architects. During World War II, it played the role of reluctant host to Nazi tanks. In 1994, the glass-roofed central hall was closed when bits of metal started falling off. After major restoration, the Palais reopened in 2005 and now hosts major exhibitions.

Musée d'Art Moderne de la Ville de Paris

11 av du Président-Wilson, 16th (01.53.67.40.00, www.mam.paris.fr). M° Alma Marceau or Iéna. **Open** 10am-6pm Tue-Sun. **Admission** free. *Temporary exhibitions* €5-€11; free-€4.50 reductions. No credit cards. **Map** p58 B4 ❼

This monumental 1930s building, housing the city's modern art collection, is strong on the Cubists, Fauves, the Delaunays, Rouault and Ecole de Paris artists Soutine and van Dongen. The museum was briefly closed in May 2010 after the theft of five masterpieces. The €100-million haul netted paintings by Picasso, Matisse, Braque, Modigliani and Léger.

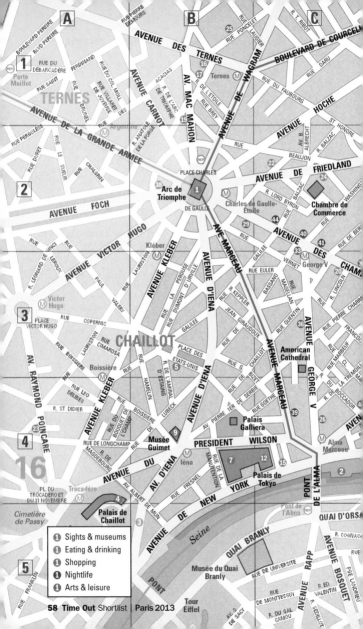

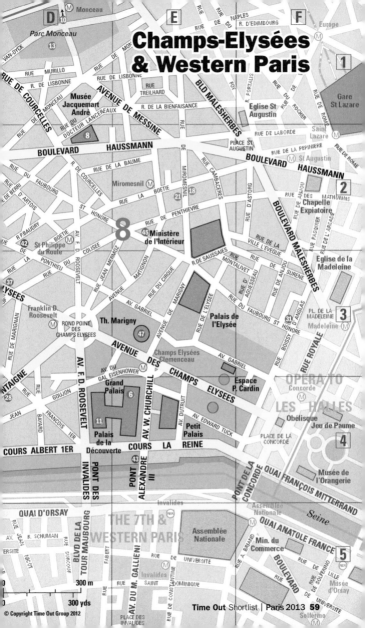

Champs-Elysées & Western Paris

© Copyright Time Out Group 2012

GAÎTÉ LYRIQUE
THE STAGE
FOR DIGITAL
EMOTIONS
IN PARIS

— exhibitions, concerts, performances, lives, multimedia shows, theatre, screenings, talks, workshops, videogames

• 3 BIS, RUE PAPIN – 75003 PARIS
• +33 1 53 01 51 51
• WWW.GAITE-LYRIQUE.NET

RÉVOLUTIONS NUMÉRIQUES

Event highlights The Art of War, 1938-1947: From Picasso to Dubuffet (12 Oct 2012-17 Feb 2013).

Musée Jacquemart-André

158 bd Haussmann, 8th (01.45.62. 11.59, www.musee-jacquemart-andre. com). M° Miromesnil or St-Philippe-du-Roule. **Open** 10am-6pm daily. **Admission** €10; free-€8.50 reductions. **Map** p59 D2 ❽

A stern pair of stone lions usher visitors into this grand 19th-century mansion, home to a collection of stately *objets d'art* and fine paintings. The collection was assembled by Edouard André and his artist wife Nélie Jacquemart, using money inherited from his rich banking family. The mansion was built to order to house their art hoard, which includes Rembrandts, Tiepolo frescoes and paintings by Italian masters Uccello, Mantegna and Carpaccio.

Musée National des Arts Asiatiques – Guimet

6 pl d'Iéna, 16th (01.56.52.53.00, www.museeguimet.fr). M° Iéna. **Open** 10am-6pm Mon, Wed-Sun. **Admission** €7.50; free-€5.50 reductions. **Map** p58 B4 ❾

The museum houses 45,000 objects from Neolithic times onwards, in a voyage across the diverse Asian religions and civilisations. Lower galleries focus on India and South-east Asia, centred on Hindu and Buddhist Khmer sculpture from Cambodia. Don't miss the Giant's Way, part of the entrance to a temple complex at Angkor Wat. Upstairs, Chinese antiquities include mysterious jade discs. Afghan glassware, Tibetan mandalas and Moghul jewellery also feature.

Musée National Jean-Jacques Henner

43 av de Villiers, 17th (01.47.63.42.73, www.musee-henner.fr). M° Malesherbes. **Open** 11am-6pm Mon, Wed-Sun. **Admission** €5; free-€3 reductions. **Map** p59 D1 ❿

The Musée Jean-Jacques Henner traces the life of one of France's most respected artists, from his humble beginnings in Alsace in 1829 to his rise as one of the most sought-after painters in Paris. On the first floor, Alsatian landscapes and family portraits are a reminder of the artist's lifelong attachment to his native region. What brought the artist most acclaim (and criticism), however, was his trademark nymph paintings.

Palais de la Découverte

Av Franklin-D-Roosevelt, 8th (01.56. 43.20.21, www.palais-decouverte.fr). M° Champs-Elysées Clemenceau or Franklin D. Roosevelt. **Open** 9.30am-6pm Tue-Sat; 10am-7pm Sun (last entry 30mins before closing). **Admission** €7; free-€4.50 reductions. *Planetarium* €3.50. **Map** p59 D4 ⓫

This science museum houses designs dating from Leonardo da Vinci's time to the present day. Models, real apparatus and audio-visual material bring the displays to life, and exhibits cover astrophysics, astronomy, biology, chemistry, physics and earth sciences. There are shows at the Planetarium, and 'live' experiments take place at weekends and during school holidays.

Palais de Tokyo: Site de Création Contemporaine

13 av du Président-Wilson, 16th (01.47.23.54.01, www.palaisdetokyo. com). M° Alma Marceau or Iéna. **Open** noon-9pm Tue-Sun. **Admission** €8; free under-18s. **Map** p58 C4 ⓬

When it opened in 2002, many thought the Palais' stripped-back interior was a design statement. In fact, it was a practical answer to tight finances. The 1937 building has now come into its own as an open-plan space, hosting exhibitions, shows and performances. Extended hours and a funky café have succeeded in drawing a younger audience, and the roll-call of artists is impressive. The Palais recently underwent a revamp, reopening in its entirety in early 2012. It's also the site of the prestigious Triennale.

Parc Monceau

Bd de Courcelles, av Hoche, rue Monceau, 8th. M° Monceau. **Open** *Nov-Mar* 7am-8pm daily. *Apr-Oct* 7am-10pm daily. **Admission** free. **Map** p59 D1 ⑬

Monceau is a favourite with well-dressed children and their nannies. It was laid out in the 18th century for the Duc de Chartres in the English style, with a lake, lawns and follies: an Egyptian pyramid, a Corinthian colonnade, Venetian bridge and sarcophagi.

Eating & drinking

Alain Ducasse au Plaza Athénée

Hôtel Plaza Athénée, 25 av Montaigne, 8th (01.53.67.65.00, www.alain-ducasse.com). M° Alma Marceau. **Open** 7.45-10.15pm Mon-Wed; 12.45-2.15pm, 7.45-10.15pm Thur, Fri. Closed mid July-mid Aug & 2wks Dec. **€€€€**. **Haute cuisine**. **Map** p58 C4 ⑭

The sheer glamour factor would be enough to recommend this restaurant, Alain Ducasse's most lofty Paris undertaking. The dining room ceiling drips with 10,000 crystals. An *amuse-bouche* of a single langoustine in a lemon cream with a touch of Iranian caviar starts the meal off beautifully, but other dishes can be inconsistent. Cheese is delicious, as is the *rum baba comme à Monte-Carlo*.

Antoine

NEW *10 av de New York, 16th (01.40.70.19.28, www.antoine-paris.fr). M° Alma-Marceau or Trocadéro.* **Open** noon-2.45pm, 7.30-10.45pm daily. **€€€**. **Seafood**. **Map** p58 C4 ⑮

Antoine is Paris's newest shrine to the sea. Chic, moneyed crowds gather to sample chef Mickaël Feval's perfect oysters and extravagant dishes like whole roasted lobster with winter vegetables *en cocotte*, plump St-Jacques scallops with creamy purée, and wonderful vanilla millefeuille. The fixed-price lunch menu is excellent value.

Le Dada

12 av des Ternes, 17th (01.43.80. 60.12). M° Ternes. **Open** 6am-2am Mon-Sat; 7am-10pm Sun. **€€**. **Café**. **Map** p58 B1 ⑯

Perhaps the hippest café in this stuffy part of town, Le Dada is best known for its well-placed, sunny terrace. Inside, the wood-block carved tables and red walls provide a warm atmosphere for a crowd that tends towards the well-heeled, well-spoken and, well, loaded. That said, the atmosphere is friendly; if terracing is your thing, you could happily spend a summer's day here.

Flute l'Etoile

19 rue de l'Etoile, 17th (01.45.72. 10.14, www.flutebar.com). M° Ternes. **Open** 5pm-2am Tue-Sat; 6am-10pm Sun. **Champagne bar**. **Map** p58 B1 ⑰

With a menu extending to some 23 different champagnes and designer decor (slick wooden panelling, blue walls, red velvet), Paris's first dedicated champagne lounge certainly looks the part. For drinkers wishing to sample different vintages without buying a whole glass (from €9), the small tasting glasses (from €5) are a nice touch. And for anyone who might be 'bored' by plain bubbly, cocktails such as champagne sangria make for a sophisticated alternative.

Granterroirs

30 rue de Miromesnil, 8th (01.47.42. 18.18, www.granterroirs.com). M° Miromesnil. **Open** 9am-8pm Mon-Fri. *Food served* noon-3pm Mon-Fri. Closed 3wks Aug. **€€**. **Bistro**. **Map** p59 E2 ⑱

The walls of this *épicerie* heave with more than 600 enticing specialities originating from southern France, including Périgord foie gras, charcuterie from Aubrac and a fine selection of wines. The make great gifts – but why not try sampling some of the goodies by enjoying the midday *table d'hôte* feast? Come in early to ensure that you can choose from the five succulent *plats du jour*.

Antoine

Master chef

Christophe Moret is cooking up a storm.

Becoming a top French chef is tough work. For a start you have to be good enough to uphold the reputation of La Gastronomie Française (the world's most famous cuisine and part of UNESCO's World Heritage List since 2010). Then there's the competition, with more aspiring masterchefs than there are dream jobs to go round.

Even if you do manage to become sous-chef to a legend like Alain Ducasse or Paul Bocuse, usually the only way to become head chef is by opening your own restaurant. Fortunately for Christophe Moret, though, Michelin-starred Jean-Louis Nomicos has left the mighty **Lasserre** (17 av Franklin-Roosevelt, 8th, 01.43.59.02.13, www.restaurant-lasserre.com), where notables such as the Duke of Windsor and Salvador Dalí once graced the tables, to open his own restaurant, Les Tablettes de Jean-Louis Nomicos (16 av Bugeaud, 16th, 01.56.28.16.16, www.lestablettesjeanlouisnomicos.com) – a move that left a vacancy which Moret was only too happy to fill.

After seven years under Ducasse at the Plaza Athénée, 'it was time to take on a new challenge,' says Moret enthusiastically. 'I'm 44 now, and I want to prove that I can do it.' Joining him in Lasserre's kitchen is pastry chef Claire Heitzler, who left her job at the Ritz to come here.

A typical meal might start with an amuse-bouche of lettuce mousse with golden caviar, followed by scallops with caramelised

Jerusalem artichokes and oodles of grated white truffles. Mains include André Malraux pigeon, a dish invented by the restaurant's founder Réné Laserre and stuffed with foie gras, or Christophe Moret's duck stuffed with truffles and turnips in lapsang souchong tea. Desserts are heavenly.

The dining room itself is a sumptuous affair, with solid silver table decorations and a retractable roof – perfect for romantic summer splurges.

Le Hide

10 rue du Général-Lanrezac, 17th (01.45.74.15.81, www.lehide.fr). M° Charles de Gaulle Etoile. **Open** noon-3pm, 7.30-10.30pm Mon-Fri; 7.30-10.30pm Sat. €€. **Bistro.** **Map** p58 B1 ⑲

This bistro is packed with a happy crowd that appreciates Japanese-born chef Hide Kobayashi's superb cooking. Expect dishes such as duck foie gras terrine with pear-and-thyme compôte to start, followed by tender faux-filet steak in a light foie gras sauce. Desserts are excellent: perfect tarte tatin comes with crème fraîche from Normandy.

Ladurée

75 av des Champs-Elysées, 8th (01.40. 75.08.75, www.laduree.fr). M° Franklin D. Roosevelt or George V. **Open** 7.30am-11.30pm Mon-Fri; 8.30am-12.30am Sat; 8.30am-11.30pm Sun. €€. **Café.** **Map** p58 C3 ⑳

Decadence permeates this elegant tea-room. While you bask in the glow of bygone wealth, indulge in tea, pastries and, above all, hot chocolate. It's a rich, velvety tar that will leave you in the requisite stupor for a lazy afternoon.

Maxan

37 rue de Miromesnil, 8th (01.42. 65.78.60, www.rest-maxan.com). M° Miromesnil. **Open** noon-2.30pm Mon; noon-2.30pm, 7.30-11.30pm Tue-Fri; 7.30-11.30pm Sat. Closed Aug. €€. **Bistro.** **Map** p59 E2 ㉑

This is a welcome new-wave bistro. Owner-chef Laurent Zajac uses quality seasonal ingredients, giving them a personal spin in dishes such as scallops with curry spices and artichoke hearts, classic veal sweetbreads with wild asparagus, and an exotic take on *île flottante.* Popular with Ministry of Interior types at lunch, quieter by night.

Stella Maris

4 rue Arsène-Houssaye, 8th (01.42.89. 16.22, www.stellamaris-paris.com). M° Charles de Gaulle Etoile. **Open** noon-2.30pm, 7.30-10.30pm Mon-Fri; 7.30-10.30pm Sat. Closed 2wks Aug. €€€€. **Haute cuisine.** **Map** p58 B2 ㉒

Trained by Robuchon and Troisgros, Tateru Yoshino turns out food that is resolutely French. You might float your way through foie gras with carrots, truffles and pistachio oil, pan-fried sea bass with saffron risotto, and perfectly lopsided Grand Marnier soufflé.

La Table Lauriston

129 rue de Lauriston, 16th (01.47.27. 00.07, www.restaurantlatablelauriston. com). M° Trocadéro. **Open** noon-2.30pm, 7-10.30pm Mon-Fri; 7-10.30pm Sat. Closed 3wks Aug & 1wk Dec. €€€. **Bistro.** **Map** p58 A4 ㉓

In spring, stalks of asparagus from the Landes are trimmed to avoid any stringiness and served with the simplest *vinaigrette d'herbes.* More extravagant is *foie gras cuit au torchon,* in which the duck liver is wrapped in a cloth and poached in a bouillon. Skip the crème brûlée and order a dessert with attitude: the giant *baba au rhum.*

Taillevent

15 rue Lamennais, 8th (01.44.95. 15.01, www.taillevent.com). M° George V. **Open** 12.15-1.30pm, 7.15-9.30pm Mon-Fri. Closed Aug. €€€€. **Haute cuisine.** **Map** p58 C2 ㉔

Rémoulade de coquilles St-Jacques is a technical feat, with slices of raw, marinated scallop wrapped in a tube shape around a diced apple filling, encircled by a *rémoulade* sauce. An earthier and lip-smacking dish is the trademark *épeautre* – an ancient wheat – cooked 'like a risotto' with bone marrow, black truffle, whipped cream and parmesan, and topped with sautéed frog's legs.

Shopping

Alléosse

13 rue Poncelet, 17th (01.46.22.50.45, www.fromage-alleosse.com). M° Ternes. **Open** 9am-1pm, 4-7pm Tue-Thur; 9am-1pm, 4.30-7pm Fri, Sat. **Map** p58 B1 ㉕

People cross town for these cheeses – wonderful farmhouse camemberts, delicate st-marcellins, a choice of *chèvres* and several rarities.

Balenciaga
10 av George V, 8th (01.47.20.21.11, www.balenciaga.com). M° Alma Marceau or George V. **Open** 10am-7pm Mon-Sat. **Map** p58 C4 ㉖
The Spanish fashion house is ahead of Japanese and Belgian designers in the hip stakes. Floating fabrics contrast with dramatic cuts, producing a sophisticated style that the fashion *haut monde* can't wait to slip into.

Balmain
44 rue François 1er, 8th (01.47.20.57.58, www.balmain.com). M° George V. **Open** 10.30am-7pm Mon-Sat. **Map** p58 C3 ㉗
A portrait of the late Pierre Balmain surveys the scene at his eponymous shop. What would he have made of the clothes around him? Long gone are the afternoon dresses with perfectly positioned waists, full skirts and trapezoidal necklines. The racks are these days lined with bondage trousers, studded jackets and animal print drainpipes. There hasn't been such a good display of grungy, punk glamour since Kensington Market closed its doors.

Dior
26-30 av Montaigne, 8th (01.40.73. 73.73, www.dior.com). M° Franklin D. Roosevelt. **Open** 10am-7pm Mon-Sat. **Map** p59 D4 ㉘
The Dior universe is here on avenue Montaigne, from the main prêt-à-porter store and jewellery, menswear and eyewear to Baby Dior, where rich infants are coochy-cooed by drooling assistants.

Drugstore Publicis
133 av des Champs-Elysées, 8th (01.44.43.79.00, www.publicis drugstore.com). M° Charles de Gaulle Etoile. **Open** 8am-2am Mon-Fri; 10am-2am Sat, Sun. **Map** p58 B2 ㉙

On the ground floor there's a newsagent, pharmacy, bookshop and upmarket deli full of quality olive oils and elegant biscuits. The basement is a macho take on Colette, keeping selected design items and lifestyle mags, and replacing high fashion with wines and a cigar cellar.

Fnac
74 av des Champs-Elysées, 8th (08.25. 02.00.20, www.fnac.com). M° George V. **Open** 10am-midnight Mon-Sat; noon-midnight Sun. **Map** p58 C3 ㉚
Fnac is a supermarket of culture: books, DVDs, CDs, audio kit, computers and photo equipment. Most branches stock everything; others specialise. All branches operate as a concert box office.

Givenchy
28 rue du Fbg-St-Honoré, 8th (01.42.68.31.00, www.givenchy.com). M° Madeleine or Concorde. **Open** 10am-7pm Mon-Sat. **Map** p59 F3 ㉛
This flagship Fbg-St-Honoré store for men's and women's prêt-à-porter and accessories incorporates surreal rooms within rooms – cut-out boxes filled with white, black or mahogany panelling – providing a contemporary art gallery setting for Givenchy's designs.

LE66
66 av des Champs-Elysées, 8th (01.53.53.33.80). M° George V. **Open** 11am-8pm Mon-Fri; 11.30am-8.30pm Sat; 2-8pm Sun. **Map** p59 D3 ㉜
This fashion concept store is youthful and accessible, with an ever-changing selection of hip brands. Assistants, who are also the buyers and designers, make for a motivated team. The store takes the form of three transparent modules, the first a bookstore run by Black Book of the Palais de Tokyo, and the second two devoted to fashion.

Louis Vuitton
101 av des Champs-Elysées, 8th (01.53.57.52.00, www.vuitton.com). M° George V. **Open** 10am-8pm Mon-Sat; 11am-7pm Sun. **Map** p58 C2 ㉝

The 'Promenade' flagship sets the tone for Vuitton's global image, from the 'bag bar', bookstore and new jewellery department to the women's and men's ready-to-wear.

Prada

10 av Montaigne, 8th (01.53.23.99.40, www.prada.com). Mº Alma Marceau. **Open** 11am-7pm Mon; 10am-7pm Tue-Sat. **Map** p58 C4 ➌➍

The high priestess of European chic, Miuccia Prada's elegant stores pull in fashion followers of all ages. Handbags of choice are complemented by the coveted ready-to-wear range.

Sephora

70 av des Champs-Elysées, 8th (01.53.93.22.50, www.sephora.fr). Mº Franklin D. Roosevelt. **Open** 10am-midnight Mon-Thur, Sun; 10am-1am Fri, Sat. **Map** p58 C3 ➌➎

The flagship of the cosmetic supermarket chain houses around 12,000 brands of scent and slap. Sephora Blanc (14 cour St-Emilion, 12th, 01.40.02.97.79) features beauty products in a minimalist interior.

Sony Style

39 av George V, 8th (09.69.39.39.39, www.boutiquegeorge5.fr). Mº George V. **Open** 10.30am-7.30pm Mon-Sat. **Map** p58 C3 ➌➏

Sony's concept store brings high-tech gadgets and zen decor together in an *hôtel particulier*. Phones, cameras, computers and PlayStations are all here, and the latest innovations from Japan are beamed in on big screens. The store also offers free IT coaching.

Virgin Megastore

52-60 av des Champs-Elysées, 8th (01.49.53.50.00, www.virginmega.fr). Mº Franklin D. Roosevelt. **Open** 10am-midnight Mon-Sat; noon-midnight Sun. **Map** p59 D3 ➌➐

The luxury of perusing CDs and DVDs until midnight makes this a choice spot, and the listening posts let you sample any CD. Tickets for concerts and sports events are available here too. This main branch has the best book selection.

Nightlife

L'Arc

12 rue de Presbourg, 16th (01.45.00.78.70, www.larc-paris.com). Mº Charles de Gaulle Etoile. **Open** *Restaurant* noon-2.30pm, 7-11pm Mon-Fri; 7-11pm Sat; 11am-4pm Sun. *Club* midnight-5am Fri, Sat. **Admission** free. **Map** p58 B2 ➌➑

Paris's jet set darlings have a new haunt in which to strut their stuff. L'Arc boldly steers away from the 'resto-lounge-club' formula that has taken Paris by storm over the last decade, instead focusing on design, discretion and a decent meal. On Fridays and Saturdays, once the plates are cleared away, it's party time in the cool 1960s-style club, awash with leather sofas and pink and blue lighting.

Le Baron

6 av Marceau, 8th (01.47.20.04.01, www.clublebaron.com). Mº Alma Marceau. **Open** 11pm-6am daily. **Admission** free. **Map** p58 C4 ➌➒

This small but supremely exclusive hangout for the international jet set only holds 150, most of whom are regulars you'll need to befriend in order to get past the door. But if you manage to get in, you'll be rubbing shoulders with celebrities and super-glossy people.

Le Lido

116bis av des Champs-Elysées, 8th (01.40.76.56.10, www.lido.fr). Mº Franklin D. Roosevelt or George V. **Lunch** 1pm. **Matinée** 3pm Tue, Sun (once a mth, dates vary). **Dinner** 7pm. **Shows** 9.30pm, 11.30pm daily. **Admission** *Matinée show* (incl champagne) €80. *Lunch & matinée show* (incl champagne) €130. *9.30pm show* (incl champagne) €100. *11.30pm show* (incl champagne) €90. *Dinner & show* €150-€280. *Show & backstage tour* €110-€120. **Map** p58 C2 ➍➓

PARIS BY AREA

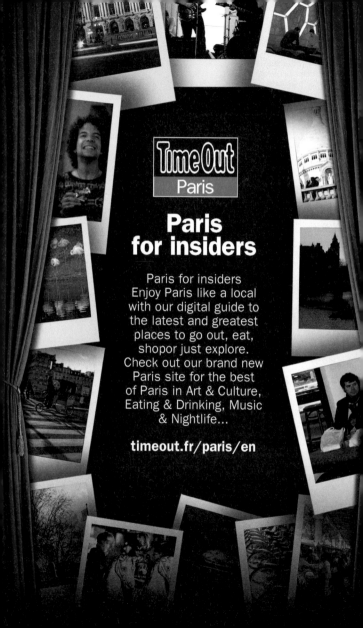

This is the largest cabaret of all: high-tech touches optimise visibility, and chef Philippe Lacroix provides fabulous gourmet nosh. On stage, 60 Bluebell Girls slink around, shaking their boobs with panache.

Queen

102 av des Champs-Elysées, 8th (01.53.89.08.90, www.queen.fr). Mº George V. **Open** midnight-7am Mon-Thur, Sun; midnight-8am Fri, Sat. **Admission** €15 Mon-Thur, Sun; €20 Fri, Sat. **Map** p58 C2 ⓸

Once the city's most fêted gay club and the only venue that could hold a torch to the Rex, with a roster of top local DJs holding court, Queen's star faded in the early noughties but is now starting to shine more brightly again.

Le Régine

49 rue de Ponthieu, 8th (01.40.39. 07.07, www.leregine.com) Mº St-Philippe-du-Roule. **Open** 7pm-5am Thur; midnight-6am Fri, Sat. **Admission** €10-€20. **Map** p59 D2 ⓺

Régine was once a key figure on the Paris nightlife scene, and the club she created is experiencing a rejuvenation. Her portrait still sits by the entrance for a touch of '70s nostalgia, but the revamped venue has shifted from disco to sophisticated electro, inviting the cream of international DJs to the decks.

Showcase

Underneath Pont Alexandre III, 8th (01.45.61.25.43, www.showcase.fr). Mº Champs-Elysées Clemenceau. **Open** 10pm-dawn Fri, Sat; 11am-3pm Sun. **Admission** free-€30. **Map** p59 E4 ⓻

This vast venue is where music-crazed insomniacs come on weekends to discover up-and-coming bands and dance until daybreak. The club has lost some of its hype over the last couple of years, but high-profile guest DJs have been setting the bar higher lately: Carol Cox, will.i.am and Calvin Harris have made appearances in the past couple of years.

Arts & leisure

Le Balzac

1 rue Balzac, 8th (01.45.61.10.60, www.cinemabalzac.com). Mº George V. **Admission** €9.50; €6-€7.50 reductions. No credit cards. **Map** p58 C2 ⓸

Built in 1935 and boasting a mock ocean-liner foyer, the Balzac scores highly for design and programming. Manager Jean-Jacques Schpoliansky often welcomes punters in person.

Salle Pleyel

252 rue du Fbg-St-Honoré, 8th (01.42.56.13.13, www.sallepleyel.fr). Mº Ternes. **Box office** noon-7pm Mon-Sat. *By phone* 11am-7pm Mon-Sat; 11am-5pm Sun. **Admission** €10-€160. **Map** p59 E2 ⓺

Home to the Orchestre de Paris, this restored concert hall has regained its prestigious status as the only venue dedicated to large-scale symphonic concerts in the capital.

Théâtre des Champs-Elysées

15 av Montaigne, 8th (01.49.52.50.50, www.theatrechampselysees.fr). Mº Alma Marceau. **Box office** noon-7pm Mon-Sat; 2hrs before show Sun. *By phone* 11am-6pm Mon-Fri, 2-6pm Sat. **Admission** €5-€160. **Map** p58 C4 ⓸

This beautiful art nouveau theatre, with bas-reliefs by Bourdelle, remains the favourite venue for touring foreign orchestras, with a prestigious line-up of visiting maestros.

Théâtre Marigny

Av de Marigny, 8th (08.92.22.23.33, www.theatremarigny.fr). Mº Champs-Elysées Clemenceau or Franklin D. Roosevelt. **Box office** 11am-6.30pm Mon-Sat; 11am-3pm Sun. **Admission** €25-€79. **Map** p59 E3 ⓻

Théâtre Marigny boasts a location off the Champs-Elysées, a deluxe interior conceived by Charles Garnier, high-profile casts and an illustrious pedigree stretching back some 150 years.

Musée du Louvre p74

Opéra to Les Halles

In centuries gone by, these two adjoining central districts – bounded by the Grands Boulevards to the north and the river to the south – were the city's commercial and provisioning powerhouses, home to most of the newspapers, banks and major mercantile institutions. Nowadays, although there is still a strong financial slant, thanks to the presence of the two stock exchanges and the Banque de France, the focus is on shopping: mass-market stuff in and around **Les Halles**, shading into more exclusive brands the further one moves west, in particular on and just off rue St-Honoré.

Les Halles itself was, famously, the city's wholesale food market until 1969, when the Second Empire iron-framed buildings that housed it were ripped out. The soulless shopping centre that filled the gap in the 1970s has been one of the city's least liked features, and is itself doomed to destruction in the next few years, to be replaced by a 21st-century glory of gardens, glass and open spaces (see box p78).

A short distance west of Les Halles is the **Louvre**, no longer the centre of French power though it still exerts considerable influence: first as a grandiose architectural ensemble, a palace within the city; and, second, as a symbol of the capital's cultural pre-eminence. Across rue de Rivoli from the Louvre stands the elegant **Palais-Royal**. After a stroll in its quiet gardens, it's hard to believe this was the starting point of the French Revolution. Today, its arcades house a mix of antiques dealers, philatelists and fashion showcases.

Sights & museums

La Collection 1900
Maxim's, 3 rue Royale, 8th (01.42.65. 30.47, www.maxims-musee-art nouveau.com). M° Madeleine. **Open** *Guided tours* (reservations essential)

2pm Wed-Sun (English); 3.15pm, 4.30pm (French). **Admission** €15. No credit cards. **Map** p72 A3 ❶

Couturier Pierre Cardin has owned belle époque restaurant Maxim's since 1981, and now he has added a museum of art nouveau, which he has been collecting since the age of 18. There are rooms and rooms of exhibits, arranged so as to evoke a 19th-century courtesan's boudoir. Read Zola's *Nana* before your visit to grasp the full effect of the dreamy lake maidens sculpted in glistening faience, pewter vanity sets in the shape of reclining nudes, and beds inlaid with opium flowers to promote sleep. Dinner settings on display include Gustav Eiffel's own chunky tureens, just crying out for turtle soup.

Eglise de la Madeleine

Pl de la Madeleine, 8th (01.44.51.69.00, www.eglise-lamadeleine.com). Mº Concorde or Madeleine. **Open** 9.30am-7pm daily. **Admission** free. **Map** p72 A2 ❷

The building of a church on this site began in 1764; in 1806 Napoleon sent instructions from Poland for Barthélémy Vignon to design a 'Temple of Glory' dedicated to his Grand Army. After the emperor's fall, construction slowed and the building, by now a church again, was finally consecrated in 1845. The exterior is ringed by fluted Corinthian columns, with a double row at the front, and a frieze of the Last Judgement above the portico. Inside are giant domes, an organ and pseudo-Grecian marble side altars.

Forum des Halles

1st. Mº Les Halles/RER Châtelet Les Halles. **Map** p73 E4 ❸

The labyrinthine mall and transport interchange extend for three levels underground and include the Ciné Cité multiplex and Forum des Images, as well as fashion chains and the Forum des Créateurs, a section dedicated to young designers. But all is changing from 2012 until 2016, with a new landscaping of the area. See box p78.

Jardin des Tuileries

Rue de Rivoli, 1st. Mº Concorde or Tuileries. **Open** *Apr, May* 7am-9pm daily; *June-Aug* 7am-11pm daily; *Sept-Mar* 7.30am-7.30pm daily. **Map** p72 B4 ❹

The gravelled alleyways of these gardens have been a chic promenade ever since they opened to the public in the 16th century. André Le Nôtre created the prototypical French garden with terraces and central vista running down the *Grand Axe* through circular and hexagonal ponds. As part of Mitterrand's Grand Louvre project, sculptures such as Coysevox's winged horses were transferred to the Louvre and replaced by copies, and the Maillol sculptures were returned to the Jardins du Carrousel; a handful of modern sculptures have been added, including bronzes by Moore, Ernst, Giacometti, and Dubuffet's *Le Bel Costumé*. A funfair sets up along the rue de Rivoli side during the summer.

Jeu de Paume

1 pl de la Concorde, 8th (01.47.03.12.50, www.jeudepaume.org). Mº Concorde. **Open** noon-9pm Tue; noon-7pm Wed-Fri; 10am-7pm Sat, Sun (last admission 30mins before closing). **Admission** €8.50; free-€5.50 reductions. **Map** p72 A3 ❺

The Centre National de la Photographie moved into this site in 2005. The building, which once served as a tennis court, has been divided into two whole, almost hangar-like galleries. It is not an intimate space, but it works well for showcase retrospectives. A video art and cinema suite in the basement shows new digital installation work.

Event highlights Manuel Álvarez Bravo (16 Oct 2012-20 Jan 2013)

Musée des Arts Décoratifs

107 rue de Rivoli, 1st (01.44.55. 57.50, www.lesartsdecoratifs.fr). Mº Palais Royal Musée du Louvre or Pyramides. **Open** 11am-6pm Tue, Wed, Fri-Sun; 11am-9pm Thur.

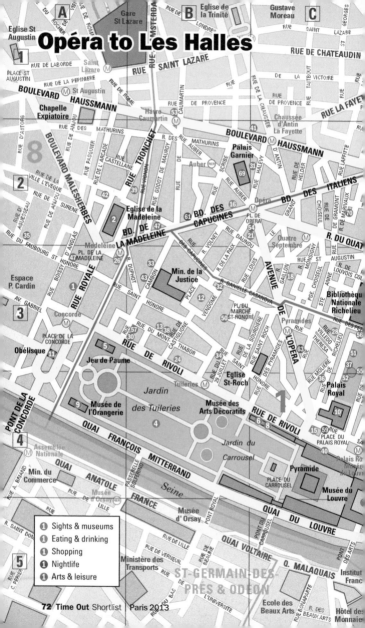

Opéra to Les Halles

Eglise St Augustin
Gare St Lazare
Eglise de la Trinité
Gustave Moreau

RUE DE CHATEAUDIN

PLACE ST AUGUSTIN

BOULEVARD HAUSSMANN

Chapelle Expiatoire

Palais Garnier

BOULEVARD HAUSSMANN

RUE LA FAYETTE

Chaussée d'Antin La Fayette

BOULEVARD MALESHERBES

Eglise de la Madeleine

BD. DES CAPUCINES

Opéra

BD. DES ITALIENS

R. DU QUAT

BD. DE LA MADELEINE

Espace P. Cardin

Min. de la Justice

Bibliothèque Nationale Richelieu

Concorde

Pyramides

Obélisque

Jeu de Paume

RUE DE RIVOLI

Eglise St-Roch

Palais Royal

Jardin des Tuileries

Musée des Arts Décoratifs

RUE DE RIVOLI

Musée de l'Orangerie

PLACE DE LA CONCORDE

Jardin du Carrousel

PLACE DU PALAIS ROYAL

QUAI FRANÇOIS MITTERRAND

Pyramide

Musée du Louvre

Assemblée Nationale

Min. du Commerce

QUAI ANATOLE FRANCE

Seine

PLACE DU CARROUSEL

QUAI DU LOUVRE

Musée d'Orsay

QUAI VOLTAIRE

Q. MALAQUAIS

Institut Franç

Ministère des Transports

ST-GERMAIN-DES-PRÈS & ODEON

Ecole des Beaux Arts

Hôtel des Monnaie

- **1** Sights & museums
- **1** Eating & drinking
- **1** Shopping
- **1** Nightlife
- **1** Arts & leisure

Admission (with Musée de la Mode & Musée de la Publicité) €9; free-€7.50 reductions. **Map** p72 C4 ❻

Taken as a whole along with the Musée de la Mode et du Textile and Musée de la Publicité, this is one of the world's major collections of design and the decorative arts. The major focus here is French furniture and tableware, from extravagant carpets to delicate crystal and porcelain. Of most obvious attraction to the layman are the reconstructed period rooms, ten in all, showing how the other half lived from the late 1400s to the early 20th century.

Musée du Louvre

Rue de Rivoli, 1st (01.40.20.50.50, www.louvre.fr). M° Palais Royal Musée du Louvre. **Open** 9am-6pm Mon, Thur, Sat, Sun; 9am-10pm Wed, Fri. **Admission** *Permanent collections* €10; free-€6 reductions. **Map** p72 C5 ❼

Some 35,000 works of art and artefacts are on show, divided into eight departments and housed in three wings: Denon, Sully and Richelieu. Treasures from the Egyptians, Etruscans, Greeks and Romans each have their own galleries in the Denon and Sully wings, as do Middle Eastern and Islamic works of art. The first floor of Richelieu is taken up with European decorative arts from the Middle Ages up to the 19th century.

The main draw, though, is the painting and sculpture. Two glass-roofed sculpture courts contain the Marly horses on the ground floor of Richelieu, with French sculpture below and Italian Renaissance pieces in the Denon wing. The Grande Galerie and Salle de la Joconde (home to the *Mona Lisa*) run the length of Denon's first floor with French Romantic painting alongside. Dutch and French painting occupies the second floor of Richelieu and Sully. Laminated panels provide a lively commentary, and the website is superb.

Work continues on the new Islamic Arts department, due to be completed in autumn 2012.

Musée de la Mode et du Textile

107 rue de Rivoli, 1st (01.44.55.57.50, www.lesartsdecoratifs.fr). M° Palais Royal Musée du Louvre or Pyramides. **Open** *Exhibitions* 11am-6pm Tue, Wed, Fri-Sun; 11am-9pm Thur. **Admission** (with Musée des Arts Décoratifs & Musée de la Publicité) €9; free-€7.50 reductions. **Map** p72 C4 ❽

This municipal fashion museum holds Elsa Schiaparelli's entire archive and hosts exciting themed exhibitions. Dramatic black-walled rooms make a fine background to the clothes, and video screens and a cinema space show how the clothes move, as well as interviews with the creators.

Event highlights Tromp l'œil – Imitations, pastiches et autres illusions (until 15 Nov 2013)

Musée de l'Orangerie

Jardin des Tuileries, 1st (01.44.77. 80.07, www.musee-orangerie.fr). M° Concorde. **Open** 9am-6pm Mon, Wed-Sun. **Admission** €7.50; free-€5 reductions. **Map** p72 A4 ❾

The look of this Monet showcase is utilitarian and fuss-free, with the museum's eight, tapestry-sized *Nymphéas* (water lilies) paintings housed in two plain oval rooms. They provide a simple backdrop for the ethereal romanticism of Monet's works, which he painted late in his life. Downstairs, the Jean Walter and Paul Guillaume collection of Impressionism and the Ecole de Paris is a mixed bag of sweet-toothed Cézanne and Renoir portraits, with works by Modigliani, Rousseau, Matisse, Picasso and Derain.

Palais-Royal

Pl du Palais-Royal, 1st. M° Palais Royal Musée du Louvre. **Open** *Gardens* 7.30am-8.30pm daily. **Admission** free. **Map** p72 C4 ❿

Built for Cardinal Richelieu by Jacques Lemercier, the building was once known as Palais Cardinal. Richelieu left it to Louis XIII, whose widow Anne d'Autriche preferred it to the Louvre

Musée de l'Orangerie

Collection
Jean Walter
et Paul Guillaume

and rechristened it when she moved in with her son, the young Louis XIV. In the 1780s, the Duc d'Orléans enclosed the gardens in a three-storey peristyle and filled it with cafés, shops, theatres, sideshows and accommodation to raise money for rebuilding the burned-down opera. Daniel Buren's striped columns grace the main courtyard.

Place de la Concorde

1st/8th. Mº Concorde. **Map** p72 A3 ⓫
This is the city's largest square, its grand east–west perspectives stretching from the Louvre to the Arc de Triomphe, and north–south from the Madeleine to the Assemblée Nationale across the Seine. In 1792, the centre statue of Louis XV was replaced with the guillotine for Louis XVI, Marie-Antoinette and many more.

Place Vendôme

1st. Mº Opéra or Tuileries.
Map p72 B3 ⓬
Elegant place Vendôme got its name from a *hôtel particulier* built by the Duc de Vendôme that stood on the site. Opened in 1699, the eight-sided square was conceived by Hardouin-Mansart to show off an equestrian statue of the Sun King, torn down in 1792 and replaced in 1806 by the Colonne de la Grande Armée. During the 1871 Commune, this symbol of 'brute force and false glory' was pulled down; the present column is a replica. At no.12, you can visit the Grand Salon where Chopin died in 1849.

Eating & drinking

L'Ardoise

28 rue du Mont-Thabor, 1st (01.42. 96.28.18, www.lardoise-paris.com). Mº Concorde or Tuileries. **Open** noon-2.30pm, 6.30-11pm Tue-Sat; 6.30-11pm Sun. Closed 1st 3wks Aug. **€€. Bistro. Map** p72 B3 ⓭
One of the city's finest modern bistros, L'Ardoise is regularly packed with gourmets eager to sample Pierre Jay's delicious cooking. A wise choice might be six oysters with warm chipolatas and pungent shallot dressing; equally attractive is a hare pie with an escalope of foie gras nestling in its centre. Unusually, it's open on Sundays.

La Bourse ou la Vie

12 rue Vivienne, 2nd (01.42.60.08.83). Mº Bourse. **Open** noon-10pm Mon-Fri. Closed 1wk Aug & 1wk Dec. **€€.**
Bistro. Map p73 D3 ⓮
After a career as an architect, the round-spectacled owner of La Bourse ou la Vie has a new mission in life: to revive the dying art of the perfect *steak-frites*. The only decision you'll need to make is which cut of beef to order with your chips, unless you pick the cod. Choose between ultra-tender *coeur de filet* or a huge, tender *bavette*. Rich, creamy pepper sauce is the speciality here, but the real surprise is the chips, which gain a distinctly animal flavour from the suet in which they are cooked.

Café Marly

93 rue de Rivoli, cour Napoléon, 1st (01.49.26.06.60). Mº Palais Royal Musée du Louvre. **Open** 8am-2am daily. **€€. Café. Map** p72 C4 ⓯
A class act, this, as you might expect of a Costes café whose lofty, arcaded terrace overlooks the Louvre's glass pyramid. It's reached through the passage Richelieu (the entrance for advance Louvre ticket holders), and the prime location comes at a price: it's €6 for a Heineken – so you might as well splash out €12 on a chocolate martini or a Shark of vodka, lemonade and grenadine. Most wines are under €10 a glass, and everything is impeccably served by razor-sharp staff.

Café de la Paix

12 bd des Capucines, 9th (01.40.07. 36.36, www.cafedelapaix.fr). Mº Opéra. **Open** 7am-midnight daily. **€€. Café. Map** p72 B2 ⓰
Lap up every detail – this is once-in-a-holiday stuff. Whether you're out on the historic terrace or looking up at the

ornate stucco ceiling, you'll be sipping in the footsteps of the likes of Oscar Wilde, Josephine Baker, Emile Zola, and Bartholdi and the Franco-American Union (as they sketched out the Statue of Liberty). Let the immaculate staff bring you a kir (€12) or, for an afternoon treat, the vanilla mille-feuille – possibly the best in Paris.

De la Ville Café

34 bd de Bonne-Nouvelle, 10th (01.48. 24.48.09, www.delavillecafe.com). M° Bonne Nouvelle. **Open** 11am-2am Mon-Sat; noon-2am Sun. **Bar**. **Map** p73 E2 **⑰**
De la Ville has brought good news to Bonne-Nouvelle. A major expansion and refurbishment have upped the ante. Inside, the distressed walls remain, but the curvy club section at the back has become very cool. A grand staircase leads to a first-floor lounge and exhibition space. The café was opened by the Café Charbon crew.

Drouant

18 pl Gaillon, 2nd (01.42.65.15.16, www.drouant.com). M° Pyramides or Quatre Septembre. **Open** noon-2.30pm, 7pm-midnight daily. **€€€**. **Brasserie**. **Map** p72 C3 **⑱**
Star chef Antoine Westermann has whisked this landmark brasserie into the 21st century with bronze-coloured banquettes and butter-yellow fabrics. Westermann has dedicated this restaurant to the art of the hors d'oeuvre, in themed sets of four ranging from global (Thai beef salad with brightly coloured vegetables) to nostalgic (silky leeks in vinaigrette). The bite-sized surprises continue with the main course accompaniments and multiple mini-desserts.

Frenchie

5 rue du Nil, 2nd (01.40.39.96.19, www.frenchie-restaurant.com). M° Sentier. **Open** 7-10.30pm Mon-Fri. **€€**. **Bistro**. **Map** p73 E3 **⑲**
Grégory Lemarchand honed his craft with Jamie Oliver in London before opening this loft-style bistro next to the

market street rue Montorgueil. It has been an instant hit, thanks to the bold flavours of dishes such as gazpacho with calamari, squash blossoms and plenty of herbs; braised lamb with roasted aubergine and spinach; and coconut tapioca with strawberry sorbet. Book several days ahead.

Le Fumoir

6 rue de l'Amiral-de-Coligny, 1st (01.42.92.00.24, www.lefumoir.fr). M° Louvre Rivoli. **Open** 11am-2am daily. Closed 2wks Aug. **Bar**. **Map** p73 D5 **⑳**
This elegant bar facing the Louvre has become a local institution: neo-colonial fans whirr lazily and oil paintings adorn the walls. A sleek crowd sips martinis or reads papers at the mahogany bar (originally from a Chicago speakeasy), giving way to young professionals in the restaurant and pretty things in the library. It can feel a touch try-hard, but expertly mixed cocktails should take the edge off any evening.

Harry's New York Bar

5 rue Daunou, 2nd (01.42.61.71.14, www.harrys-bar.fr). M° Opéra. **Open** noon-2am Mon-Thur, Sun; noon-3am Fri, Sat. **Bar**. **Map** p72 B2 **㉑**
The city's most stylish American bar is beloved of expats, visitors and hard-drinking Parisians. The bartenders mix some of the most sophisticated cocktails in town, from the trademark bloody mary (invented here, so they say) to the *Pétrifiant*, an elixir of half a dozen spirits splashed into a beer mug. Gershwin composed *An American in Paris* in the piano bar here.

Kaï

18 rue du Louvre, 1st (01.40.15.01.99). M° Louvre Rivoli. **Open** 12.30-2.15pm, 7.30-10.30pm Tue-Sat; 7.30-10.30pm Sun. Closed 1wk Apr & 3wks Aug. **€€€**. **Japanese**. **Map** p73 D4 **㉒**
This restaurant has developed a following among fashionable diners. The 'Kaï-style' sushi is a zesty take on a classic: marinated and lightly grilled yellowtail

All change at Les Halles

Mayor Delanoë's plans for the shopping mall are under way.

Forum des Halles

On the night of 4 March 1969, Les Halles' wholesale food market transplanted to the suburb of Rungis, turning the 'belly' of Paris into its '*trou*'. Left with a giant hole in the middle of the city, Paris's then mayor, Jacques Chirac, could have done something great. But he created an urban nightmare – a sprawling underground shopping mall covered with a park that became the haunt of drug addicts. Now it's Mayor Bertrand Delanoë's turn to put it right.

Eight years of public consultations have dragged out the affair, but in 2010 work tentatively began with the laying out of a children's playground. The horrendous, mirror-fronted Willerval pavilions, a pastiche of the old Baltard pavilions housing a variety of public services, were destroyed the following year and work began on revamping the underground traffic tunnels that alienate pedestrians and cyclists. But the new Les Halles has really started to take shape in 2012, with a revamp of the park and the building of a canopy over the shopping mall that will allow in natural light and air. The project is due to be completed in 2016.

Despite the hype, though, Parisians seem unexcited. Rebuilding something approximating the old Baltard market pavilions could have restored the heart that is now lacking in the neighbourhood. And a larger park is great, but how will it be policed at night? And, notwithstanding the addition of a hip hop studio, the five subterranean floors of shopping will remain the preserve of *banlieusards*, shooting in on the RER to buy a new pair of trainers. Despite his good intentions, Delanoë may rue the day he tried to revive Chirac's white elephant.

is pressed on to a roll of shiso-scented rice. Not to be outdone, grilled aubergine with miso, seemingly simple, turns out to be a smoky, luscious experience. A main of breaded pork lacks the finesse of the starters, but is still satisfying.

Liza

14 rue de la Banque, 2nd (01.55.35. 00.66, www.restaurant-liza.com). M° Bourse. **Open** 12.30-2pm, 8-10.30pm Mon-Thur; 12.30-2pm, 8-11pm Fri; 8-11pm Sat; noon-4pm Sun. **€€**. **Lebanese**. Map p73 D3 ㉓
Liza Soughayar's eatery showcases the style and superb food of Beirut. Lentil, fried onion and orange salad is delicious, as are the *kebbe* (minced seasoned raw lamb) and grilled halloumi cheese with home-made apricot preserve. Main courses such as minced lamb with coriander-spiced spinach and rice are light, flavoursome and well presented.

Le Meurice

Hôtel Meurice, 228 rue de Rivoli, 1st (01.44.58.10.55, www.meuricehotel.com). M° Tuileries. **Open** 7-10.30am, 12.30-2pm, 7.30-10pm Mon-Fri; 7-11am Sat, Sun. Closed 2wks Feb & Aug. **€€€€**. **Haute cuisine**. Map p72 B3 ㉔
Chef Yannick Alléno produces some glorious, if rather understated, dishes, teasing the flavour out of every leaf, frond, fin or fillet. A fine cheese tray comes from Quatrehomme, and the pastry chef amazes with his signature millefeuille.

Ô Château

🆕 *68 rue Jean-Jacques Rousseau, 1st (01.44.73.97.80, www.o-chateau.com). M° Les Halles.* **Open** noon-midnight Mon-Wed, Sun; noon-2am Thur-Sat. **Wine bar**. Map p73 D4 ㉕
Sommelier Olivier Magny's spacious, convivial wine bar has been a great success since opening in 2011. There are no fewer than 40 wines available by the glass here, with the chance to taste some very rare bottles in *soupçon*-sized quantities. Thrice-daily tastings take place in the intimate tasting rooms.

Senderens

9 pl de la Madeleine, 8th (01.42.65. 22.90, www.senderens.fr). M° Madeleine. **Open** noon-2.45pm, 7.30-11pm daily. Closed 3wks Aug. **€€€€**. **Haute cuisine**. Map p72 A3 ㉖
Alain Senderens reinvented his art nouveau institution (formerly Lucas Carton) a few years ago with a *Star Trek* interior and a mind-boggling fusion menu. You might find dishes such as roast duck foie gras with a warm salad of black figs and liquorice powder. Each dish comes with a suggested wine, whisky, sherry or punch.

Le Tambour

41 rue Montmartre, 2nd (01.42.33. 06.90). M° Sentier. **Open** 8am-6am daily. **Bar**. Map p73 D3 ㉗
The Tambour is a classic nighthawk's bar decked with vintage public transport paraphernalia, its slatted wooden banquettes and bus stop-sign bar stools occupied by chatty regulars who give the 24-hour clock their best shot. Neither tatty nor threatening, there's a long dining room memorable for its métro map from Stalingrad station.

Thaïm

46 rue de Richelieu, 1st (01.42.96. 54.67). M° Bourse or Palais Royal. **Open** noon-3pm, 7-11.30pm Mon-Fri; 7-11pm Sat. **€**. **Thai**. Map p72 C3 ㉘
Thaïm has an elegant decor of dark wood and plum fabrics. Particularly good value is the three-course lunch menu, which might bring crisp fried parcels filled with spiced vegetables, an aromatic green fish curry (there is a choice of fish, meat or poultry every day), and coconut-pumpkin soup. There is a vast choice of teas, including an iced ginger-coconut version.

Shopping

Agnès b

2, 3, 6 & 19 rue du Jour, 1st (men 01.42.33.04.13, women 01.45.08. 56.56, www.agnesb.com). M° Les

Halles. **Open** *Oct-Apr* 10am-7pm Mon-Sat. *May-Sept* 10am-7.30pm Mon-Sat. **Map** p73 D4 ㉙

Agnès b rarely wavers from her design vision: pure lines in fine quality cotton, merino wool and silk. Best buys are shirts, pullovers and cardigans. Her mini-empire of men's, women's, children's, travel and sportswear shops is compact; see the website for details.

Alice Cadolle

4 rue Cambon, 1st (01.42.60.94.22, www.cadolle.com). M° Concorde or Madeleine. **Open** 10am-6.30pm Mon-Sat. Closed Aug. **Map** p72 B3 ㉚

Five generations of lingerie-makers are behind this boutique, founded by Hermine Cadolle, who claimed to be the inventor of the bra. Poupie Cadolle continues the tradition in a cosy space devoted to a luxury ready-to-wear line of bras, panties and corsets. For a special treat, Cadolle Couture (255 rue St-Honoré, 1st, 01.42.60.94.94) will create bespoke lingerie (by appointment only).

Apple Store

12 rue Halévy, 9th (01.44.83.42.00, www.apple.com). M° Opéra. **Open** 9am-8pm Mon-Wed; 9am-9pm Thur-Sat. **Map** p72 C2 ㉛

Apple's second Paris store opened in 2010 in a stunning belle époque former bank facing the Opéra Garnier. To fit in with such hallowed surroundings, Apple strayed from its standard model, retaining the original carved wooden staircase, wrought-iron railings, marble columns and mosaic tile floor.

Boucheron

26 pl Vendôme, 1st (01.42.61.58.16, www.boucheron.com). M° Opéra. **Open** 10.30am-7pm Mon-Sat. **Map** p72 B3 ㉜

Boucheron was the first to set up shop on place Vendôme, attracting celebrity custom from the nearby Ritz hotel. Owned by Gucci, the grand jeweller produces stunning pieces, using traditional motifs with new accents: take, for example, its chocolate-coloured gold watch.

Chanel

31 rue Cambon, 1st (01.42.86.26.00, www.chanel.com). M° Concorde or Madeleine. **Open** 10am-7pm Mon-Sat. **Map** p72 B3 ㉝

Fashion legend Chanel has managed to stay relevant, thanks to Karl Lagerfeld. Coco opened her first boutique in this street, at no.21, in 1910, and the tradition continues in this elegant interior. Lagerfeld has been designing for Chanel since 1983, and keeps on revamping the classics – the little black dress and the Chanel suit – with great success.

Colette

213 rue St-Honoré, 1st (01.55.35.33.90, www.colette.fr). M° Pyramides or Tuileries. **Open** 11am-7pm Mon-Sat. **Map** p72 B3 ㉞

The renowned one-stop concept and lifestyle store features a highly eclectic selection of accessories, fashion, books, media, gadgets, and hair and beauty brands, all in a swanky space.

Comme des Garçons

54 rue du Fbg-St-Honoré, 8th (01.53.30.27.27). M° Concorde or Madeleine. **Open** 11am-7pm Mon-Sat. **Map** p72 A2 ㉟

Rei Kawakubo's design ideas and revolutionary mix of materials have influenced fashions of the past two decades, and are showcased in this fibreglass store. Comme des Garçons Parfums (23 pl du Marché-St-Honoré, 1st, 01.47.03.15.03) provides a futuristic setting for the brand's fragrances.

Designpack Gallery

24 rue de Richelieu, 1st (01.44.85.86.00, www.designpackgallery.fr). M° Palais Royal Musée du Louvre. **Open** 11am-7pm Mon-Fri; noon-7.30pm Sat. **Map** p72 C4 ㊱

Fabrice Peltier is passionate about the art of *emballage*, to the extent of opening his own gallery-boutique. Once a Tetrapak designer, he now recycles his own used packaging into desirable objects: red plastic bottles become lighting and clothes hangers, and bottle tops are melted down to become a multi-coloured armchair. African tin trinkets, Austrian vases made from cut-down bottles, and other ingenious recycling is also on sale.

Didier Ludot

20-24 galerie de Montpensier, 1st (01.42.96.06.56, www.didierludot.fr). Mº Palais Royal Musée du Louvre. **Open** 11am-7pm Mon-Sat. **Map** p72 C3 ③

Didier Ludot's temples to vintage haute couture appear in Printemps, Harrods and New York's Barneys. The pieces are stunning: Dior, Molyneux, Balenciaga, Pucci, Féraud and Chanel, from the 1920s onwards. Ludot also curates exhibitions, using the shop windows around the Palais-Royal as a gallery. La Petite Robe Noire (125 galerie de Valois, 1st, 01.40.15.01.04) stocks Ludot's own line of vintage little black dresses.

Eglé Bespoke

26 rue du Mont-Thabor, 1st (01.44.15.98.31, www.eglebespoke. com). Mº Concorde. **Open** 11am-7pm Mon-Sat. **Map** p72 B3 ③

Two young entrepreneurs are reviving bespoke for a new generation. Custom shirts start from €119 and can be delivered in a week or so; they will also make or copy shirts for women and produce made-to-order jeans for both sexes.

Erès

2 rue Tronchet, 8th (01.47.42.28.82, www.eres.fr). Mº Madeleine. **Open** 10am-7pm Mon-Sat. **Map** p72 B2 ③

Erès's beautifully cut swimwear has embraced a sexy '60s look, with buttons on low-cut briefs. The top and bottom can be purchased in different sizes, or you can buy one piece of a bikini.

La Galerie du Carrousel du Louvre

99 rue de Rivoli, 1st (01.43.16.47.10, www.lecarrouseldulouvre.com). Mº Palais Royal Musée du Louvre. **Open** 10am-8pm daily. **Map** p72 C4 ④

This massive underground centre – open every day of the year – is home to more than 35 shops, mostly big-name chains vying for your attention and cash. Options include the Apple Store, Virgin Megastore, Swatch Store and L'Occitane en Provence.

Galeries Lafayette

40 bd Haussmann, 9th (01.42.82. 34.56, fashion shows 01.42.82.30.25, fashion advice 01.42.82.35.50, www. galerieslafayette.com). Mº Chaussée d'Antin/RER Auber. **Open** 9.30am-8pm Mon-Wed, Fri, Sat; 9.30am-9pm Thur. **Map** p72 C2 ④

Espace Luxe on the first floor features luxury prêt-à-porter and accessories and nine avant-garde designers, and a vast shoe department is home to some 150 brands. The men's fashion space on the third floor, Lafayette Homme, has natty designer corners and a 'Club' area with internet access. On the first floor, Lafayette Gourmet has exotic foods galore, and a wine cellar. Lafayette Maison over the road has five floors of home furnishings and design.

Hédiard

21 pl de la Madeleine, 8th (01.43.12. 88.88, www.hediard.fr). Mº Madeleine. **Open** 9am-8.30pm Mon-Sat. **Map** p72 A2 ④

Hédiard's charming shop dates back to 1880, when it was the first to introduce exotic foods to Paris, specialising in rare teas and coffees, spices, jams and candied fruits. Pop upstairs for a cuppa in the shop's posh tearoom.

Hervé Léger

24 rue Cambon, 1st (01.42.60.02.00, www.herveleger.com). Mº Concorde. **Open** 10am-7pm Mon-Sat. **Map** p72 B3 ④

A couple of decades ago, Hervé Léger's silhouette-cinching bandage dresses were as evocative of the era as supermodels Linda, Christy, Naomi and Cindy. But somewhere in the mid-'90s women lost their love of Lycra. In the

Colette p80

past few seasons, however, updated reinterpretations of Léger's style, by the likes of Christopher Kane and Marios Schwab, have been nothing short of a fashion phenomenon. Less modified versions, sold by the Léger label itself (now owned and designed by Max Azria of BCBG fame), have been less critically acclaimed.

Jean-Paul Gaultier

6 rue Vivienne, 2nd (01.42.86.05.05, www.jeanpaulgaultier.com). M° Bourse. **Open** 10.30am-7pm Mon-Fri; 11am-7pm Sat. **Map** p73 D3 ㊹
Having celebrated his 30th year in the fashion business, Gaultier is still going strong. His boudoir boutique stocks men's and women's ready-to-wear and the reasonably priced JPG Jeans lines. The haute couture department is by appointment only.

Kiliwatch

64 rue Tiquetonne, 2nd (01.42.21. 17.37, www.espacekiliwatch.fr). M° Etienne Marcel. **Open** 2-7.15pm Mon; 11am-7.45pm Tue-Sat. **Map** p73 E3 ㊺
The trailblazer of the rue Etienne-Marcel revival is filled with hoodies, casual shirts and jeans. Brands include Gas, Edwin and Pepe Jeans.

Kokon To Zai

48 rue Tiquetonne, 2nd (01.42.36. 92.41, www.kokontozai.co.uk). M° Etienne Marcel. **Open** 11.30am-7.30pm Mon-Sat. **Map** p73 E4 ㊻
This tiny style emporium is sister to the Kokon To Zai in London. The neon-lit club feel of the mirrored interior matches the dark glamour of the designs. Unique pieces straight off the catwalk share space with creations by Marjan Peijoski, Noki, Raf Simons, Ziad Ghanem and new Norwegian designers.

Lanvin

22 rue du Fbg St-Honoré, 8th (01.44.71. 31.73, www.lanvin.com). M° Concorde or Madeleine. **Open** 10.30am-7pm daily. **Map** p72 A3 ㊼

The couture house that began in the 1920s with Jeanne Lanvin has been reinvented by the indefatigable Albert Elbaz. In October 2007, he unveiled this revamped showroom that set new aesthetic standards for luxury fashion retailing. Lanvin has an exhibition room devoted to her in the Musée des Arts Décoratifs, and this apartment-boutique also incorporates original furniture from the Lanvin archive. All this would be nothing, of course, if the clothes themselves were not exquisite.

Lavinia

3 bd de la Madeleine, 1st (01.42.97.20. 20, www.lavinia.fr). M° Madeleine. **Open** 10am-8pm Mon-Sat. **Map** p72 B2 ㊽
Lavinia stocks a broad selection of French and non-French wines; its *cave* has everything from a 1945 Mouton-Rothschild at €22,000 to trendy and 'fragile' wines for under €10. Have fun tasting wine with the *dégustation* machines on the ground floor, which allow customers to taste a sip of up to ten different wines each week for €10.

Legrand Filles et Fils

1 rue de la Banque, 2nd (01.42.60. 07.12, www.caves-legrand.com). M° Bourse. **Open** 11am-7pm Mon; 10am-7.30pm Tue-Fri; 10am-7pm Sat. Closed Mon in July & Aug. **Map** p73 D3 ㊾
Fine wines, teas and *bonbons*, and a showroom for regular wine tastings.

Marc by Marc Jacobs

19 pl du Marché-Saint-Honoré, 1st (01.40.20.11.30, www.marcjacobs.com). M° Tuileries. **Open** 11am-7pm Mon-Sat. **Map** p72 B3 ㊿
The store for Jacobs' casual, punky line has fashionistas clustering like bees round a honeypot, not least for the fabulously inexpensive accessories that add spice to a tired outfit. A skateboard table and giant pedalo in the form of a swan are the centrepieces of the store, which stocks men's and women's prêt-à-porter, shoes and special editions.

Marc Jacobs

34 galerie de Montpensier, 1st (01.55.35.02.60, www.marcjacobs.com). M° Palais Royal Musée du Louvre. **Open** 11am-7pm Mon-Sat. **Map** p72 C3 (51)

Marc Jacobs brought new life and verve – and an influx of fashionistas – to these elegant cloisters. Stocking womenswear, menswear, accessories and shoes, the shop has become a place of pilgrimage for the designer's legion of admirers.

Martin Margiela

23 & 25bis rue de Montpensier, 1st (womenswear 01.40.15.07.55, menswear 01.40.15.06.44, www.maisonmartinmargiela.com). M° Palais Royal Musée du Louvre. **Open** 11am-7pm Mon-Sat. **Map** p72 C4 (52)

This Paris outlet is a pristine, white, unlabelled space. Martin Margiela's collection for women (Line 1) has a blank label but is recognisable by external white stitching. You'll also find Line 6 (women's basics) and Line 10 (menswear), plus accessories for men and women and shoes.

Printemps

64 bd Haussmann, 9th (01.42.82.50.00, www.printemps.com). M° Havre Caumartin/RER Auber. **Open** 9.35am-8pm Mon-Wed, Fri, Sat; 9.35am-10pm Thur. **Map** p72 B1 (53)

Fashion is where Printemps excels; an entire floor is devoted to shoes, and the beauty department stocks more than 200 brands. In Printemps de la Mode, French designers sit alongside the big international designers. The Fashion Loft offers a younger take on current trends. Printemps de la Maison stocks everything from everyday tableware to design classics. For refuelling, there's a tearoom, sushi bar and Café Be, an Alain Ducasse bakery.

Repetto

22 rue de la Paix, 2nd (01.44.71.83.12, www.repetto.com). M° Opéra. **Open** 9.30am-7.30pm Mon-Sat. **Map** p72 B2 (54)

This ballet shoe-maker struck gold when it decided to reissue its dance shoes with pavement soles several years ago. The prowly *ballerines* and showbiz dance boots in black, metallic and spangly finishes are fun, timelessly stylish and exceptionally comfortable. The shoes are sold alongside the full range of real balletwear; what's more. you can try out your *pointes* on a red carpet with a *barre* if you want to show off.

Salons du Palais-Royal Shiseido

Jardins du Palais-Royal, 142 galerie de Valois, 1st (01.49.27.09.09, www.sergelutens.com). M° Palais Royal Musée du Louvre. **Open** 10am-7pm Mon-Sat. **Map** p72 C3 (55)

Under the arcades of the Palais-Royal, Shiseido's perfumier Serge Lutens practises his aromatic arts. A former photographer at Paris *Vogue* and artistic director of make-up at Christian Dior, Lutens is a maestro of rare taste. Bottles of his concoctions – Tubéreuse Criminelle, Rahat Loukoum and Ambre Sultan – can be sampled by visitors. Look out for Fleurs d'Oranger, which the great man defines as the smell of happiness itself. Many of the perfumes are exclusive to the Salons; prices start at around €100.

Stella McCartney

114-121 galerie du Valois, Jardin du Palais-Royal, 1st (01.47.03.03.80, www.stellamccartney.com). M° Palais Royal Musée du Louvre. **Open** 10.30am-7pm Mon-Sat. **Map** p72 C3 (56)

Stella McCartney is crazy about the 'clash of history, fashion and contemporary art' at the Palais-Royal, where she has opened her sumptuous boutique. Thick carpets, maplewood and metal sculptures create a rarefied setting for women's prêt-à-porter, bags, shoes, sunglasses and her range of simple but stylish lingerie, as well as the perfume and skincare lines.

Yohji Yamamoto

4 rue Cambon, 1st (01.40.20.00.71, www.yohjiyamamoto.co.jp). M° Concorde. **Open** 10.30am-7pm Mon-Sat. **Map** p72 B3 ⑤⑦
Yamamoto has achieved his dream of having a flagship store on rue Cambon. This temple to the creator is as impressive as those in New York and Antwerp, a pristine white gallery space. Behind an origami-screen window mannequins clothed in his showpieces seem to float in the air. A grand staircase leads to womenswear on the first floor, while menswear is on the lower ground.

Nightlife

Au Duc des Lombards

42 rue des Lombards, 1st (01.42.33. 22.88, www.ducdeslombards.com). M° Châtelet. **Open** *Concerts* 8pm Mon-Sat. Closed mid Aug. **Admission** €18-€25. **Map** p73 E5 ⑤⑧
Some of the capital's venerated jazz spots have lost the fight for survival in recent years. But this one has endured, and attracts a high class of performer and a savvy crowd.

Le Cab

2 pl du Palais-Royal, 1st (01.58.62. 56.25, www.cabaret.fr). M° Palais Royal Musée du Louvre. **Open** 11.30pm-5am Thur-Sat. *Restaurant* 8-11.30pm Tue-Sat. **Admission** free Tue, Wed; €20 Thur-Sat. **Map** p72 C4 ⑤⑨
Le Cab is owned by the management behind Club Mix and Queen, and R&B and commercial house dominate the playlist. The doormen are tough, and if they don't like you, you won't get in (unless you've booked for dinner).

Chacha Club

47 rue Berger, 1st (01.40.13.12.12, www.chachaclub.fr). M° Châtelet. **Open** 8pm-6am Tue-Sat. **Admission** varies. **Map** p73 D4 ⑥⓪
Paris's fetishistic obsession with the cigarette has produced a new nightlife phenomenon: the fumoir. The Chacha Club was the first high-profile establishment to open one, and it forms just one of the sexy attributes of this hot haunt near Les Halles. It combines restaurant, bar and club in a suite of rooms with 1930s-inspired decor.

Olympia

28 bd des Capucines, 9th (08.92. 68.33.68, www.olympiahall.com). M° Opéra. **Open** *Box office* noon-7pm daily. *Concerts* times vary. **Map** p72 B2 ⑥①
The Beatles, Frank Sinatra, Jimi Hendrix and Edith Piaf have all performed here over the years. Now it's mostly home to nostalgia and *variété*.

Rex

5 bd Poissonnière, 2nd (01.42.36. 10.96, www.rexclub.com). M° Bonne Nouvelle. **Open** 11.30pm-6am Wed-Sat. **Admission** free-€15. **Map** p73 E2 ⑥②
The Rex's sound system puts over 40 different sound configurations at the DJ's fingertips. Once associated with techno pioneer Laurent Garnier, the Rex still occupies an unassailable position as the city's serious club music venue.

Le Scop'Club

NEW *5 av de l'Opéra, 8th (01.42.60. 64.45, www.scopitoneclub.com). M° Pyramides.* **Open** from 7pm Tue-Sat. *Club* midnight-5am Thur-Sat. **Admission** free. **Map** p72 C3 ⑥③
This small club is all about electro-rock, with black-painted walls and live acts taking to the stage at weekends. Gigs aren't free, but DJ sets by the likes of MGMT and 'music label battles' are interesting alternatives on other nights. The crowd is young and dressed to impress, but the Scop'Club is easier to get into than when it was Paris Paris.

Silencio

142 rue de Montmartre, 2nd (www.silencio-club.com). M° Bourse or Grands Boulevards. **Open** 6pm-6am Tue-Sun. **Admission** varies. **Map** p73 D3 ⑥④

David Lynch's first Paris joint, named after the cult setting in his 2001 movie *Mulholland Drive*, is mainly for private members. The director designed every aspect of the decor, from the gold-leaf walls to the 1950s-style furniture.

Théâtre du Châtelet

1 pl du Châtelet, 1st (01.40.28.28.40, www.chatelet-theatre.com). M° Châtelet. **Open** times vary. **Admission** €25-€150. **Map** p73 E5 **65**

This venerable theatre and classic music hall has another life as a jazz and *chanson* venue, with performances by top-notch international musicians.

Toro

74 rue Jean-Jacques-Rousseau, 1st (01.44.76.00.03, www.toroparis.com). M° Les Halles. **Open** *DJ sets* 10pm-2am Thur-Sun. **Admission** free. **Map** p73 D4 **66**

This no-frills tapas bar hides a small but wonderfully wacky dancefloor down in the basement where DJs mix up house music with flamenco tunes.

Arts & leisure

Châtelet – Théâtre Musical de Paris

1 pl du Châtelet, 1st (01.40.28.28.40, www.chatelet-theatre.com). M° Châtelet. **Box office** 10am-7pm Mon-Sat; 1hr before performance Sun. *By phone* 10am-7pm Mon-Sat. Closed July, Aug. **Admission** €20-€111.50. **Map** p73 E5 **67**

The Châtelet is fast becoming Paris's main venue for musicals hailing from Broadway and the West End – such as *The Sound of Music* – which are usually performed in the original language by visiting companies.

Forum des Images

2 Grande Galerie, Porte St-Eustache, Forum des Halles, 1st (01.44.76.63.00, www.forumdesimages.net). M° Les Halles. **Admission** (per day) €4-€5. **Map** p73 E4 **68**

The Forum was conceived partly as a screening venue for old and little-known movies, and partly as an archive centre for every kind of moving picture featuring Paris; today, the collection numbers over 6,500 documentaries, adverts, newsreels and films.

Opéra National de Paris, Palais Garnier

Pl de l'Opéra, 9th (08.92.89.90.90, www.operadeparis.fr). M° Opéra. **Box office** 11.30am-6.30pm Mon-Sat. *By phone* 9am-6pm Mon-Fri; 9am-1pm Sat. **Admission** €8-€180. **Map** p72 B2 **69**

The Palais Garnier is the jewel in the crown of Paris music-making. The Opéra National often favours the high-tech Bastille for new productions, but the matchless acoustics of the Palais Garnier are superior to the new house.

Théâtre National de l'Opéra Comique

Pl Boïeldieu, 2nd (01.42.44.45.40, www.opera-comique.com). M° Richelieu Drouot. **Box office** 11am-7pm Mon-Sat; 11am-5pm Sun. *By phone* 11am-7pm Mon-Sat; 11am-5pm Sun. **Admission** €6-€115. **Map** p72 C2 **70**

Its promotion to national theatre status has brought this jewel box of a theatre back to life and the opening seasons, exploring a specifically French repertoire often ignored by larger houses, have been welcomed with enthusiasm. Event highlights Marc-Antoine Charpentier's David et Jonathas (Jan 2013)

Théâtre de la Ville

2 pl du Châtelet, 4th (01.42.74.22.77, www.theatredelaville-paris.com). M° Châtelet. **Box office** 11am-7pm Mon; 11am-8pm Tue-Sat. **Admission** €10-€34. **Map** p73 E5 **71**

Programming features hip chamber music outfits such as the Kronos and Takács Quartets, Early Music pioneer Fabio Biondi, and soloists like pianist Aleksandar Madzar.

Montmartre & Pigalle

Perched on a hill (or *butte*), Montmartre is the highest point in Paris, its tightly packed houses spiralling round the mound below the dome of **Sacré-Coeur**. Despite the many tourists, it's surprisingly easy to fall under the spell of this romantic district. Climb stairways, peer down alleys and into ivy-covered houses and quiet squares, and explore streets such as rue des Abbesses, rue des Trois-Frères and rue des Martyrs, with their cafés, boutiques and bohemian residents.

At the bottom of the hill, in once-notorious Pigalle, the seediness of yesteryear's sex clubs and brothels is steadily being replaced by hot music venues and nightspots.

Sights & museums

Cimetière de Montmartre
20 av Rachel, access by staircase from rue Caulaincourt, 18th

(01.53.42.36.30). M° Blanche or Place de Clichy. **Open** *6 Nov-15 Mar* 8am-5.30pm Mon-Fri; 8.30am-5.30pm Sat; 9am-5.30pm Sun, public hols. *16 Mar-5 Nov* 8am-6pm Mon-Fri; 8.30am-6pm Sat; 9am-6pm Sun, public hols. **Admission** free. **Map** p89 A1 ❶
Truffaut, Nijinsky, Berlioz, Degas, Offenbach and German poet Heine are all buried here. So, too, are La Goulue, the first great cancan star, and consumptive heroine Alphonsine Plessis, inspiration for *La Traviata*. Flowers are still left on the grave of diva Dalida.

Musée d'Art Halle St-Pierre
2 rue Ronsard, 18th (01.42.58.72.89, www.hallesaintpierre.org). M° Anvers. **Open** *Jan-July, Sept-Dec* 10am-6pm Mon-Fri; 10am-7pm Sat; 11am-6pm Sun. *Aug* noon-6pm Mon-Fri. **Admission** prices vary. **Map** p89 C2 ❷
The former market in the shadow of Sacré-Coeur specialises in *art brut, art outsider* and *art singulier* from its own and other collections.

Mummy's boys

A restaurant offering tasty bites of French *jeunesse*.

Four thirtysomething friends, all formerly club-night promoters for Wagg, are behind a nostalgic concept that has led to the opening of five separate restaurants in Paris – all offering simple, hearty food, like their mothers used to make.

The mothership is **Les Fils à Maman** (see p91) in the newly bobo 9th arrondissement. The vibe in both rooms of the restaurant is *géniale*, with a party atmosphere in the first room and comic books and board games lining the second space. Foodwise, begin with the signature Babybel fried with three different coatings, or plump for the standout goat's cheese and aubergine starter. The *cordon blue* of *magret de canard* (duck breast) and Beaufort cheese is also top-notch, while desserts are noticeably in keeping with the teenage theme – think Kinder eggs on an apple nest – although slightly more grown-up choices, such as apple tart, are also available.

Aside from Les Fils à Maman, there is **Le Club des 5** in Batignolles; **Le Clan de Jules**, also in the 17th, with speakeasy overtones; **Les Athlètes**, evoking a boy's bedroom with boxing gloves and football annuals; and – perhaps most inexplicably to the English – **Le Petit Resto dans la Prairie**; the cult series it mimics is adored by the French.

Musée de l'Erotisme

72 bd de Clichy, 18th (01.42.58.28.73, www.musee-erotisme.com). Mº Blanche. **Open** 10am-2am daily. **Admission** €9; €6 reductions. **Map** p89 A2 ❸
Seven floors of erotic art and artefacts. The first three run from first-century Peruvian phallic pottery through Etruscan fertility symbols to Yoni sculptures from Nepal; the fourth gives a history of Paris brothels; the top floors host exhibitions of erotic art.

Musée de Montmartre

12 rue Cortot, 18th (01.49.25.89.37, www.museedemontmartre.fr). Mº Abbesses. **Open** 10am-6pm daily. **Admission** €8; free-€6 reductions. **Map** p89 B1 ❹
At the back of a garden, this 17th-century manor house displays the history of the hilltop, with rooms devoted to composer Gustave Charpentier and a tribute to the Lapin Agile cabaret, with Toulouse-Lautrec posters.

Musée National Gustave Moreau

14 rue de la Rochefoucauld, 9th (01.48.74.38.50, www.musee-moreau.fr). Mº Trinité. **Open** 10am-12.45pm, 2-5.15pm Mon, Wed, Thur; 10am-5.15pm Fri-Sun. **Admission** €5; free-€3 reductions. **Map** p89 A4 ❺
This wonderful museum combines the private apartment of Symbolist painter Gustave Moreau (1825-98) with the vast gallery he built to display his work. Don't miss the trippy masterpiece *Jupiter et Sémélé* on the second floor.

Musée de la Vie Romantique

Hôtel Scheffer-Renan, 16 rue Chaptal, 9th (01.55.31.95.67, www.vie-romantique.paris.fr). Mº Blanche or St-Georges. **Open** 10am-6pm Tue-Sun. **Admission** free. **Exhibitions** €9; free-€3.30 reductions. **Map** p89 A3 ❻
When Dutch artist Ary Scheffer lived in this small villa, the area teemed with composers, writers and artists. Aurore

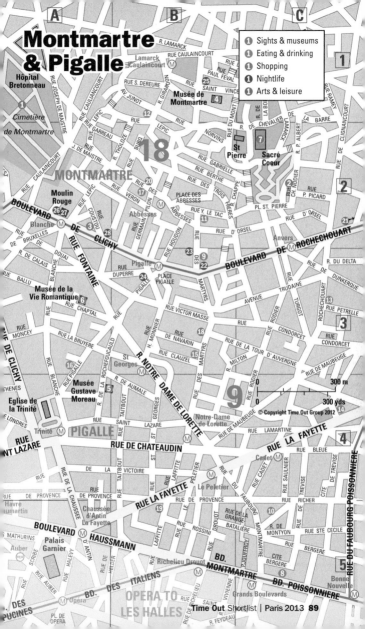

Montmartre
& Pigalle

❶ Sights & museums
❶ Eating & drinking
❶ Shopping
❶ Nightlife
❶ Arts & leisure

Cimetière de Montmartre p87

Dupin, Baronne Dudevant (George Sand) was a guest at Scheffer's soirées and the museum is devoted to Sand, although the watercolours, lockets, jewels and plastercast of her right arm that she left behind reveal little of her ideas or affairs.

Sacré-Coeur

35 rue du Chevalier-de-la-Barre, 18th (01.53.41.89.00, www.sacre-coeur-montmartre.com). Mᵒ Abbesses or Anvers. **Open** *Basilica* 6am-11pm daily. *Crypt & dome* Winter 10am-5.45pm daily. Summer 9am-6.45pm daily. **Admission** free. *Crypt & dome* €5. **Map** p89 C2 ⑦

Work on this enormous mock Romano-Byzantine edifice began in 1877. It was commissioned after the nation's defeat by Prussia in 1870, voted for by the Assemblée Nationale and built from public subscription. Finally completed in 1914, it was consecrated in 1919. The interior boasts lavish mosaics.

Eating & drinking

Le Brébant

32 bd Poissonnière, 9th (01.47.70.01.02). Mᵒ Grands Boulevards. **Open** 7.30am-6am daily. **Bar**. **Map** p89 C5 ⑧

This prominent, round-the-clock bar-bistro has a busy terrace below a colourful, stripy awning, and the split-level interior is all bare bulbs and wrought iron. Prices are steep, so push the boat out and opt for an expertly prepared fruit daiquiri.

La Fourmi

74 rue des Martyrs, 18th (01.42.64.70.35). Mᵒ Pigalle. **Open** 8am-2am Mon-Thur; 8am-4am Fri, Sat; 10am-2am Sun. **Bar**. **Map** p89 B3 ⑨

La Fourmi is an old bistro that has been converted for today's tastes, with picture windows lighting the spacious interior. The classic zinc bar counter is crowned with industrial lights, and an excellent music policy and cool clientele (although they'd have to go some to beat the bar staff) ensure a pile of flyers.

Les Fils à Maman

7 bis Rue Geoffroy-Marie, 9th (01.48.24.59.39, www.lesfilsamaman.com). Mᵒ Grands Boulevards. **Open** 11.30am-3pm, 7-10.30pm Mon-Sat; 7-10.30pm Sun. €€. **Bistro**. **Map** p89 C5 ⑩ See box p88.

Le Miroir

94 rue des Martyrs, 18th (01.46.06.50.73). Mᵒ Abbesses. **Open** noon-3pm, 7-11pm Tue-Sat; noon-3pm Sun. €€. **Bistro**. **Map** p89 B2 ⑪

This friendly bistro is a welcome addition to the neighbourhood. Big mirrors, red banquettes and a glass ceiling at the back give it character, while the professional food and service reflect the owners' haute cuisine training. Expect dishes such as salad of whelks with white beans, crisp-skinned duck and chanterelle mushrooms.

Le Moulin de la Galette

83 rue Lepic, 18th (01.46.06.84.77, www.lemoulindelagalette.eu). Mᵒ Abbesses. **Open** noon-11pm daily. Closed Aug. €€€. **Bistro**. **Map** p89 B1 ⑫

The Butte Montmartre was once dotted with windmills, and this survivor houses a chic restaurant. It's hard to imagine a more picturesque setting in Montmartre. The kitchen makes an effort with dishes such as foie gras with melting beetroot cooked in lemon balm and juniper or suckling pig alongside potato purée.

Pétrelle

34 rue Pétrelle, 9th (01.42.82.11.02, www.petrelle.fr). Mᵒ Anvers. **Open** 8-10pm Tue-Sat. Closed 4wks July/Aug & 1wk Dec. €€. **Bistro**. **Map** p89 C3 ⑬

Jean-Luc André is as inspired a decorator as he is a cook, and the quirky charm of his dining room has made it popular with fashion designers and film stars. The €29 no-choice menu is huge value (marinated sardines with tomato relish, rosemary-scented rabbit with roasted vegetables, deep purple poached figs).

Poussette Café

*6 rue Pierre Sémard, 9th (01.78.10.
49.00, www.lepoussettecafe.com). M°
Poissonnière.* **Open** 10.30am-6.30pm
Tue-Sat. No credit cards. **€**. **Café**.
Map p89 C4 ⓮

Fed up with the impracticalities of
pushing her pram (*poussette*) into the
local café, mother of two Laurence
Constant designed her own parent-
friendly establishment. This upmarket
salon de thé caters for the harassed par-
ent (herbal teas, smoothies, quiches and
salads) and demanding baby (purées,
solids and cuddly toys). You can sign
up for magic shows and parenting
workshops via the café's website.

Rose Bakery

*46 rue des Martyrs, 9th (01.42.82.
12.80). M° Notre-Dame-de-Lorette.*
Open 9am-7pm Tue-Fri; 9am-5pm
Sat, Sun. Closed 2wks Aug & 1wk
Dec. **€**. **Café**. **Map** p89 B3 ⓯

This English-themed café run by a
Franco-British couple stands out for
the quality of its ingredients – organic
or from small producers – as well as the
too-good-to-be-true puddings. The DIY
salad plate is crunchily satisfying, but
the *pizzettes*, daily soups and occasional risottos are equally good.

Rouge Passion

*14 rue Jean-Baptiste Pigalle, 9th (www.
rouge-passion.fr). M° Pigalle or St
Georges.* **Open** noon-3pm, 7pm-midnight
Mon-Fri; 7pm-midnight Sat; 11.30am-
4pm Sun. **Wine bar**. **Map** p89 A3 ⓰

Two bright upstarts are behind this
venture. Offering a long list of wines
(from just €3), free *assiettes apéros*
(peanuts, olives and tapenades on
toast) and decor that is satisfyingly
vintage (red banquettes and beige
walls), the formula is spot on.

Le Sancerre

*35 rue des Abbesses, 18th (01.42.58.
08.20). M° Abbesses.* **Open** 7am-2am
Mon-Thur; 7am-4am Fri, Sat; 9am-2am
Sun. **Bar**. **Map** p89 B2 ⓱

This popular Montmartre institution is
home to a frenzied mix of alcohol-
fuelled transvestites, tourists, lovers
and bobo (bohemian-bourgeois) locals,
who all come for the cheap beer (under
€4), trashy music and buzzy terrace.
The decor inside is scruffy, the service
slow and the food (omelettes, *steak-
frites*) nothing special; yet there is
something irresistibly refreshing about
the no-frills approach.

Shopping

Arnaud Delmontel

*39 rue des Martyrs, 9th (01.48.78.29.33,
www.arnaud-delmontel.com). M° St-
Georges.* **Open** 7am-8.30pm Mon, Wed-
Sun. No credit cards. **Map** p89 B3 ⓲

With its crisp crust and chewy crumb
shot through with irregular holes,
Delmontel's Renaissance bread is one
of the finest in Paris. He puts the same
skill into his almond croissants and
tarte au citron à l'ancienne.

Galeries Laffitte

*27 rue Laffitte, 9th (01.47.70.38.83,
www.galerieslaffitte.fr). M° Notre-Dame-
de-Lorette.* **Open** 9am-7pm Mon-Fri;
10am-7pm Sat. **Map** p89 B5 ⓳

The basement space here houses a regular *papeterie* filled with pens and note-
books, while the ground floor has art
supplies and a selection of gifts, from
quality leather bags to Italian pastel-
coloured diary covers.

Le Grenier à Pain

*38 rue des Abbesses, 18th (01.46.06.
41.81). M° Abbesses.* **Open** 7.30am-
8pm Mon, Wed-Sun. No credit cards.
Map p89 B2 ⓴

Expect queues at this Montmartre
bakery, 2010 winner of the Grand Prix
de la Baguette de Tradition Française
de la Ville de Paris. As well as gaining
plenty of new customers, Baker
Djibril Bodian also picked up a cash
prize of €4,000 and a contract to keep
President Nicolas Sarkozy in bread
for a year.

Tati

*4 bd de Rochechouart, 18th (01.55.
29.52.20, www.tati.fr). Mº Barbès
Rochechouart.* **Open** 10am-7pm Mon-
Fri; 9.30am-7pm Sat. **Map** p89 C2 ㉑

Expect to find anything from T-shirts
to wedding dresses, as well as bargain
children's clothes and household
goods, at this discount heaven.

Nightlife

La Cigale/La Boule Noire

*120 bd de Rochechouart,18th
(01.49.25.81.75, www.lacigale.fr).
Mº Anvers or Pigalle.* **Open** times
vary. **Map** p89 B3 ㉒

One of Paris's finest venues, the horseshoe shaped theatre La Cigale is linked
to more cosy venue La Boule Noire,
good for catching cult-ish visiting acts.

Le Divan du Monde

*75 rue des Martyrs, 18th (01.40.05.
06.99, www.divandumonde.com).
Mº Abbesses or Pigalle.* **Open** 8pm-
2am Tue-Thur; 7.30pm-5am Fri, Sat.
Admission €5-€30. **Map** p89 B3 ㉓

After a drink in the Fourmi opposite,
pop over to the Divan for one-off parties and regular events. The upstairs
specialises in VJ events, and downstairs holds dub, reggae, funk and
world music club nights.

Le Folie's Pigalle

*11 pl Pigalle, 9th (01.48.78.55.25,
www.lefoliespigalle.com). Mº Pigalle.*
Open midnight-dawn Mon-Thur;
midnight-noon Fri, Sat; 6pm-midnight
Sun. **Admission** €20 (incl 1 drink);
€7 Sun eve. **Map** p89 B3 ㉔

The racy Folie's Pigalle's programme
includes everything from dancehall
and hip hop to techno and electro, go-
go dancers, striptease and Paris's only
transsexual spectacle.

Au Lapin Agile

*22 rue des Saules, 18th (01.46.06.
85.87, www.au-lapin-agile.com).
Mº Lamarck Caulaincourt.* **Shows**

9pm-1am Tue-Sun. **Admission** Show
(incl 1 drink) €24; €17 reductions
(except Sat & public hols). No credit
cards. **Map** p89 B1 ㉕

The prices have gone up, tourists outnumber the locals and they sell their
own compilation CDs these days, but
that's all that seems to have changed
since this bar first opened in 1860.

La Machine du Moulin Rouge

NEW *90 bd de Clichy, 18th (01.53.41.
88.89, www.lamachinedumoulinrouge.
com). Mº Blanche.* **Open** 7pm-6am
Wed-Sat. **Admission** free until 11pm,
then €10-€20. **Map** p89 A2 ㉖

This three-floor bar/club/live venue
has had a substantial makeover and is
now reborn with a dash of decadence.
The main dancefloor, La Chaufferie,
used to be the Moulin Rouge's boiler
room and the old pipes remain, but the
new *Alice in Wonderland*-style decor is
a breath of fresh air.

Moulin Rouge

*82 bd de Clichy, 18th (01.53.09.82.82,
www.moulin-rouge.com). Mº Blanche.*
Dinner 7pm. **Shows** 9pm, 11pm
daily. **Admission** *9pm show* (incl
champagne) €102. *11pm show* (incl
champagne) €92. *Dinner & show*
€150-€180. **Map** p89 A2 ㉗

Toulouse-Lautrec posters, glittery
lampposts and fake trees lend tacky
charm to this revue, while 60 Doriss
dancers cavort with faultless synchronisation. Costumes are flamboyant and
the *entr'acte* acts funny.

Les Trois Baudets

*64 bd de Clichy, 18th (01.42.62.33.33,
www.lestroisbaudets.com). Mº Pigalle.*
Open 6pm-1.30am Tue-Sat. Closed Aug.
Admission €5-€20. **Map** p89 A2 ㉘

With a 250-seater theatre, an enviable
sound system, two bars and a restaurant, this new concert hall encourages
chanson française and other musical
genres (rock, electro, folk and slam), as
long as they're in French.

Point Ephemere p99

North-east Paris

In the city's folklore, north-east Paris is working-class Paris – and although patches are gentrifying and little actual industry remains, the area still has a rough and ready vibe. Many of the streets here are somewhat on the tatty side, but others are artsy and fashionable, especially those close to the Canal St-Martin; and large swathes of the north-east are excitingly multi-ethnic, with thriving North African, Turkish and Caribbean enclaves.

Sights & museums

Canauxrama
13 quai de la Loire, 19th (01.42. 39.15.00, www.canauxrama.fr).
Tickets €16; free-€8.50 reductions.
Map p97 C1 ❶
Take a trip up the city's second water-way, the Canal St-Martin. The tree-lined canal is a pretty sight, and the trip even goes underground, where the tun-nel walls are enlivened by a light show.

Gare du Nord
Rue de Dunkerque, 10th (08.91. 36.20.20). Mº Gare du Nord.
Map p97 A2 ❷
The grandest of the great 19th-century train stations (and Eurostar terminal since 1994) was designed by Hittorff between 1861 and 1864. The stone façade, with Ionic capitals and statues representing towns served by the sta-tion, hides a vast iron-and-glass vault.

Musée de la Musique
Cité de la Musique, 221 av Jean-Jaurès, 19th (01.44.84.44.84, www.citedela musique.fr). Mº Porte de Pantin.
Open noon-6pm Tue-Sat; 10am-6pm Sun. **Admission** €8; free-€6.40 reductions. **Map** p97 E1 ❸
This innovative museum houses a collection of instruments from the old Conservatoire, interactive computers and scale models of opera houses and concert halls. Visitors are supplied with an audio guide in a choice of languages, and the musical commentary is a joy,

playing the appropriate instrument as you approach each exhibit.

Event highlights Festival de Jerusalem (2-3 Feb 2013).

Parc des Buttes-Chaumont

Rue Botzaris, rue Manin, rue de Crimée, 19th. M° Buttes Chaumont. **Open** *Oct-Apr* 7am-8pm daily. *May-Sept* 7am-10pm daily. **Map** p97 E2 ❹ See box p98.

Eating & drinking

Bar Ourcq

*68 quai de la Loire, 19th (01.42.40. 12.26). M° Laumière .***Open** 3pm-midnight Wed, Thur; 3pm-2am Fri, Sat; 3-10pm Sun. No credit cards. **Bar**. **Map** p97 D1 ❺

This was one of the first hip joints to hit the Canal de l'Ourcq, with an embankment broad enough to accommodate *pétanque* games (ask at the bar) and a cluster of deckchairs. The cabin-like interior is pretty cosy, and drinks are listed in a hit parade of prices, starting with €2.50 for a *demi* or glass of red.

A la Bière

*104 av Simon-Bolivar, 19th (01.42.39. 83.25). M° Colonel Fabien .***Open** noon-3pm, 7pm-1.30am daily. **€**. **Brasserie**. **Map** p97 D2 ❻

A la Bière looks like one of those non-descript corner brasseries with noisy pop music, but what makes it stand out is an amazingly good-value prix fixe full of fine bistro favourites: home-made rabbit terrine, charcoal-grilled entrecôte with hand-cut chips, juicy Lyonnais sausages with potatoes drenched in olive oil, garlic and parsley. This is one of the few bargains left in Paris.

Chez Jeanette

47 rue du Fbg-St Denis, 10th (01.47.70.30.89). M° Château d'Eau or Strasbourg St-Denis. **Open** 8am-2am daily. **€**. **Café**. **Map** p97 A3 ❼

When she sold her café back in March 2007, Jeanette handed over to the young team from Chez Justine. Now the awful 1940s lights, tobacco-stained wallpaper depicting the Moulin Rouge and PVC-covered banquettes have been rewarded with a Fooding prize for decor, and the café is fast becoming one of Paris's hippest spots for an aperitif.

Chez Prune

36 rue Beaurepaire, 10th (01.42.41. 30.47). M° Jacques Bonsergent. **Open** 8am-2am Mon-Sat; 10am-2am Sun. **Bar**. **Map** p97 B3 ❽

This supremely hip retro café, with high ceilings and low lighting, sticks to a simple formula: groups of friends crowd around the cosily ordered banquettes, picking at moderately priced cheese or meat platters. Mostly, though, they come for a few leisurely drinks or an *apéro* before heading to one of the late-night venues in the area.

La Fidélité

12 rue de la Fidélité, 10th (01.47. 70.19.34, www.lafidelite.com). M° Gare de L'Est. **Open** 8pm-1am Mon-Sat. **€€**. **Brasserie**. **Map** p97 A3 ❾

There was a huge buzz when La Clique took this place over, and so far the brasserie is setting a high standard with its elegant styling. The neighbourhood is arguably one of the least attractive in the capital, but La Fidélité has become a place of pilgrimage not only for A-listers, but also for lovers of good, well-priced food – the lunchtime prix fixe is a bargain and the *joue de boeuf* is sublime. On Thursdays and Fridays, the basement morphs into the Cave de la Fidélité, a jukebox bar.

Le Verre Volé

67 rue de Lancry, 10th (01.48.03. 17.34). M° Jacques Bonsergent. **Open** 10.30am-2.30pm, 7.30pm-2am Tue-Sun. Closed Aug. **€€**. **Bistro**. **Map** p97 B3 ❿

This organic-only *cave à vins* doubles up as a minuscule wine bar and restaurant. Although wine (around €4 per

North-east Paris

RUE DE CRIMÉE

Parc des Buttes Chaumont

© Copyright Time Out Group 2012

300 m
300 yds

Sights & museums
Eating & drinking
Shopping
Nightlife
Arts & leisure

RUE CARDUCCI
RUE DES ALOUETTES
RUE MEUNINGE
RUE FESSART
Pyrénées

Buttes Chaumont

RUE DU PLATEAU
RUE BOTZARIS
RUE DU PLATEAU
RUE FESSART
RUE PRADIER
RUE FESSART

AVENUE DU GAL. S. MARTIN
AVENUE SIMON BOLIVAR
BOLIVAR
RUE LAUZIN
RUE J. ROMAIN
AVENUE SIMON

RUE MANIN
RUE MEYNADIER
RUE MANIN
RUE PETIT
RUE DU RHIN
AV. DE LAUMIÈRE
RUE CARREL
RUE CAVENDISH
RUE ARMAND CARREL
RUE MANIN
RUE EDOUARD PAILLERON
RUE SECRÉTAN

Laumière

R. DE LA MOSELLE
RUE DE MEAUX
RUE BOURET
AVENUE SECRÉTAN
AVENUE SIMON BOLIVAR
AVENUE MATHURIN MOREAU

19

RUE DE L'ATLAS
CITÉ ST. CHAUMONT
RUE BURNOUF
RUE REBEVAL

AVENUE JEAN JAURÈS
AVENUE DE LA LOIRE

Jaurès

QUAI DE LA SEINE
QUAI DE LA LOIRE

RUE DE FLANDRE

Stalingrad

LA VILLETTE

Colonel Fabien

PLACE DU COLONEL FABIEN

RUE DE MEAUX
CITÉ LEPAGE
RUE BOURET
RUE SECRÉTAN
AVENUE SECRÉTAN

R. VICQ D'AZIR
RUE D'AZIR
RUE CLAUDE VELLEFAUX
RUE SAMBRE ET MEUSE
RUE JULIETTE DODU
AUX BELLES
RUE ST. MARTIN
R. STE. MARTHE
R. DU CHALET
BD. DE LA VILLETTE

C

Hôpital St Louis

RUE BICHAT
RUE ALIBERT

QUAI DE JEMMAPES
QUAI DE VALMY
RUE LOUIS BLANC
RUE BLANC

Louis Blanc

PLAGE ROBERT DESNOS

RUE DES ÉCLUSES ST. MARTIN
QUAI DE JEMMAPES
QUAI DE VALMY

RUE DE LA GRANGE AUX BELLES
RUE BICHAT
RUE DE L'HÔPITAL ST. LOUIS

RUE DE TAN...
RUE DU CHÂTEAU LANDON
RUE CHAUDRON
RUE D'AUBERVILLIERS
RUE PHILIPPE DE GIRARD
RUE LOUIS BLANC
RUE A. PARODI
RUE F. DUPONT
RUE E. VARLIN
RUE E. VARLIN

ILIPPE
RUE CAIL
Hôpital Fernand Widal

RUE LA FAYETTE
ST MARTIN
RUE DU FAUBOURG

RUE DE TERRAGE
RUE DU TERRAGE
RUE VERDUN
RUE DE VERDUN
RUE DES RÉCOLLETS
R. DES VINAIGRIERS
R. DU FAUBOURG ST MARTIN

10

RUE DEMARQUAY
Château Landon
RUE D'ALSACE
RUE DU 8 MAI 1945

Gare de l'Est

Gare de l'Est

La Chapelle

BLVD DE LA CHAPELLE
BLD DE LA CHAPELLE

Hôpital Lariboisière
Gare du Nord

RUE DU FAUBOURG SAINT DENIS
RUE LA FAYETTE
DENIS

BLVD DE MAGENTA
BD DE STRASBOURG
Château d'Eau

Party in the park

Skip the Tuileries and head for the 19th instead.

Rosa Bonheur

There are plenty of handsomely ordered opportunities to indulge in a bit of park life in Paris, from the gravelled pathways of the Jardin des Tuileries to the ornamental ponds of the Jardin du Luxembourg. But if you're looking for something a little less formal, one patch of greenery which is definitely worth a stroll is the **Parc des Buttes-Chaumont** (see p96). Set high up in Belleville and too often overlooked by weekenders keen not to stray too far from the tourist loop, this 19th arrondissement gem is one of the city's most magical spots. When the city's boundaries were expanded in 1860, Belleville – once a village that provided Paris

with fruit, wine and weekend escapes – was absorbed and the Buttes-Chaumont was created on the site of a former gypsum and limestone quarry. The park, with its meandering paths, waterfalls, temples and vertical cliffs, was designed by Adolphe Alphand for Haussmann, and was opened as part of the celebrations for the Universal Exhibition in 1867.

After lounging with the locals for a few hours, head for the park's hugely hip hangout, the wonderfully jolly **Rosa Bonheur** *guinguette* (www.rosabonheur.fr). Open until midnight, it makes the perfect place to sip an *apéro* and take in the stunning views of the city stretching out below.

glass) is the focus, you're obliged to eat; a hearty sausage and mash will set you back around €15. Purists who would prefer a simple snack to complement their *bon vin* should opt for a plate of charcuterie and cheese at €12. It's good to know that staff will sell a bottle of wine (and open it) to drink by the canal.

Shopping

Antoine et Lili
95 quai de Valmy, 10th (01.40.37. 41.55, www.antoineetlili.com). Mº Jacques Bonsergent. **Open** 11am-7pm Mon, Sun; 11am-8pm Tue-Fri; 10am-8pm Sat. **Map** p97 B3 ⑪
Antoine et Lili's fuchsia-pink, custard-yellow and apple-green shopfronts are a new raver's dream. The Canal St-Martin 'village' comprises womenswear, a kitsch home decoration boutique and childrenswear.

Culture(s)
46 rue de Lancry, 10th (01.48. 03.58.71). Mº Jacques Bonsergent or République. **Open** 11am-2pm, 3-7pm Tue-Sat. **Map** p97 B3 ⑫
In a loft-style studio, this unusual florist combines exotic flowers, trees and garden-themed items, such as floral printed rain hats. Truly original.

Nightlife

Le Cabaret Sauvage
59 Bd Macdonald, 19th (01.42.09. 03.09, www.cabaretsauvage.com). Mº Porte de la Villette. **Open** 11pm-dawn, days vary. **Admission** €10-€20. **Map** p97 E1 (off map) ⑬
A stylish venue that's taken over by outside promoters for occasional club nights. The world music focus has recently been superseded by electronic and drum 'n' bass nights.

Café Chéri(e)
44 bd de la Villette, 19th (01.42.02. 02.05). Mº Belleville. **Open** 8am-2am daily. **Admission** free. **Map** p97 D3 ⑭

A popular DJ bar, especially in summer when people flock to the terrace. Expect anything from DJ Jet Boy's electro punk to rock, funk, hip hop, rare groove, indie, dance, jazz, and '80s classics.

New Morning
7-9 rue des Petites-Ecuries, 10th (01.45.23.51.41, www.newmorning.com). **Admission** approx €10. **Map** p97 A3 ⑮
One of the best places for the latest cutting-edge jazz exponents, with a policy that also embraces *chanson*, blues, world and sophisticated pop.

Point Ephémère
200 quai de Valmy, 10th (01.40.34. 02.48, www.pointephemere.org). Mº Jaurès or Louis Blanc. **Open** 10am-2am daily. **Admission** varies. **Map** p97 C2 ⑯
This is a classy affair, bringing together local rock, jazz and world gigs with a decent restaurant, dance and recording studios and exhibitions.

Arts & leisure

Hammam Med Centre
43-45 rue Petit, 19th (01.42.02.31.05, www.hammammed.com). Mº Ourcq. **Open** *Women* 11am-10pm Mon-Fri; 9am-7pm Sun. *Mixed (swimwear required)* 10am-9pm Sat. **Map** p97 E1 ⑰
This hammam is hard to beat – spotless mosaic-tiled surroundings, flowered sarongs and a relaxing pool. The 'Forfait florale' option (€139) will have you enveloped in rose petals and massaged with *huile d'Argan* from Morocco.

MK2 Bibliothèque
14 quai de la Seine, 19th (08.92.69. 84.84, www.mk2.fr). Mº Stalingrad. **Open** times vary. **Admission** €10.50; €5-€7 reductions. **Map** p97 C1 ⑱
MK2's mini multiplex on the quai de la Loire was seen as a key factor in the social rise of what had previously been a scuzzy part of town. Now the chain has opened another multiplex across the water, with a boat from one to the other.

La Promenade Plantée p106

The Marais & Eastern Paris

PARIS BY AREA

Whereas historic *quartiers* like Montmartre and St-Germain-des-Prés are well past their heyday, the Marais has been luckier, and for the last two decades has been one of the hippest parts of the city, stuffed with modish hotels, boutiques and restaurants – in no small part due to its popularity with the gay crowd. It's also prime territory for arts lovers, thanks to its generous quotient of museums, and its tightly knit street plan – largely untouched by Haussmann – makes it a charming place in which to get lost. The Marais' neighbour to the west is Beaubourg, whose focal point is the iconic Centre Pompidou, with the city's all-important Hôtel de Ville a stone's throw to the south.

A little further east is the Oberkampf district, home to some of the city's best bars and a nightlife hub for the last decade.

Sights & museums

Atelier Brancusi

Piazza Beaubourg, 4th (01.44.78.12.33, www.centrepompidou.fr). M° Hôtel de Ville or Rambuteau. **Open** 2-6pm Mon, Wed-Sun. **Admission** free. **Map** p102 A2 ❶
When Constantin Brancusi died in 1957, he left his studio and its contents to the state, and it was later moved and rebuilt by the Centre Pompidou. His fragile works in wood and plaster, the endless columns and streamlined bird forms show how Brancusi revolutionised sculpture.

Centre Pompidou (Musée National d'Art Moderne)

Rue St-Martin, 4th (01.44.78.12.33, www.centrepompidou.fr). M° Hôtel de Ville or Rambuteau. **Open** 11am-9pm (last entry 8pm) Mon, Wed, Fri-Sun (until 11pm some exhibitions); 11am-11pm Thur. **Admission** *Museum & exhibitions* €10-€12; free-€9 reductions. **Map** p102 A2 ❷

The Centre Pompidou (or 'Beaubourg') holds the largest collection of modern art in Europe. For the main collection, buy tickets on the ground floor and take the escalators to level four for post-1960s art. Level five spans 1905 to 1960. Masterful ensembles let you see the span of Matisse's career on canvas and in bronze, the variety of Picasso's invention, and the development of cubic orphism by Sonia and Robert Delaunay. Others on the hits list include Braque, Duchamp, Mondrian, Malevich, Kandinsky, Dalí, Giacometti, Ernst, Miró, Calder, Magritte, Rothko and Pollock. Recent acquisitions line the central corridor on level four, and at the far end you can find architecture and design. Video art and installations by the likes of Mathieu Mercier and Dominique Gonzalez-Foerster are in a room given over to *nouvelle création*. Centre Pompidou's Metz outpost opened in May 2010.

Cimetière du Père-Lachaise

Bd de Ménilmontant, 20th (01.55. 25.82.10). M° Père-Lachaise. **Open** *6 Nov-15 Mar* 8am-5.30pm Mon-Fri; 8.30am-5.30pm Sat; 9am-5.30pm Sun. *16 Mar-5 Nov* 8am-6pm Mon-Fri; 8.30am-6pm Sat; 9am-6pm Sun & public hols. **Map** p103 F2 ❸

Père-Lachaise is the celebrity cemetery – it has the mortal remains of almost anyone French, talented and dead that you care to mention. Not even French, for that matter. Creed and nationality have never prevented entry: you just had to have lived or died in Paris or have an allotted space in a family tomb. Finding a particular grave can be tricky, so buy a €2 map from the hawkers at the Père-Lachaise métro or from shops nearby. Highlights include Chopin's medallion portrait and the muse of Music, Jim Morrison's grave, plus famous neighbours La Fontaine and Molière, who knew each other in real life and now share the same fenced-off plot.

Hôtel de Sully

62 rue St-Antoine, 4th (01.42.74.47.75, www.jeudepaume.org). M° St-Paul. **Open** noon-7pm Tue-Fri; 10am-7pm Sat, Sun. **Admission** €5; €2.50 reductions. **Map** p102 C4 ❹

With the Jeu de Paume, the former Patrimoine Photographique forms part of the two-site home for the Centre National de la Photographie.

Hôtel de Ville

29 rue de Rivoli, 4th (01.42.76.40.40, www.paris.fr). M° Hôtel de Ville. **Open** 10am-7pm Mon-Sat. Tours by appointment only. **Map** p102 A3 ❺

The palatial, multi-purpose Hôtel de Ville is the heart of the city administration. Free exhibitions are held in the Salon d'Accueil (10am-6pm Mon-Fri). The rest of the building, accessible by weekly tours (book in advance), has parquet floors, marble statues and painted ceilings.

Maison Européenne de la Photographie

5-7 rue de Fourcy, 4th (01.44.78. 75.00, www.mep-fr.org). M° St-Paul. **Open** 11am-8pm Wed-Sun (last entry 7.30pm). **Admission** €7; free-€4 reductions. **Map** p102 B4 ❻

Probably the capital's best photography exhibition space, hosting retrospectives by Larry Clark and Martine Barrat, along with work by emerging photographers. The building, an airy mansion with a modern extension, contains a huge permanent collection.

Maison de Victor Hugo

Hôtel de Rohan-Guéménée, 6 pl des Vosges, 4th (01.42.72.10.16, www.musee-hugo.paris.fr). M° Bastille or St-Paul. **Open** 10am-6pm Tue-Sun. **Admission** free. *Exhibitions* prices vary. **Map** p102 C4 ❼

Victor Hugo lived here from 1833 to 1848, and today the house is a museum devoted to the great man. On display are his first editions, nearly 500 drawings and Hugo's home-made furniture.

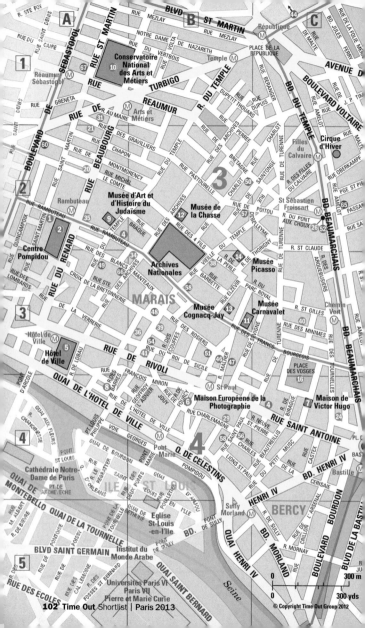

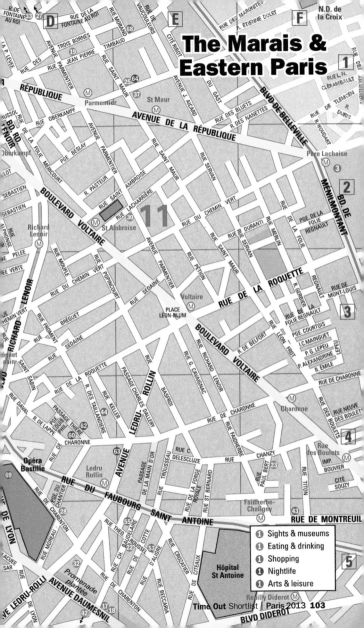

The Marais & Eastern Paris

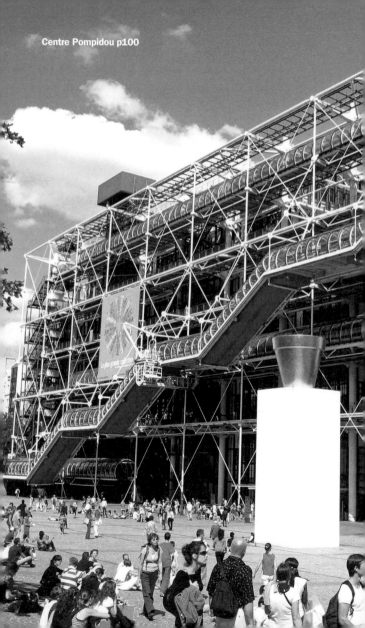

Le Mémorial de la Shoah

17 rue Geoffroy-l'Asnier, 4th (01.42.77. 44.72, www.memorialdelashoah.org). Mº Pont Marie or St-Paul. **Open** 10am-6pm Mon-Wed, Fri, Sun; 10am-10pm Thur. *Research centre* 10am-5.30pm Mon-Wed, Fri, Sun; 10am-7.30pm Thur. **Admission** free. **Map** p102 A4 ❽

Airport-style security checks mean queues, but don't let that put you off: the Mémorial du Martyr Juif Inconnu is an impressively presented and moving memorial to the Holocaust. Enter via the Wall of Names, where limestone slabs are engraved with the first and last names of each of the 76,000 Jews deported from France from 1942 to 1944 with, as an inscription reminds the visitor, the say-so of the Vichy government. The basement-level exhibition documents the plight of French and European Jews.

Musée d'Art et d'Histoire du Judaïsme

Hôtel de St-Aignan, 71 rue du Temple, 3rd (01.53.01.86.53, www.mahj.org). Mº Rambuteau. **Open** 11am-6pm Mon-Fri; 10am-6pm Sun. Closed Jewish hols. **Admission** €6.80; free-€4.50 reductions. **Map** p102 A2 ❾

This museum sprang from the collection of a private association formed in 1948 to safeguard Jewish heritage after the Holocaust. Displays illustrate ceremonies, rites and learning, and show how styles were adapted across the globe through examples of Jewish decorative arts. Photographic portraits of modern French Jews, with audio soundtrack, bring a contemporary edge. The Holocaust is marked by Boris Taslitzky's stark sketches from Buchenwald and Christian Boltanski's courtyard memorial to the Jews who lived in the building in 1939, 13 of whom died in the camps.

Musée des Arts et Métiers

60 rue Réaumur, 3rd (01.53.01.82.00, www.arts-et-metiers.net). Mº Arts et Métiers. **Open** 10am-6pm Tue,

Wed, Fri-Sun; 10am-9.30pm Thur. **Admission** €6.50; free-€4.50 reductions. **Map** p102 A1 ❿

Europe's oldest science museum is a fascinating, well laid out and vast collection of treasures. Here are beautiful astrolabes, celestial spheres, barometers, clocks, some of Pascal's calculating devices, the Lumière brothers' cinematograph, an enormous 1938 TV set, and still larger exhibits like Cugnot's 1770 'Fardier' (the first ever powered vehicle) and Clément Ader's steam-powered Avion 3. The visit concludes in the chapel, which contains old cars, a scale model of the Statue of Liberty and the monoplane in which Blériot crossed the Channel in

Musée Carnavalet

23 rue de Sévigné, 3rd (01.44.5̶ 58, www.carnavalet.paris.fr). Mº St̶ . **Open** 10am-6pm Tue-Sun. Ad̶ on free. *Exhibitions* prices vary. **Map** p102 B3 ⓫

Here, 140 rooms depict the history of Paris, from pre-Roman Gaul to the 20th century. Original 16th-century rooms house Renaissance collections, with portraits by Clouet and furniture and pictures relating to the Wars of Religion. The first floor covers the period up to 1789 and neighbouring Hôtel Le Peletier de St-Fargeau covers the period from 1789 onwards. Displays relating to 1789 detail that year's convoluted politics and bloodshed, with prints and memorabilia, including a chunk of the Bastille. There are items belonging to Napoleon, a cradle given by the city to Napoleon III, and a reconstruction of Proust's bedroom.

Musée de la Chasse et de la Nature

Hôtel Guénégaud, 62 rue des Archives, 3rd (01.53.01.92.40, www.chasse nature.org). Mº Rambuteau. **Open** 11am-6pm Tue-Sun. **Admission** €6; free-€4.50 reductions. **Map** p102 B2 ⓬

A two-year overhaul turned the three-floor hunting museum from a musty old-timer into something really rather special. The history of hunting and man's larger relationship with the natural world are examined in such things as a series of wooden cabinets devoted to the owl, wolf, boar and stag, each equipped with a bleached skull, small drawers you can open to reveal droppings and footprint casts, and a binocular eyepiece you can peer into for footage of the animal in the wild.

Musée Cognacq-Jay

Hôtel Donon, 8 rue Elzévir, 3rd (01.40.27.07.21, www.paris.fr/musees). Mº St-Paul. **Open** 10am-6pm Tue-Sun. **Admission** free. **Map** p102 B3 ⓬
This museum houses a collection put together in the early 1900s by La Samaritaine founder Ernest Cognacq and his wife Marie-Louise Jay. They stuck mainly to 18th-century French works (Watteau, Fragonard, Boucher, Greuze and pastellist Quentin de la Tour), though some English artists (Reynolds, Romney, Lawrence) and Dutch and Flemish names (an early Rembrandt, Ruysdael, Rubens), plus Canalettos and Guardis, have managed to slip in. Pictures are displayed in panelled rooms with furniture, porcelain, tapestries and sculpture of the period.

Musée National Picasso

Hôtel Salé, 5 rue de Thorigny, 3rd (01.42.71.25.21, www.musee-picasso.fr). Mº Chemin Vert or St-Paul. **Map** p102 B3 ⓮
The Musée Picasso is currently closed for restoration, and is due to reopen in summer 2013. Check the website for details. In the meantime, the Centre Pompidou and Musée de l'Orangerie both contain Picasso collections.

Place de la Bastille

4th/11th/12th. Mº Bastille. **Map** p102 C4 ⓯
Nothing remains of the prison that, on 14 July 1789, was stormed by revolutionary forces. Parts of the foundations can be seen in the métro. The Colonne de Juillet, topped by a gilded *génie* of Liberty, is a monument to Parisians who fell during the revolutions of July 1830 and 1848.

Place des Vosges

4th. Mº St-Paul. **Map** p102 C4 ⓰
Paris's first planned square was commissioned in 1605 by Henri IV and inaugurated by his son Louis XIII in 1612. With harmonious red-brick and stone arcaded façades and pitched slate roofs, it differs from the later pomp of the Bourbons. Mme de Sévigné, salon hostess and letter-writer, was born at no.1bis in 1626. At that time the garden hosted duels and trysts.

La Promenade Plantée

Av Daumesnil, 12th. Mº Gare de Lyon or Ledru-Rollin. **Map** p103 D5 ⓱
The railway tracks atop the Viaduc des Arts were replaced in the late 1980s by a promenade planted with roses, shrubs and rosemary. It continues at ground level through the Jardin de Reuilly and the Jardin Charles Péguy on to the Bois de Vincennes.

Le Viaduc des Arts

15-121 av Daumesnil, 12th (www. viaduc-des-arts.com). Mº Gare de Lyon or Ledru-Rollin. **Map** p103 D5 ⓲
Glass-fronted workshops in the arches beneath the Promenade Plantée provide showrooms for furniture and fashion designers, picture-frame gilders, tapestry restorers, porcelain decorators, and chandelier, violin and flute makers.

Eating & drinking

L'Alimentation Générale

64 rue Jean-Pierre-Timbaud, 11th (01.43.55.42.50, www.alimentation-generale.net). Mº Parmentier. **Open** 7pm-2am Wed-Sun; 7pm-4am Thur-Sat. **Bar.** **Map** p103 D1 ⓳
The 'Grocery Store' is rue Jean-Pierre-Timbaud's answer to La Mercerie: it, too, is a big old space filled with junk. Cupboards of kitsch china and lampshades made from kitchen sponges are

an inspired touch. The beer is equally well chosen – Flag, Sagres, Picon and Orval by the bottle – and the unusual €8 house cocktail involves basil and figs. DJs rock the joint.

L'Ambassade d'Auvergne

22 rue du Grenier-St-Lazare, 3rd (01.42.72.31.22, www.ambassade-auvergne.com). Mº Arts et Métiers. **Open** noon-2pm, 7.30-10pm daily. €€. **Bistro**. Map p102 A2 ⓴

This rustic *auberge* is a fitting embassy for the hearty fare of central France. An order of cured ham comes as two hefty, plate-filling slices, and the salad bowl is chock-full of green lentils cooked in goose fat, studded with bacon and shallots. The *rôti d'agneau* arrives as a pot of melting chunks of lamb in a rich, meaty sauce with a helping of tender white beans. Dishes arrive with the flagship *aligot*, the creamy, elastic mash-and-cheese concoction.

Andy Whaloo

69 rue des Gravilliers, 3rd (01.42.71.20.38). Mº Arts et Métiers. **Open** 6pm-2am Tue-Sat. **Bar**. Map p102 A2 ㉑

Andy Whaloo, created by the people behind its neighbour 404 and London's Momo and Sketch, is Arabic for 'I have nothing'. Bijou? This place brings new meaning to the word. The formidably fashionable crowd fights for coveted 'seats' on upturned paint cans; it's a beautifully designed venue, crammed with Moroccan artefacts and a spice rack of colours. It's quiet early on, with a surge around 9pm.

Le Baron Rouge

1 rue Théophile-Roussel, 12th (01.43.43.14.32). Mº Ledru-Rollin. **Open** 10am-3pm, 5-10pm Tue-Fri; 10am-10pm Sat; 10am-4pm Sun. **Bar**. Map p103 E5 ㉒

It sells wine, certainly – great barrels of the stuff are piled high and sold by the glass at very reasonable prices. But the Red Baron is not just a wine bar – more a local chat room, where regulars congregate to yak over their *vin*, along with a few draught beers and perhaps a snack of sausages or oysters. Despite its lack of seating (there are only four tables), it's a popular pre-dinner spot.

Le Bistrot Paul Bert

18 rue Paul-Bert, 11th (01.43.72.24.01). Mº Charonne or Faidherbe Chaligny. **Open** noon-2pm, 7.30-11pm Tue-Sat. Closed Aug. €€. **Bistro**. Map p103 F4 ㉓

This heart-warming bistro gets it right almost down to the last crumb. A starter salad of *ris de veau* illustrates the point, with lightly browned veal sweetbreads perched on a bed of green beans and baby carrots with a sauce of sherry vinegar and deglazed cooking juices. A roast shoulder of suckling pig and a thick steak with a raft of golden, thick-cut *frites* look inviting indeed. Desserts are superb too, including what may well be the best *île flottante* in Paris. If you happen to be in the area at lunchtime, bear in mind that the prix fixe menu is remarkable value.

Bofinger

5-7 rue de la Bastille, 4th (01.42.72.87.82, www.bofingerparis.com). Mº Bastille. **Open** noon-3pm, 6.30pm-midnight daily. €€. **Brasserie**. Map p102 C4 ㉔

Bofinger draws big crowds for its art nouveau setting and brasserie atmosphere. Downstairs is the prettiest place in which to eat, but the upstairs room is air-conditioned. An à la carte selection might start with garlicky snails or a well-made langoustine terrine, followed by an intensely seasoned salmon tartare, a generous (if unremarkable) cod steak, or calf's liver accompanied by cooked melon. Alternatively, you could have the foolproof brasserie meal of oysters and fillet steak, washed down by the fine Gigondas.

Café Charbon

109 rue Oberkampf, 11th (01.43.57.55.13, www.lecafecharbon.com). Mº Ménilmontant or Parmentier. **Open**

9am-2am Mon-Thur, Sun; 9am-4am Fri, Sat. Closed Aug-mid Sept. **Bar**. Map p103 E1 ㉕

The bar within this restored belle époque building sparked the Oberkampf nightlife boom. Its booths, mirrors and adventurous music policy put trendy locals at ease, capturing the essence of café culture spanning each end of the 20th century. After more than 15 years, the formula still works.

Cantine Merci

111 bd Beaumarchais, 3rd (01.42. 77.78.92). M° St-Sébastien Froissart. **Open** noon-3pm Mon-Sat. €. **Café**. Map p102 C2 ㉖

Concept store Merci is all about feeling virtuous even as you indulge, and its basement canteen is a perfect example. Salads, soup and risotto of the day, an organic salmon plate, and the *assiette merci* (perhaps chicken kefta with two salads) make up the brief menu, complete with invigorating teas and juices.

Le Chateaubriand

129 av Parmentier, 11th (01.43.57. 45.95). M° Goncourt. **Open** noon-2pm, 8-11pm Tue-Fri; 8-11pm Sat. Closed 3wks Aug, 2wks Dec. €€. **Bistro**. Map p103 D1 ㉗

Basque chef Iñaki Aizpitarte runs this stylish bistro. Come at dinner to try the cooking at its most adventurous, as a much simpler menu is served at lunch. Dishes have been deconstructed down to their very essence and put back together again. You'll understand if you try starters such as steak tartare garnished with a quail's egg or asparagus with tahini foam and little splinters of sesame-seed brittle. The cooking's not always so cerebral – goat's cheese with stewed apple jam is brilliant.

China

50 rue de Charenton, 12th (01.43. 46.08.09, www.lechina.eu). M° Bastille or Ledru Rollin. **Open** noon-2am Mon-Fri; 5pm-2am Sat, Sun. Closed Aug. **Bar**. Map p103 D5 ㉘

This sexy take on a 1930s Shanghai gentleman's club, with red walls, leather chesterfields and the longest bar in Paris, serves some of the finest cocktails in town (including its signature singapore sling). The Cantonese cuisine is pricey, so skip dinner and head upstairs to the cigar bar (if you're romantically inclined) or downstairs to the cellar for weekly jazz, pop and world music concerts.

Cru

7 rue Charlemagne, 4th (01.40.27. 81.84, www.restaurantcru.fr). M° St-Paul. **Open** 12.30-2.30pm, 7.30-11pm Tue-Sat; 12.30-2.30pm Sun. €€. **Bistro**. Map p102 B4 ㉙

Opening a raw-food restaurant is a gamble, so the owners of Cru cheat here and there, offering root vegetable 'chips' and a few *plancha* dishes. Still, the menu has plenty for the crudivore, such as some unusual carpaccios (the veal with preserved lemon is particularly good) and intriguing 'red' and 'green' plates, variations on the tomato and cucumber.

Le Dauphin

31 av Parmentier, 11th (01.48.06. 58.41). M° Goncourt. **Open** 11am-2pm, 7-11pm Tue-Fri; 7-11pm Sat. Closed 3wks Aug, 2wks Dec. €. **Wine bar**. Map p103 D1 ㉚

Iñaki Aizpitarte's recently opened Le Dauphin, a Rem Koolhaas-designed tapas-style place a few doors from Le Chateaubriand, offers sub-€10 dishes such as *magret séché*, *tempura de gambas* and *tarte au citron meringuée*. As at Le Chateaubriand, sourcing is all-important – bread comes from Du Pain et des Idées, which was voted best baker in Paris in 2008 by Gault Millau.

Derrière

69 rue des Gravilliers, 3rd (01.44.61. 91.95). M° Arts et Métiers. **Open** noon-2.30pm, 8-11pm Mon-Fri; 8-11.30pm Sat; noon-4.30pm, 8-11pm Sun. €€. **Bistro**. Map p102 A1 ㉛

Mourad Mazouz, the man behind Momo and Sketch in London, has hit on another winning formula with this apartment-restaurant in the same street as his restaurant 404 and bar Andy Wahloo. The cluttered-chic look mixes contemporary fixtures and antique furniture. It attracts a young, hip crowd that appreciates the high-calorie comfort food, such as roast chicken with buttery mashed potatoes.

L'Encrier

55 rue Traversière, 12th (01.44.68. 08.16). M° Gare de Lyon or Ledru-Rollin. **Open** noon-2.30pm, 7.30-11pm Mon-Fri; 7.30-11pm Sat. Closed Aug & Christmas wk. €. **Bistro**. Map p103 D5 ㉜
Through the door and past the velvet curtain, you find yourself face to face with the kitchen – and a crowd of locals, many of whom seem to know the charming boss personally. Start with fried rabbit kidneys on a bed of salad dressed with raspberry vinegar, an original and wholly successful combination, and follow with goose *magret* with honey served with sautéed potatoes. To end, share a chocolate cake or try the popular profiteroles.

Le Floréal

73 rue du Fbg-du-Temple, 10th (01.42.08.81.03). M° Goncourt. **Open** 7am-7pm Mon; 7am-2am Tue-Sat; 8am-7pm Sun. €. **Diner**. Map p103 D1 ㉝
The proprietors of Chez Jeanette and Chez Justine have chosen a site opposite Le Chateaubriand and Le Dauphin for their new venture, Le Floréal – an American-style diner serving hamburgers and cupcakes (and favourite of Matthieu Almeric, Daniel Craig's good-looking nemesis in *Quantum of Solace*).

Le Gaigne

12 rue Pecquay, 4th (01.44.59. 86.72, www.restaurantlegaigne.fr). M° Rambuteau. **Open** 12.15-2pm, 7.30-10.30pm Tue-Thur; 12.15-2pm, 7.30-11pm Fri, Sat. €€. **Bistro**. Map p102 B3 ㉞

It's a familiar story: young chef with haute cuisine credentials opens a small bistro in an out-of-the-way street. Here, the restaurant is even tinier than usual, with only 20 seats, and the cooking is unusually inventive. Chef Mickaël Gaignon worked with Pierre Gagnaire, and it shows in dishes such as *l'oeuf bio* – three open eggshells filled with creamed spinach, carrot and celeriac – or roast monkfish with broccoli purée and a redcurrant emulsion. The dining room is pleasantly modern.

Le Hangar

12 impasse Berthaud, 3rd (01.42.74. 55.44). M° Rambuteau. **Open** noon-2.30pm, 7.30-11pm Tue-Sat. Closed Aug. €. No credit cards. **Bistro**. Map p102 A2 ㉟
It's worth making the effort to find this bistro by the Centre Pompidou, with its terrace tucked away in a hidden alley and excellent cooking. A bowl of tapenade and toast are supplied to keep you going while choosing from the comprehensive *carte*. It yields, for starters, tasty and grease-free *rillettes de lapereau* (rabbit) alongside perfectly balanced pumpkin and chestnut soup. Main courses include pan-fried foie gras on a smooth potato purée made with olive oil.

Lizard Lounge

18 rue du Bourg-Tibourg, 4th (01.42. 72.81.34, www.cheapblonde.com). M° Hôtel de Ville. **Open** noon-2am daily. **Bar**. Map p102 B3 ㊱
An anglophone favourite deep in the Marais, this loud and lively joint provides lager in pints (€6), plus cocktails (€7) and a viewing platform for beer-goggled oglers. Bargain boozing (cocktails €5) kicks off at 5pm; from 8pm to 10pm there's another happy hour in the cellar bar; on Mondays, it lasts all day.

La Mercerie

98 rue Oberkampf, 11th (01.56.98.14.10). M° Parmentier. **Open** 5pm-Mon-Fri; 3pm-2am Sat, Sun. **Bar**. Map p103 E1 ㊲

PARIS BY AREA

Café Charbon p107

The spacious Mercerie has bare walls (bare everything, in fact) and room for the usual Oberkampf shenanigans of death-wish drinking against a backdrop of loud, eclectic music. A DJ programme is lipsticked on the back bar mirror. Happy hour is from 7pm to 9pm, so you can cane the house vodkas and still have enough euros to finish the job. The back area provides intimacy.

La Perle

78 rue Vieille-du-Temple, 3rd (01.42. 72.69.93). M° Chemin Vert or St-Paul. **Open** 6am-2am Mon-Fri; 8am-2am Sat, Sun. **Bar**. **Map** p102 B3 ③⑧
The Pearl achieves a rare balance between all-day and late-night venue, and also has a good hetero/homo mix. It feels like a neighbourhood bar; labourers and screenwriters rub elbows with young dandies, keeping one eye on the mirror and an ear on the electro-rock.

Le Petit Fer à Cheval

30 rue Vieille-du-Temple, 4th (01.42. 72.47.47, www.cafeine.com). M° St-Paul. **Open** 9am-2am daily. **Bar**. **Map** p102 B3 ③⑨
Even a miniature Shetland pony would be pushed to squeeze his hoof into this fer à cheval (horseshoe) – this adorable little café has one of France's smallest bars. Tucked in behind the glassy façade is a friendly dining room lined with reclaimed métro benches; if you want scenery, the tables out front overlook the bustle of rue Vieille-du-Temple. In business for more than 100 years, the café enjoyed a retro makeover by Xavier Denamur in the 1990s, and today sports vintage film posters.

Le Petit Marché

9 rue de Béarn, 3rd (01.42.72.06.67). M° Chemin Vert. **Open** noon-4pm, 7.45pm-midnight daily. **€€**. **Bistro**. **Map** p102 C3 ④⓪
Petit Marché's menu is short and modern with Asian touches. Raw tuna is flash-fried in sesame seeds and served

with a Thai sauce, making for a refreshing starter; crispy-coated deep-fried king prawns have a similar oriental lightness. The main vegetarian risotto is rich in basil, coriander, cream and green beans. Pan-fried scallops with lime are precision-cooked and accompanied by a good purée and more beans. There's a short wine list.

Stolly's

16 rue Cloche-Perce, 4th (01.42.76. 06.76, www.cheapblonde.com). M° Hôtel de Ville or St-Paul. **Open** 4.30pm-2am daily. **Bar**. **Map** p102 B3 ④①
This seen-it-all drinking den has been serving a mainly anglophone crowd for nights immemorial. The staff make the place what it is, and a summer terrace eases libation, as do the long happy hours; but don't expect anyone at Stolly's to faff about with food.

Le Train Bleu

Gare de Lyon, pl Louis-Armand, 12th (01.43.43.09.06, www.le-train-bleu.com). M° Gare de Lyon. **Open** 11.30am-3pm, 7-11pm daily. **€€€**. **Brasserie**. **Map** p103 D5 ④②
This listed dining room – with vintage frescoes and big oak benches – exudes a pleasant air of expectation. Don't expect cutting-edge cooking, but rather fine renderings of French classics. Lobster served on walnut oil-dressed salad leaves is a generous, beautifully prepared starter. Mains of veal chop topped with a cap of cheese, and sandre (pike-perch) coupled with a 'risotto' of crozettes are also pleasant. A few reasonably priced wines would be a welcome addition.

Shopping

L'Autre Boulange

43 rue de Montreuil, 11th (01.43.72. 86.04, www.lautreboulange.com). M° Faidherbe Chaligny or Nation. **Open** 7.30am-1.30pm, 3-7.30pm Mon-Fri; 7.30am-1pm Sat. Closed Aug. **Map** p103 F5 ④③

PARIS BY AREA

Michel Cousin bakes up to 23 types of organic loaf in his wood-fired oven – varieties include the *flutiot* (rye bread with raisins, walnuts and hazelnuts), the *sarment de Bourgogne* (sourdough and a little rye) and a spiced cornmeal bread.

Come On Eileen
16-18 rue des Taillandiers, 11th (01.43.38.12.11). M° Ledru-Rollin. **Open** *Sept-July* 11am-8.30pm Mon-Fri; 2-8pm Sun. *Aug* 2-8pm Mon-Fri. **Map** p103 D4 **44**
The owners of this three-floor vintage wonderland have an eye for what's funky, from cowboy gear to 1960s debutantes' frocks. The stock is in good condition, but prices are high.

Du Pain et des Idées
34 rue Yves Toudic, 10th (01.42.40. 44.52, www.dupainetdesidees.com). M° Jacques Bonsergent. **Open** 6.45am-8pm Mon-Fri. **No credit cards. Map** p102 C1 **45**
Christophe Vasseur is a previous winner of the Gault-Millau prize for Best Bakery. Among his specialities are Le Rabelais – *pain brioché* with saffron, honey and nuts; and Le Pagnol aux Pommes, a bread studded with royal gala apple (with its skin on), raisins and orange flower water.

L'Eclaireur
40 rue de Sévigné, 4th (01.48.87.10.22, www.leclaireur.com). M° St-Paul. **Open** 11am-7pm Mon-Sat. **Map** p102 B3 **46**
Sophisticated, avant-garde L'Eclaireur stocks designs by Comme des Garçons, Martin Margiela and Dries van Noten. Among its finds, check out smocks by Finnish designer Jasmin Santanen.

L'Eclaireur Homme
12 rue Malher, 4th (01.44.54.22.11, www.leclaireur.com). M° St-Paul. **Open** 11am-7pm Mon-Sat. **Map** p102 B3 **47**
Amid the exposed ducts of this old printworks you'll find items by Prada, Comme des Garçons, Dries van Noten and Martin Margiela. The star is Italian

Stone Island, whose radical clothing features parkas with a steel shell to counteract pollution.

Free 'P' Star
8 rue Ste-Croix-de-la-Bretonnerie, 4th (01.42.76.03.72, www.freepstar.com). M° St-Paul. **Open** 11am-9pm Mon-Sat; noon-9pm Sun. **Map** p102 B3 **48**
Late-night shopping is fun at this Aladdin's cave of retro glitz, ex-army wear and glad rags that has provided fancy dress for many a Paris party.

I Love My Blender
36 rue du Temple, 3rd (01.42.77. 50.32, www.ilovemyblender.fr). M° Hôtel de Ville. **Open** 10am-7pm Tue-Sat; 10am-5pm Sun. **Map** p102 A3 **49**
Christophe Persouyre left a career in advertising to share his passion for English and American literature: all the books he stocks were penned in English, and here you can find their mother-tongue and translated versions.

Julien, Caviste
50 rue Charlot, 3rd (01.42.72.00.94). M° Filles du Calvaire. **Open** 9am-1.30pm, 3.30-7.30pm Tue-Sat; 10.30am-1.30pm Sun. Closed 3rd wk Aug. **Map** p102 B2 **50**
Julien promotes the small producers he has discovered, and often holds wine tastings on Saturdays.

K Jacques
16 rue Pavée, 4th (01.40.27.03.57, www.kjacques.fr). M° St-Paul. **Open** 10am-7.30pm daily. **Map** p102 B3 **51**
Set up in Saint-Tropez in 1933 by Jacques Keklikian and his wife, the K Jacques workshop started life stitching together basic leather sandals for visitors to the Med resort. The Homère (or Homer) was, and still is, the signature piece – Picasso loved them, and over the years they've counted the likes of Colette and Brigitte Bardot among their fans. Now the company offers a range of around 60 styles.

Merci

*111 bd Beaumarchais, 3rd (01.42.77.
00.33, www.merci-merci.com). M° St-
Sébastien Froissart.* **Open** 10am-7pm
Mon-Sat. **Map** p102 C2 ⑤
Concept store Merci is housed in an
elaborately reconfigured 19th-century
fabric factory. Inside, three loft-like
floors heave with furniture, jewellery,
stationery, fashion, household products, kidswear and a haberdashery.

Moisan

*5 pl d'Aligre, 12th (01.43.45.46.60,
www.painmoisan.fr). M° Ledru-Rollin.*
Open 7am-8pm Tue-Sat; 7am-2pm
Sun. No credit cards. **Map** p103 E5 ⑤
Moisan's organic bread, *viennoiseries*
and rustic tarts are outstanding. At this
branch there's always a healthy queue.

Nodus

*22 rue Vieille-du-Temple, 4th (01.42.
77.07.96, www.nodus.fr). M° Hôtel de
Ville or St-Paul.* **Open** 10.45am-2pm,
3-7.30pm Mon-Sat; 1-7.30pm Sun.
Map p102 B3 ⑤
Under the wooden beams of this cosy
men's shirt specialist are rows of
striped, checked and plain dress shirts,
stylish silk ties with subtle designs,
and silver-plated crystal cufflinks.

Première Pression Provence

*3 rue Antoine Vollon, 12th (01.53.33.
03.59, www.premiere-pression-provence.
com). M° Ledru Rollin.* **Open** noon-2.30pm,
3.30-7.30pm Tue-Fri; 10.30am-2.30pm,
3.30-7.30pm Sat. **Map** p103 E5 ⑤
This is L'Occitane creator Olivier
Baussan's latest project, where you are
encouraged to taste spoonfuls of single-
producer olive oil to educate your palate
about the nuances of *vert*, *mûr* and *noir*
(known as the '*fruités*') before buying.

Red Wheelbarrow

*22 rue St-Paul, 4th (01.48.04.75.08,
www.theredwheelbarrow.com). M° St
Paul.* **Open** 10am-6pm Mon; 10am-7pm
Tue-Sat; 2-6pm Sun. **Map** p102 B4 ⑤

This friendly bookshop in the Marais
has an excellent children's section.

Shine

*15 rue de Poitou, 3rd (01.48.05.
80.10). M° Filles du Calvaire.* **Open**
11am-7.30pm Mon-Sat; 1-7pm Sun.
Map p102 B2 ⑤
See by Chloé, Marc by Marc Jacobs and
Acne Jeans, plus Repetto shoes and
Véronique Branquino, are among the
goodies in this glossy showcase.

Le Village St-Paul

*Rue St-Paul, rue Charlemagne & quai
des Célestins, 4th (www.levillagesaint
paul.com). M° St-Paul.* **Open** 10am-
7pm Mon-Sat. No credit cards. **Map**
p102 B4 ⑤
This colony of antiques sellers, housed in
small, linking courtyards, is a source of
furniture, kitchenware and wine gadgets.

Zadig & Voltaire

*42 rue des Francs-Bourgeois,
3rd (01.44.54.00.60, www.zadig-et-
voltaire.com). M° Hôtel de Ville or St-
Paul.* **Open** 10.30am-7.30pm Mon-Sat;
1.30-7.30pm Sun. **Map** p102 B3 ⑤
Zadig & Voltaire's relaxed collection is
a winner. Popular separates include
cotton tops, shirts and faded jeans; its
cashmere jumpers are superb.

Nightlife

Ateliers de Charonne

*21 rue de Charonne, 11th (01.40.21.
83.35, www.ateliercharonne.com).
M° Charonne or Ledru-Rollin.* **Open**
8pm-1am Tue-Sat. **Admission** free.
Map p103 D4 ⑥
This jazz club is the place to see the
rising stars of gypsy jazz (*jazz
manouche*). If you want to grab a good
spot near the front of the stage, reserve
for dinner and the show.

Le Bataclan

*50 bd Voltaire, 11th (01.43.14.00.30,
www.le-bataclan.com). M° Oberkampf.*
Open times vary. **Map** p103 D2 ⑥

Cultural download

Digital design comes to the Gaîté Lyrique.

After a ten-year revamp, the belle époque **Gaîté Lyrique** theatre (see p115), built in 1862, has been turned into Paris's first digital cultural centre; a seven-floor, multidisciplinary concert hall-cum-gallery that thrusts visitors deep into the realms of digital art, music, graphics, film, fashion, design, video games and even sushi-shaped memory sticks, on sale in the Gaîté Lyrique's quirky boutique.

It's not the first time the building has undergone a transformation. After being an *haut-lieu* of operetta and Russian ballet, it was pillaged by the Nazis, only to become a circus school in the 1970s and a mini-theme park in the 1980s. But this time its multi-million euro interior, which combines the original belle époque foyer with starkly modern spaces by architect Manuelle Gautrand, is set to become a permanent fixture on the city's cultural scene.

The opening schedule in late 2010 featured events and installations at the forefront of technology and creation. There are no fewer than three electronic music concerts each week and around 120 live multimedia performances a year, along with guest appearances by artists, musicians and DJs (including Gilles Petersen three weekends a year) and film projections. You can even just pop into the funky space for a decent cup of coffee and a flick through the magazines.

Exhibition-wise, expect interactivity and the best of Europe's cutting-edge art scene – a highlight for spring 2012 was April's 'Keep Portland Weird' season, celebrating the eclectic contemporary sounds coming out of Portland, Oregon.

Established in 1864, this highly distinctive venue remains admirably discerning in its booking of rock, world, jazz and hip hop acts.

La Mécanique Ondulatoire

8 passage Thière, 11th (01.43.55.16.74, www.myspace.com/lamecanique). Mº Bastille or Ledru Rollin. **Open** 6pm-2am Mon-Sat. Concerts from 8pm Tue-Sat. **Admission** €4-€7. **Map** p103 D4 🖲
Cementing Bastille's status as Paris's prime hangout for rockers, this exciting venue has three levels and alternates eclectic DJs with live acts in the cellar, plus there's jazz on Tuesday nights.

Le Motel

8 passage Josset, 11th (01.58.30.88.52, www.myspace.com/lemotel). Mº Ledru Rollin. **Open** 6pm-1.45am Tue-Sun. Closed Aug. **Map** p103 E4 🖲
This most Anglophile of Paris bars, with Stone Roses and Smiths posters adorning the walls, manages to fit plenty of live bands, including some of the best local talent, on to its tiny stage.

Nouveau Casino

109 rue Oberkampf, 11th (01.43.57. 57.40, www.nouveaucasino.net). Mº Parmentier. **Open** *Concerts* times vary. **Map** p103 E1 🖲
Nouveau Casino is a concert venue that also hosts some of the city's liveliest club nights. Local collectives, international names and record labels, such as Versatile, regularly host nights here; check the website for one-off parties.

Panic Room

101 rue Amelot, 11th (01.58.30.93.43, www.panicroomparis.com). Mº St-Sébastien Froissart. **Open** 6pm-2am Tue-Sat. Closed 2wks Aug. **Admission** free. **Map** p102 C2 🖲
This bar quickly carved out a niche on the rock scene. The excellent Goldrush collective has live acts and DJs blasting the sound system in the basement, while upstairs friendly barmen serve affordable cocktails behind a concrete counter.

Arts & leisure

Les Bains du Marais

31-33 rue des Blancs-Manteaux, 4th (01.44.61.02.02, www.lesbains dumarais.com). Mº St-Paul. **Open** *Men* 10am-11pm Thur; 10am-8pm Fri. *Women* 11am-8pm Mon; 10am-8pm Tue; 10am-7pm Wed. *Mixed (swimwear required)* 7-11pm Wed; 10am-8pm Sat; 10am-11pm Sun. Closed Aug. **Map** p102 A3 🖲
This hammam and spa mixes the modern and traditional (lounging beds and mint tea). Facials, waxing and essential oil massages (€70) are also available. The hammam is €35.

Gaîté Lyrique

3bis rue Papin, 3rd (01.53.01. 51.51, www.gaite-lyrique.net). Mº Réaumur Sébastapol. **Box office** 2-8pm Tue-Sat; 2-6pm Sun. **Map** p102 A1 🖲
See box p114.

Maison des Métallos

94 rue Jean-Pierre Timbaud, 11th (01.48.05.88.27, www.maisondes metallos.org). Mº Parmentier or Couronnes. **Map** p103 E1 🖲
This cutting-edge cultural showcase for contemporary artists offers up an ambitious multicultural programme of concerts, dance, film screenings, exhibitions, and popular debates.

Opéra National de Paris, Bastille

Pl de la Bastille, 12th (08.92.89. 90.90, from abroad 01.71.25.24.23, www.operadeparis.fr). Mº Bastille. **Box office** (130 rue de Lyon, 12th) 11.30am-6.30pm Mon-Sat. *By phone* 9am-6pm Mon-Fri; 9am-1pm Sat. **Admission** €5-€180. **Map** p103 D4 🖲
Despite the unflattering acoustics, the standard of performance here is high and there are some exciting evenings planned under director Nicolas Joel.
Event highlights Mozart's Le Nozze di Figaro (15 Sept-25 Oct); Bizet's Carmen (4-29 Dec).

PARIS BY AREA

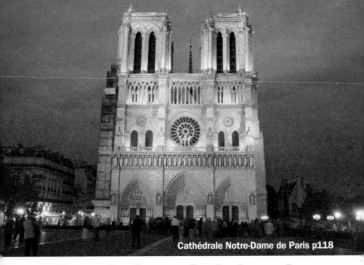

Cathédrale Notre-Dame de Paris p118

The Seine & Islands

The Seine

It's perhaps surprising that it took so long for the Seine to become a tourist magnet. For much of the 19th and 20th centuries, the Seine was barely given a second thought by anyone who wasn't working on it or driving along its quayside roads. But in 1994, UNESCO added 12 kilometres (7.5 miles) of Paris riverbank to its World Heritage register. Floating venues such as Batofar became super-trendy; and in the last ten years, it's been one new attraction after another.

It's at its best in summer. Port de Javel and Jardin Tino-Rossi become open-air dancehalls; and there's the jamboree of Paris-Plage, Mayor Delanoë's city beach that brings sand, palm trees, loungers and free entertainment to both sides of the Seine. Come on Sundays, and stretches of riverside roads will be closed for the benefit of cyclists and

rollerskaters. And, of course, there's a wealth of boat tours on offer.

In the next few years, Delanoë hopes to take the experiment one step further by redesigning the Left Bank and banning cars completely. His ambitious plans for a stretch of road between the Musée d'Orsay and Pont de l'Alma involve a long promenade dotted with parks, cafés and possibly a floating cinema.

Sights & museums

Vedettes du Pont-Neuf

Square du Vert-Galant, 1st (01.46.33. 98.38, www.vedettesdupontneuf.com). M° Pont Neuf. **Tickets** €13; free-€6 reductions. **Map** p117 B1 ❶
The hour-long cruise takes in all the big sights, from the Eiffel Tower to Notre-Dame. You can sit inside just a foot or two above water level or outside on the top deck – where you may get drenched by pranksters throwing water from bridges as you pass underneath.

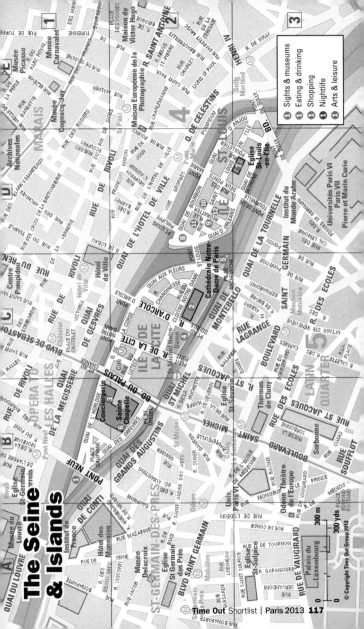

The Seine & Islands

Sights & museums
Eating & drinking
Shopping
Nightlife
Arts & leisure

300 m
300 yds

© Copyright Time Out Group 2012

The bridges

From the honeyed arches of the oldest, the Pont Neuf, to the swooping lines of the newest, the Passerelle Simone-de-Beauvoir, the city's 37 bridges are among the best-known landmarks in the city, and enjoy some of its best views.

Over the years, the city's *ponts* have been bombed, bashed by buses and boats, weather-beaten and even trampled to destruction: in 1634, the Pont St-Louis collapsed under the weight of a religious procession.

The 19th century was boom time for bridge-building: 21 were built in all, including the city's first steel, iron and suspension bridges. The Pont de la Concorde used up what was left of the Bastille after the storming of 1789; the romantic Pont des Arts was the capital's first solely pedestrian crossing (built in 1803 and rebuilt in the 1980s). The most glitteringly exuberant bridge is the Pont Alexandre III, with its bronze and glass, garlanding and gilded embellishments. More practical is the Pont de l'Alma, with its Zouave statue that has long been a flood monitor: when the statue's toes get wet, the state raises the flood alert and starts to close the quayside roads; when he's up to his ankles in Seine, it's no longer possible to navigate the river by boat. This offers some indication of how devastating the great 1910 flood was, when the plucky Zouave disappeared up to his neck – as did parts of central Paris.

The 20th century brought some spectacular additions. Pont Charles-de-Gaulle, for example, stretches like the wing of a huge aeroplane, and iron Viaduc d'Austerlitz (1905) is striking yet elegant as it cradles métro line 5. The city's newest crossing, the Passerelle Simone-de-Beauvoir, links the Bibliothèque Nationale to the Parc de Bercy.

Ile de la Cité

The Ile de la Cité is where Paris was born around 250 BC, when the Parisii, a tribe of Celtic Gauls, founded a settlement on this convenient bridging point of the Seine. Romans, Merovingians and Capetians followed, in what became a centre of political and religious power right into the Middle Ages: royal authority at one end, around the Capetian palace; the Church at the other, by **Notre-Dame**.

Perhaps the most charming spot on the island is the western tip, where Pont Neuf spans the Seine. Despite its name, it is the oldest bridge in Paris. Its arches are lined with grimacing faces, said to be modelled on some of the courtiers of Henri III. Down the steps is leafy square du Vert-Galant. In the centre of the bridge is an equestrian statue of Henri IV; the original went up in 1635, was melted down to make cannons during the Revolution, and replaced in 1818.

Sights & museums

Cathédrale Notre-Dame de Paris

Pl du Parvis-Notre-Dame, 4th (01.42. 34.56.10, www.cathedraledeparis.com). M° Cité/RER St-Michel Notre-Dame. **Open** 8am-6.45pm Mon-Fri; 8am-7.15pm Sat, Sun. *Towers* Apr-Sept 10am-6.30pm daily (June, Aug until 11pm Sat, Sun). Oct-Mar 10am-5.30pm daily. **Admission** free. *Towers* €8; free-€5 reductions. **Map** p117 C2 ❷
Notre-Dame was constructed between 1163 and 1334, and the amount of time and money spent on it reflected the city's growing prestige. The west front remains a high point of Gothic art for the balanced proportions of its twin towers and rose window, and the three doorways with their rows of saints and sculpted tympanums: the *Last Judgement* (centre), *Life of the Virgin*

Sainte-Chapelle p120

(left) and *Life of St Anne* (right). Inside, take a moment to admire the long nave with its solid foliate capitals and high altar with a marble *Pietà* by Coustou.

Climb up the towers to appreciate the masonry. The route runs up the north tower and down the south. Between the two you get a close-up view of the gallery of chimeras – the fantastic birds and hybrid beasts designed by Viollet-le-Duc along the balustrade. After a detour to see the massive bell, a staircase leads to the top of the south tower.

La Conciergerie

*2 bd du Palais, 1st (01.53.40.60.80). M°
Cité/RER St-Michel Notre-Dame.* **Open**
Mar-Oct 9.30am-6pm daily. *Nov-Feb*
9am-5pm daily. **Admission** €7; free-
€4.50 reductions. *With Sainte-Chapelle*
€11; €7.50 reductions. **Map** p117 B1 ❸
The Conciergerie looks every inch the forbidding medieval fortress. However, much of the façade was added in the 1850s, long after Marie-Antoinette, Danton and Robespierre had been imprisoned here. The visit takes you through the Salle des Gardes, the medieval kitchens with their four huge chimneys, and the Salle des Gens d'Armes, a vaulted Gothic hall built between 1301 and 1315. After the royals moved to the Louvre, the fortress became a prison under the watch of the Concierge. The wealthy had private cells with their own furniture, which they paid for; others had to make do with straw beds. A list of Revolutionary prisoners, including a hairdresser, shows that not all victims were nobles. In Marie-Antoinette's cell, the Chapelle des Girondins, are her crucifix, some portraits and a guillotine blade.

La Crypte Archéologique

*Pl Jean-Paul II, 4th (01.55.42.50.10).
M° Cité/RER St-Michel Notre-Dame.*
Open 10am-6pm Tue-Sun. **Admission**
€4; free-€3 reductions. **Map** p117 C2 ❹
Hidden under the forecourt in front of the cathedral is a large void containing pieces of Roman quaysides, ramparts and hypocausts, medieval cellars, shops and pavements, the foundations of the Eglise Ste-Geneviève-des-Ardens (the church where Geneviève's remains were stored during the Norman invasions), an 18th-century foundling hospital and a 19th-century sewer. It's not easy to work out which wall, column or staircase is which – but you do get a vivid sense of the layers of history piled one atop another during 16 centuries.

Mémorial des Martyrs de la Déportation

*Sq de l'Ile de France, 4th
(01.46.33.87.56). M° Cité/RER Châtelet
or St-Michel Notre-Dame.* **Open** *Oct-
Mar* 10am-noon, 2-5pm daily. *Apr-Sept*
10am-noon, 2-7pm daily. **Admission**
free. **Map** p117 C2 ❺
This tribute to the 200,000 Jews, Communists, homosexuals and *résistants* deported to concentration camps from France in World War II stands on the eastern tip of the island. A blind staircase descends to river level, where chambers are lined with tiny lights and the walls are inscribed with verse. A barred window looks on to the Seine.

Sainte-Chapelle

*6 bd du Palais, 1st (01.53.40.60.80).
M° Cité/RER St-Michel Notre-Dame.*
Open *Mar-Oct* 9.30am-6pm daily. *Nov-
Feb* 9am-5pm daily. **Admission** €8;
free-€5 reductions. *With Conciergerie*
€11; €7.50 reductions. **Map** p117 B2 ❻
Devout King Louis IX (St Louis, 1226-70) had a hobby of accumulating holy relics (and children: he fathered 11). In the 1240s, he bought what was advertised as the Crown of Thorns, and ordered Pierre de Montreuil to design a shrine. The result was the exquisite Flamboyant Gothic Sainte-Chapelle. With 15m (49ft) windows, the upper level, intended for the royal family and the canons, appears to consist almost entirely of stained glass. The windows depict hundreds of scenes from the Old and New Testaments, culminating with the Apocalypse in the rose window.

Ile St-Louis

The Ile St-Louis is one of the most exclusive residential addresses in the city. Delightfully unspoiled, it has fine architecture, narrow streets and pretty views from the tree-lined quays, and still retains the air of a tranquil backwater.

Rue St-Louis-en-l'Ile – lined with fine historic buildings that now house gift shops and gourmet food stores (many open on Sunday), quaint tearooms, stone-walled bars, restaurants and hotels – runs the length of the island. The grandiose Hôtel Lambert at no.2 was built by Le Vau in 1641 for Louis XIII's secretary, and has sumptuous interiors by Le Sueur, Perrier and Le Brun. At no.51 – Hôtel Chenizot – look out for the bearded faun adorning the florid doorway, which is flanked by stern dragons supporting the balcony.

At the western end there are great views of the buttresses of Notre-Dame from the terrace of the Brasserie de l'Ile St-Louis.

Sights & museums

Eglise St-Louis-en-l'Ile

19bis rue St-Louis-en-l'Ile, 4th (01.46. 34.11.60, www.saintlouisenlile.catholique. fr). M° *Pont Marie.* **Open** 9.30am-1pm, 2-7pm daily. **Map** p117 D3 **7**

The island's church was built between 1664 and 1765, following plans by Louis Le Vau and later completed by Gabriel Le Duc. The interior boasts Corinthian columns and a sunburst over the altar, and sometimes hosts classical music concerts.

Eating & drinking

Brasserie de l'Ile St-Louis

55 quai de Bourbon, 4th (01.43.54. 02.59). M° *Pont Marie.* **Open** noon-11.30pm Mon, Tue, Thur-Sun. Closed Aug. €€. **Brasserie**. **Map** p117 D2 **8**

Happily, this old-fashioned brasserie soldiers on while exotic juice bars on the Ile St-Louis come and go. The terrace has one of the best summer views in Paris and is invariably packed. The dining room exudes shabby chic, though nothing here is gastronomically gripping: a well-dressed *frisée aux lardons*, perhaps, or a pan of warming tripe.

Mon Vieil Ami

69 rue St-Louis-en-l'Ile, 4th (01.40.46. 01.35, www.mon-vieil-ami.com). M° *Pont Marie.* **Open** noon-2.30pm, 6.30-11pm Wed-Sun. Closed 3wks Jan & 1st 3wks Aug. €€. **Bistro**. **Map** p117 D2 **9**

Antoine Westermann has created a true foodie destination here. Starters such as tartare of diced raw vegetables with sautéed baby squid on top impress with deft seasoning. Typical of the mains is a casserole of roast duck with caramelised turnips and couscous.

Shopping

Arche de Noé

70 rue St-Louis-en-l'Ile, 4th (01.46.34. 61.60). M° *Pont Marie.* **Open** 10.30am-1pm, 2-7pm daily. **Map** p117 D2 **10**

'Noah's Ark' is a great place for Christmas shopping, with traditional wooden toys from eastern Europe, games, jigsaws and finger puppets.

Cacao et Chocolat

63 rue St-Louis-en-l'Ile, 4th (01.46.33.33.33, www.cacaoetchocolat. com). M° *Pont Marie.* **Open** 10.30am-7.30pm daily. **Map** p117 D2 **11**

This shop recalls chocolate's Aztec origins, with its choice of spicy fillings (honey and chilli, nutmeg, clove and citrus), chocolate masks and pyramids.

L'Occitane

1 rue d'Arcole, 4th (01.55.42.06.11, www.loccitane.com). M° *Cité.* **Open** 10.30am-7pm daily. **Map** p117 C2 **12**

The many branches of this popular Provençal chain offer natural beauty products in neat packaging.

Les Invalides p124

The 7th & Western Paris

The seventh arrondissement is one large workshop, dotted with the machinery of state and diplomacy: this is the home of parliament, several ministries and a gaggle of foreign embassies, as well as the headquarters of UNESCO. Visually speaking, much of the district is formal and aloof, albeit smart, and there are few attractions to draw the visitor – with the sizeable exceptions, naturally, of **Les Invalides**, the **Rodin Musée** and a certain A-shaped assembly of 19th-century iron lattice beside the river. Another major nearby attraction, the **Musée d'Orsay**, is gleaming after renovation (see p133).

Sights & museums

Les Égouts de Paris

Opposite 93 quai d'Orsay, by Pont de l'Alma, 7th (01.53.68.27.81). Mº Alma Marceau/RER Pont de l'Alma. **Open**
11am-4pm (until 5pm May-Sept) Mon-Wed, Sat, Sun. Closed 2wks Jan. **Admission** €4.30; free-€3.50 reductions. No credit cards. **Map** p123 B1 ❶
For centuries, the main source of drinking water in Paris was the Seine, which was also the main sewer. Construction of an underground sewerage system began at the time of Napoleon. Today, the Égouts de Paris constitutes a smelly museum; each sewer in the 2,100km (1,305-mile) system is marked with a replica of the street sign above.

Eiffel Tower

Champ de Mars, 7th (08.92.70.12.39, www.tour-eiffel.fr). Mº Bir-Hakeim/RER Champ de Mars Tour Eiffel. **Open** *By lift* Mid June-Aug 9am-12.45am daily (last ascent 11pm). Sept-mid June 9.30am-11.45pm daily (last ascent 10.30pm). *By stairs* (1st & 2nd levels) Mid June-Aug 9am-12.45am (last ascent midnight). Sept-mid June 9.30am-6.30pm (last ascent 6pm). **Admission**

122 Time Out Shortlist | Paris 2013

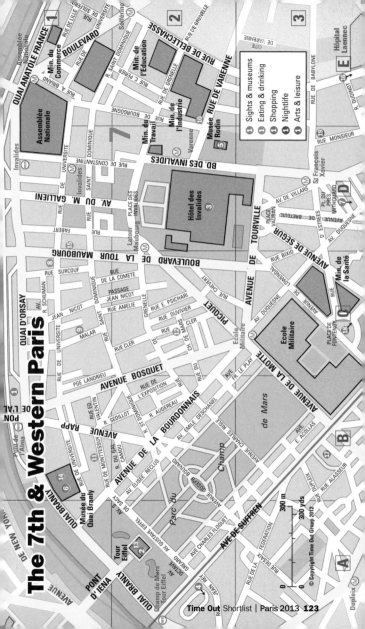

The 7th & Western Paris

1	Sights & museums
1	Eating & drinking
1	Shopping
1	Nightlife
1	Arts & leisure

© Copyright Time Out Group 2012

By stairs €4.70; €3.20-€3.70 reductions; free under-4s. *By lift* (1st & 2nd level) €8.20; €4.10-€6.60 reductions; (3rd level) €13.40; €9.30-€11.80 reductions; free under-4s. **Map** p123 A2 ❷

No building better symbolises Paris than the Tour Eiffel. Construction took more than two years and used some 18,000 pieces of metal and 2,500,000 rivets. Vintage double-decker lifts ply their way up and down; you can walk as far as the second level. There are souvenir shops, an exhibition space, café and even a post office on the first and second levels. At the top (third level), there's Eiffel's cosy salon and a viewing platform with panels pointing out what to see. Views can reach 65km (40 miles) on a good day.

Les Invalides & Musée de l'Armée

Esplanade des Invalides, 7th (08.10.11.33.99, www.invalides.org). M° La Tour-Maubourg or Les Invalides. **Open** *Apr-Sept* 10am-6pm Mon, Wed-Sat; 10am-9pm Tue; 10am-6.30pm Sun. *Oct-Mar* 10am-5pm Mon-Sat; 10am-5.30pm Sun. Closed 1st Mon of mth. **Admission** *Musée de l'Armée & Eglise du Dôme* €9; free-€7 reductions. **Map** p123 D2 ❸

Topped by its gilded dome, the Hôtel des Invalides was (and in part still is) a hospital. Commissioned by Louis XIV for wounded soldiers, it once housed up to 6,000 invalids. The complex contains two churches – the Eglise St-Louis was for the soldiers, the Eglise du Dôme for the king.

The Invalides complex also houses the enormous Musée de l'Armée. The Antique Armour wing is packed full of armour and weapons that look as good as new. The Plans-Reliefs section is a collection of gorgeous 18th- and 19th-century scale models of French cities, used for military strategy. The World War I rooms are moving, with the conflict brought into focus by uniforms, paintings, a scale model of a trench on the western front and, most sobering of all, white plastercasts of the hideously mutilated faces of two soldiers. The World War II wing takes in not just the Resistance, but also the Battle of Britain and the war in the Pacific (there's a replica of Little Boy, the bomb dropped on Hiroshima). Included in the entry price is the Historial Charles de Gaulle.

Maison de la Culture du Japon

101bis quai Branly, 15th (01.44.37. 95.01, www.mcjp.asso.fr). M° Bir-Hakeim/RER Champ de Mars Tour Eiffel. **Open** noon-7pm Tue, Wed, Fri, Sat; noon-8pm Thur. Closed Aug. **Admission** free. **Map** p123 A2 ❹

This glass-fronted Japanese cultural centre screens films and puts on exhibitions and plays. It also contains a library, an authentic tea pavilion on the roof and a well-stocked shop.

Musée National Rodin

Hôtel Biron, 79 rue de Varenne, 7th (01.44.18.61.10, www.musee-rodin.fr). M° Varenne. **Open** 10am-5.45pm Tue-Sun (gardens until 6pm). **Admission** €6; free-€5 reductions. *Exhibitions* €7; free-€5 reductions. *Gardens* free-€1. **Map** p123 D2 ❺

The Rodin museum occupies the *hôtel particulier* where the sculptor lived in the final years of his life. The *Kiss*, the *Cathedral*, the *Walking Man*, portrait busts and early terracottas are exhibited indoors. Rodin's works are accompanied by pieces by his mistress and pupil, Camille Claudel. The walls are hung with paintings by Van Gogh, Monet, Renoir, Carrière and Rodin himself. Most visitors have greatest affection for the gardens: look out for the *Burghers of Calais*, the elaborate *Gates of Hell*, and the *Thinker*.

Musée du Quai Branly

37-55 quai Branly, 7th (01.56.61.70.00, www.quaibranly.fr). RER Pont de l'Alma. **Open** 11am-7pm Tue, Wed, Sun; 11am-9pm Thur-Sat. **Admission** €8.50; free-€6 reductions. **Map** p123 B1 ❻

Built to last

Paris's World Fairs have produced some iconic buildings.

What do the Eiffel Tower, the Palais de Chaillot and the Grand Palais have in common? Beyond the obvious fact that they are major Paris monuments, these buildings share another key trait: they were all built for the World Fair.

Best known these days simply as 'Expo', the World Fair was conceived as an international showcase for technological innovations and cultural exchange, with London welcoming the first Fair in 1851. Between 1855 and 1937, Paris hosted the Exposition Universelle six times, with each successive show offering the city a plethora of new architectural landmarks. Most structures were designed for a lifespan of just a few months and dismantled at the end of the Fair, but others have survived. The Grand Palais and Petit Palais were both built as exhibition halls for the 1900 World Fair, while the colonnaded Palais de Chaillot and Palais de Tokyo were erected for the 1937 Fair.

The Champ de Mars was given a whole series of facelifts during the golden years of the Paris World Fairs. For some 50 years, its centrepiece was the Palais de l'Industrie, a huge arena-like hall constructed in 1855 to rival London's Crystal Palace. Most famously, the Eiffel Tower was originally erected here as a temporary exhibit for the 1889 World Fair. It was spared subsequent dismantling thanks to the birth of radio communication: the tower's height made it a first-rate location for an antenna.

Less well-known vestiges of the Fairs are littered all around the city. La Ruche ('The Beehive') in the 15th arrondissement was designed as a wine rotunda by Gustave Eiffel in 1900 and subsequently became one of the city's most famous artists' studios, inhabited by the likes of Chagall, Modigliani and Brancusi. Many other monuments have been relocated – the Japanese Tower and Chinese Pavilion (1900) were transported all the way to Brussels, while the Chalet Suisse (1867) was rebuilt on the Ile Reuilly in the Bois de Vincennes and is now a well respected restaurant (www.lechaletdesiles.com).

In another corner of the Bois de Vincennes, the Jardin Tropical is a rather sadder Expo leftover. Built for the Exposition Coloniale of 1907, a showcase for France's colonial dominance, its once grandiose pavilions have since fallen into disrepair, and today the crumbling ruins are a rather forlorn tribute to a bygone era.

Musée du Quai Branly p124

Surrounded by trees on the banks of the Seine, this museum is a showcase for non-European cultures. Treasures include a tenth-century anthropomorphic Dogon statue from Mali, Aztec statues, Gabonese masks, Vietnamese costumes and Peruvian feather tunics. Event highlights Sources of Aboriginal Painting (9 Oct 2012-20 Jan 2013).

Musée Valentin Haüy
5 rue Duroc, 7th (01.44.49.27.27, www.avh.asso.fr). M° Duroc. **Open** times vary. **Admission** free. **Map** p123 D3 **7**

This tiny museum is devoted to the history of braille. You can explore on your own with the aid of French, English or braille explanatory texts, or allow the curator, Noële Roy, to show you round. She will give a tour in English if preferred. The first exhibit is a shocking print, depicting the fairground freak show that inspired Valentin Haüy to devote his life to educating not only the blind, but also the backward public who came to laugh at the likes of this blind orchestra forced to perform in dunce's hats. Next begins the tactile tour, with a chance to touch books printed in embossed letters.

Eating & drinking

Le 144 Petrossian
18 bd de La Tour-Maubourg, 7th (01.44.11.32.32, www.petrossian.fr). M° La Tour Maubourg. **Open** 12.15-2.30pm, 7.30-10.30pm Tue-Sat. €€€. **Russian**. **Map** p123 C1 **8**

Senegalese-French chef Rougui Dia directs the kitchen of this famed caviar house. You'll find Russian specialities such as blinis, salmon and caviar from the Petrossian boutique downstairs, but Dia has added preparations and spices from all over the world.

L'Ami Jean
27 rue Malar, 7th (01.47.05.86.89, www.amijean.eu). M° Ecole Militaire.

Open noon-2pm, 7pm-midnight Tue-Sat. Closed Aug. €€. **Bistro**. **Map** p123 C1 **9**

This long-running Basque address is an ongoing hit thanks to chef Stéphane Jégo. Tender veal shank comes deboned with a side of baby onions and broad beans with tiny cubes of ham, and house-salted cod is soaked, sautéed and doused with an elegant vinaigrette.

L'Arpège
84 rue de Varenne, 7th (01.47.05. 09.06, www.alain-passard.com). M° Varenne. **Open** noon-2.30pm, 8-10.30pm Mon-Fri. €€€€. **Haute cuisine**. **Map** p123 E2 **10**

Assuming that you can swallow an exceptionally high bill – we're talking €42 for a potato starter – chances are you'll have a spectacular time at chef Alain Passard's Left Bank establishment. A main course of sautéed free-range chicken with a roasted shallot, an onion, potato *mousseline* and pan juices is the apotheosis of comfort food.

Au Bon Accueil
14 rue de Monttessuy, 7th (01.47.05. 46.11, www.aubonaccueilparis.com). M° Alma Marceau. **Open** noon-2.30pm, 7-10.30pm Mon-Fri. Closed 2wks Aug. €€. **Bistro**. **Map** p123 B1 **11**

Jacques Lacipière runs Au Bon Accueil, and Naobuni Sasaki turns out the beautiful food. Perhaps most impressive is his elegant use of little-known fish such as grey mullet and meagre (*maigre*), rather than the usual endangered species. The €27 lunch menu might highlight such ingredients as *suprême de poulet noir du Cros de la Géline*, free-range chicken raised on a farm run by two former cabaret singers. But the biggest surprise comes with desserts, worthy of the finest pastry shops.

Le Café du Marché
38 rue Cler, 7th (01.47.05.51.27). M° Ecole Militaire. **Open** 7am-1am Mon-Sat; 7am-4pm Sun. €. **Café**. **Map** p123 C2 **12**

This address is frequented by trendy locals, shoppers hunting down a particular type of cheese and tourists who've managed to make it this far from the Eiffel Tower. Its *pichets* of decent house plonk go down a treat, and mention must be made of the food – such as the huge house salad served with lashings of foie gras and parma ham.

Jules Verne

Pilier Sud, Eiffel Tower, 7th (01.45.55.61.44, www.lejulesverne-paris.com). M° Bir Hakeim or RER Tour Eiffel. **Open** 12.15-1.30pm, 7-9.30pm daily. **€€€€. Haute cuisine. Map** p123 A2 ⓱

You have to have courage to take on an icon like the Eiffel Tower, but Alain Ducasse has done just that in taking over the Jules Verne. He has transformed the cuisine and brought in designer Patrick Jouin. Pascal Féraud updates French classics with dishes like turbot with champagne zabaglione.

Les Ombres

27 quai Branly, 7th (01.47.53.68.00, www.lesombres-restaurant.com). M° Alma-Marceau. **Open** noon-2.30pm, 7-10.30pm daily. **€€€. Bistro. Map** p123 B1 ⓮

The full-on view of the Eiffel Tower at night would be reason enough to come to this restaurant on the top floor of the Musée du Quai Branly, but young chef Arnaud Busquet's food also demands that you take notice. His talent shows in dishes such as thin green asparagus curved into a nest with tiny *lardons* and topped with a breaded poached egg, ribbons of parmesan and meat *jus*.

Il Vino

13 bd de La Tour-Maubourg, 7th (01.44.11.72.00, www.ilvinobyenrico bernardo.com). M° La Tour-Maubourg. **Open** noon-2pm, 7pm-midnight daily. **€€€€. Italian. Map** p123 D1 ⓯

Enrico Bernardo, winner of the World's Best Sommelier award, runs this restaurant where, for once, food plays second fiddle to wine. You are given nothing more than a wine list. Each of 15 wines by the glass is matched with a surprise dish, or the chef can build a meal around the bottle of your choice. The impeccably prepared food shows a strong Italian influence.

Shopping

Fromagerie Quatrehomme

62 rue de Sèvres, 7th (01.47.34.33.45). M° Duroc or Vaneau. **Open** 8.45am-1pm, 4-7.45pm Tue-Thur; 8.45am-7.45pm Fri, Sat. **Map** p123 E3 ⓰

Marie Quatrehomme runs this *fromagerie*. Justly famous for her comté fruité, beaufort and st-marcellin, she also sells specialities such as goat's cheese with pesto.

Marie-Anne Cantin

12 rue du Champ-de-Mars, 7th (01.45. 50.43.94, www.cantin.fr). M° Ecole Militaire or La Tour Maubourg. **Open** 2-7.30pm Mon; 8.30am-7.30pm Tue-Sat; 8.30am-1pm Sun. **Map** p123 B3 ⓱

Cantin, supplier to posh Paris restaurants, offers aged *chèvres* and amazing morbier, mont d'or and comté.

Saxe-Breteuil

Av de Saxe, 7th. M° Ségur. **Open** 7am-2.30pm Thur; 7am-3pm Sat. **Map** p123 C3 ⓲

Saxe-Breteuil has an unrivalled setting facing the Eiffel Tower, as well as the city's most chic produce. Look for farmer's goat's cheese, abundant oysters and a handful of small producers.

Arts & leisure

La Pagode

57bis rue de Babylone, 7th (01.45.55. 48.48, www.allocine.fr). M° St-François-Xavier. **Admission** €9; €7.50 reductions. No credit cards. **Map** p123 D3 ⓳

This glorious edifice is a 19th-century replica of a pagoda. Renovated in the 1990s, this is one of the loveliest cinemas in the world.

Jardin du Luxembourg p130

St-Germain-des-Prés & Odéon

Like the Latin Quarter, St-Germain-des-Prés is another area that no longer quite lives up to its legend. In the middle third of the 20th century, the area was prime arts and *intello* territory, a place known as much for its high jinks as its lofty thinking: the haunt of Picasso, Giacometti, Camus, Prévert and, *bien sûr*, the Bonnie and Clyde of French philosophy, Jean-Paul Sartre and Simone de Beauvoir; the hotspot of the Paris jazz boom after World War II; and the heart of the Paris book trade. This is where the cliché of café terrace intellectualising was coined, but nowadays most of the patrons of the Flore and the Deux Magots are in the fashion business, and couturiers have largely replaced publishers. Never mind: it's a smart and attractive part of the city to wander around in, and also has some very good restaurants.

St-Germain-des-Prés grew up around the medieval abbey, the oldest church in Paris and site of an annual fair that drew merchants from across Europe. There are traces of its cloister and part of the abbot's palace behind the church on rue de l'Abbaye. Constructed in 1586 in red brick with stone facing, the palace prefigured the architecture of place des Vosges. Charming place de Furstemberg (once the palace stables) is home to the house and studio where the elderly Delacroix lived when painting the murals in St-Sulpice; it now houses the **Musée National Delacroix**. Wagner, Ingres and Colette all lived on nearby rue Jacob; its elegant 17th-century *hôtels particuliers* now contain specialist book, design and antiques shops and a few pleasant hotels. Further east, rue de Buci hosts a market and upmarket food shops.

Ecole Nationale Supérieure des Beaux-Arts (Ensb-a)

14 rue Bonaparte, 6th (01.47.03.50.00, www.ensba.fr). M° St-Germain-des-Prés. **Open** 1-7pm Tue-Sun. **Admission** €4; €2 reductions. *Exhibitions* prices vary. **Map** p131 C1 ❶

The city's most prestigious fine arts school resides in what remains of the 17th-century Couvent des Petits-Augustins, the 18th-century Hôtel de Chimay, some 19th-century additions and chunks of various French châteaux moved here after the Revolution (when the buildings briefly served as a museum of French monuments).

Eglise St-Germain-des-Prés

3 pl St-Germain-des-Prés, 6th (01.55.42.81.33, www.eglise-sgp.org). M° St-Germain-des-Prés. **Open** 8am-7.45pm Mon-Sat; 9am-8pm Sun. **Admission** free. **Map** p131 C2 ❷

The oldest church in Paris. On the advice of Germain (later Bishop of Paris), Childebert, son of Clovis, had a basilica and monastery built here around 543. It was first dedicated to St Vincent, and came to be known as St-Germain-le-Doré because of its copper roof, then later as St-Germain-des-Prés ('of the fields'). During the Revolution the abbey was burned and a saltpetre refinery installed; the spire was added in a 19th-century restoration. Still, most of the present structure is 12th century, and ornate carved capitals and the tower remain from the 11th. Tombs include those of Jean-Casimir, deposed King of Poland who became Abbot of St-Germain in 1669, and Scots nobleman William Douglas.

Eglise St-Sulpice

Pl St-Sulpice, 6th (01.42.34.59.98, www. paroisse-saint-sulpice-paris.org). M° St-Sulpice. **Open** 7.30am-7.30pm daily. **Admission** free. **Map** p131 C3 ❸

It took 120 years (starting in 1646) and six architects to finish St-Sulpice. The grandiose Italianate façade, with its two-tier colonnade, was designed by Jean-Baptiste Servandoni. He died in 1766 before the second tower was finished, leaving one tower five metres shorter than the other. The trio of murals by Delacroix in the first chapel – *Jacob's Fight with the Angel, Heliodorus Chased from the Temple* and *St Michael Killing the Dragon* – create a suitably sombre atmosphere.

Jardin & Palais du Luxembourg

Pl Auguste-Comte, pl Edmond-Rostand or rue de Vaugirard, 6th (01.44.54.19.49, www.senat.fr/ visite). M° Odéon/RER Luxembourg. **Open** *Jardin* summer 7.30am-dusk daily; winter 8am-dusk daily. **Map** p131 C4 ❹

The palace itself was built in the 1620s for Marie de Médicis, widow of Henri IV, by Salomon de Brosse on the site of the former mansion of the Duke of Luxembourg. Its Italianate style was intended to remind her of the Pitti Palace in her native Florence. The palace now houses the French parliament's upper house, the Sénat.

The mansion next door (Le Petit Luxembourg) is the residence of the Sénat's president. The gardens, though, are the real draw: part formal (terraces and gravel paths), part 'English garden' (lawns and mature trees), they are the quintessential Paris park. The garden is crowded with sculptures: a looming Cyclops, queens of France, a miniature Statue of Liberty, wild animals, busts of Flaubert and Baudelaire, and a monument to Delacroix. There are orchards and an apiary. The Musée National du Luxembourg hosts prestigious exhibitions. Most interesting, though, are the people: an international mixture of *flâneurs* and *dragueurs*, chess players and martial-arts practitioners, as well as children on ponies, in sandpits and playing with sailing boats on the pond.

PARIS BY AREA

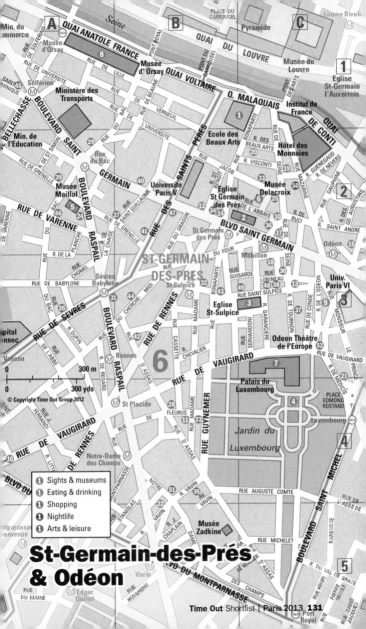

St-Germain-des-Prés & Odéon

Bread & Roses p134

Musée Maillol

59-61 rue de Grenelle, 7th (01.42. 22.59.58, www.museemaillol.com). Mº Rue du Bac. **Open** 10.30am-7pm (last admission 6.15pm) Mon-Thur, Sat, Sun; 10.30am-9.30pm (last admission 8.45pm) Fri. **Admission** €11; free-€9 reductions. **Map** p131 A2 ❺

Dina Vierny was 15 when she met Aristide Maillol (1861-1944) and became his principal model for the next decade, idealised in such sculptures as *Spring, Air* and *Harmony*. In 1995, she opened this delightful museum, exhibiting Maillol's drawings, engravings, pastels, tapestry panels, ceramics and early Nabis-related paintings, as well as the sculptures and terracottas that epitomise his calm, modern classicism. The venue has works by Picasso, Rodin, Gauguin, Degas and Cézanne, a room of Matisse drawings, rare Surrealist documents and works by naïve artists. Vierny has also championed Kandinsky and Ilya Kabakov, whose *Communal Kitchen* installation recreates the atmosphere of Soviet domesticity. Monographic exhibitions are devoted to contemporary artists.

Musée National Delacroix

6 rue de Furstemberg, 6th (01.44.41.86.50, www.musee-delacroix.fr). Mº St-Germain-des-Prés. **Open** 9.30am-5pm Mon, Wed-Sun. **Admission** €5; free reductions. **Map** p131 C2 ❻

Eugène Delacroix moved to this apartment and studio in 1857 to be near the Eglise St-Sulpice, where he was painting murals. This collection includes small oil paintings, free pastel studies of skies, sketches and lithographs.

Musée du Luxembourg

19 rue de Vaugirard, 6th (01.40.13. 62.00, www.museeduluxembourg.fr). Mº Cluny La Sorbonne or Odéon/ RER Luxembourg. **Open** 9am-10pm

Mon, Fri-Sun; 10am-8pm Tue-Thur. **Admission** €12; free-€7.50 reductions. **Map** p131 C3 ❼

When it opened in 1750, this small museum was the first public gallery in France. After major renovations, the museum reopened its doors in early 2011 with an exhibition devoted to German artist Lucas Cranach.

Event highlights The Circle of Modern Art – Le Havre Collectors (19 Sept 2012-6 Jan 2013)

Musée d'Orsay

1 rue de la Légion-d'Honneur, 7th (01.40.49.48.14, www.musee-orsay.fr). Mº Solférino/RER Musée d'Orsay. **Open** 9.30am-6pm Tue, Wed, Fri-Sun; 9.30am-9.45pm Thur. **Admission** €8; free-€5.50 reductions. **Map** p131 A1 ❽

The Musée d'Orsay's famed upper galleries recently underwent a serious brush-up, with the museum reopening its doors in October 2011 after an 18-month revamp to gasps of admiration. The museum, originally a train station designed by Victor Laloux in 1900, houses a huge collection spanning the period between 1848 and 1914, and is home to a profusion of works by Delacroix, Manet, Renoir, Pissarro, Gauguin, Monet, Cézanne, Van Gogh, and others. The results of the renovations are a better display of artworks, more spacious exhibition areas, fine Solux lighting, and Tokujin Yoshioka-designed chairs.

Eating & drinking

Le Bar Dix

10 rue de l'Odéon, 6th (01.43.26. 66.83, www.le10bar.com). Mº Odéon. **Open** 6pm-2am daily. No credit cards. **Bar.** **Map** p131 C3 ❾

Generations of students have glugged back jugs of the celebrated home-made sangría (€3 a glass in happy hour) while squeezed into the cramped upper bar, tattily authentic with its Jacques Brel record sleeves, Yves Montand handbills and pre-war light fittings.

Spelunkers and hopeless romantics negotiate the hazardous stone staircase to drink in the cellar bar, with its candlelight and old advertising murals. Can someone please come and slap a preservation order on the place?

Le Bar du Marché
75 rue de Seine, 6th (01.43.26.55.15). Mº Mabillon or Odéon. **Open** 8am-2am daily. No credit cards. **Bar**. **Map** p131 C2 ⑩
The market in question is the Cours des Halles, the bar a convivial corner café opening on to the pleasing bustle of St-Germain-des-Prés. Simple dishes like a ham omelette or a plate of herring in the €7 range, and Brouilly or muscadet at €4-€5 a glass, are proffered by beret-topped waiters. Locals easily outnumber tourists, confirming Rod Stewart's astute observation that Paris gives the impression that no one is ever working.

Bread & Roses
7 rue de Fleurus, 6th (01.42.22.06.06, www.breadandroses.fr). Mº St-Placide. **Open** 8am-8pm Mon-Sat. Closed Aug & 1wk Dec. €€. **Café**. **Map** p131 B4 ⑪
Giant wedges of cheesecake sit alongside French pastries, and huge savoury puff-pastry tarts are perched on the counter. Attention to detail shows even in the taramasalata, which is matched with buckwheat-and-seaweed bread. Prices reflect the quality of the often organic ingredients.

Café de Flore
172 bd St-Germain, 6th (01.45.48. 55.26, www.cafe-de-flore.com). Mº St-Germain-des-Prés. **Open** 7am-2am daily. €€. **Café**. **Map** p131 B2 ⑫
Bourgeois locals crowd the terrace tables at lunch, eating club sandwiches with knives and forks as anxious waiters frown at couples with pushchairs or single diners occupying tables for four. This historic café, former HQ of the Lost Generation intelligentsia, attracts tourists, and celebrities from time to time. But a *café crème* is €4.60, and the

omelettes and *croques* are best eschewed in favour of the better dishes on the menu (€15-€25). There are play readings on Mondays and philosophy debates on the first Wednesday of the month, both at 8pm, in English.

Le Comptoir
Hôtel Le Relais Saint-Germain, 9 carrefour de l'Odéon, 6th (01.43.29. 12.05). Mº Odéon. **Open** noon-6pm, 8.30-11pm (last orders 9pm) Mon-Fri; noon-11pm Sat, Sun. Closed 3wks Aug. €€. **Brasserie**. **Map** p131 C3 ⑬
Yves Camdeborde runs the bijou 17th-century Hôtel Le Relais Saint-Germain, whose art deco dining room, modestly dubbed Le Comptoir, serves brasserie fare from noon to 6pm and on weekend nights, and a five-course prix fixe feast on weekday evenings. The single dinner sitting lets the chef take real pleasure in his work. On the daily menu, you might find dishes like rolled saddle of lamb with vegetable-stuffed 'Basque ravioli'. The catch? The prix fixe dinner can be booked up six months in advance.

Les Deux Magots
6 pl St-Germain-des-Prés, 6th (01.45. 48.55.25, www.lesdeuxmagots.com). Mº St-Germain-des-Prés. **Open** 7.30am-1am daily. €€. **Café**. **Map** p131 B2 ⑭
If you stand outside Les Deux Magots, you have to be prepared to photograph tourists wanting proof of their encounter with French philosophy. The former haunt of Sartre and de Beauvoir now draws a less pensive crowd that can be all too *m'as-tu vu*, particularly at weekends. The hot chocolate is still good, though. Visit on a weekday afternoon when the editors return, manuscripts in hand, to the inside tables, leaving enough elbow room to engage in some serious discussion.

L'Epigramme
9 rue de l'Eperon, 6th (01.44.41.00.09). Mº Odéon. **Open** noon-2.30pm, 7-11.30pm Tue-Sat. €. **Bistro**. **Map** p131 C2 ⑮

L'Epigramme is a pleasantly bourgeois dining room with terracotta floor tiles, wood beams, a glassed-in kitchen and comfortable chairs. Like the decor, the food doesn't aim to innovate but sticks to tried and true classics with the occasional twist. Marinated mackerel in a mustardy dressing on toasted country bread gets things off to a promising start, but the chef's skill really comes through in main courses such as perfectly seared lamb with glazed root vegetables and intense *jus*. It's rare to find such a high standard of cooking at this price. Be sure to book.

La Ferrandaise

8 rue de Vaugirard, 6th (01.43.26. 36.36, www.laferrandaise.com). M° Odéon/RER Luxembourg. **Open** 7-10.30pm Mon; noon-2.30pm, 7-10.30pm Tue-Thur; noon-2.30pm, 7pm-midnight Fri; 7pm-midnight Sat. **€€. Bistro. Map** p131 A4 **16**

This bistro has quickly established a faithful following. A platter of excellent ham, sausage and terrine arrives as you study the blackboard menu, and the bread is crisp-crusted, thickly sliced sourdough. Two specialities are the potato stuffed with escargots in a camembert sauce, and a wonderfully flavoured, slightly rosé slice of veal. Desserts might include intense chocolate with rum-soaked bananas.

Germain

NEW *25-27 rue de Buci, 6th (01.43.26. 02.93). M° Mabillon or Odéon.* **Open** noon-midnight daily. **€€. Brasserie. Map** p131 C2 **17**

Quaint rue de Buci has been shaken up by the extravagance of Germain, a versatile brasserie halfway between *Alice in Wonderland* and London's Sketch. The heated terrace is great for people watching, and the main ground-floor room, which features the lower part of a vast yellow statue piercing through the ceiling above, is perfect for a quick lunch. There's also a cosy salon for cocktails, a more conservative dining room at the back, and a private room on the first floor with a snooker table and the top half of the yellow statue. The food is almost childishly classic, but always with a twist (ham and butter macaroni with truffle) and not as expensive as you might expect.

J'Go

Rue Clément, 6th (01.43.26.19.02, www.lejgo.com). M° Mabillon or Odéon. **Open** 11am-midnight daily. **€€.** **Wine bar. Map** p131 C3 **18**

As its name suggests, J'Go (pronounced gigot) is all about lamb – well, meat of various kinds, actually: a buzzing wine bar by day, it becomes a *rôtisserie* at meal times, serving its speciality spit-roasted lamb from Quercy, black pig from Bigorre, and whole roasted chickens. The €28 set menu is well worth it, offering a whole jar of pâté, a giant salad, and lamb with creamy stewed *haricots blancs*. If you'd rather stick to wine and tapas, sidle up to one of the wooden barrels, choose your poison (at €4 a glass all wines are good) and share a plate of charcuterie or foie gras *tartines* (€10).

La Palette

43 rue de Seine, 6th (01.43.26.68.15). M° Odéon. **Open** 9am-2am Mon-Sat. Closed Aug. **€. Café. Map** p131 C2 **19**

La Palette is the café-bar of choice for the Beaux-Arts students who study at the venerable institution around the corner, and young couples who steal kisses in the wonderfully preserved art-deco back room decorated with illustrations. Grab a spot on the leafy terrace if you can.

Le Restaurant

L'Hôtel, 13 rue des Beaux-Arts, 6th (01.44.41.99.01, www.l-hotel.com). M° St-Germain-des-Prés. **Open** 12.30-2.30pm, 7.30-10pm Tue-Sat. **€€€.** **Haute cuisine. Map** p131 C2 **20**

L'Hôtel has the talented Philippe Bélisse in charge of the kitchen. You can choose from a short seasonal menu with such dishes as pan-fried tuna, John Dory or

Dive in

Hermès' stunning store is set in an old swimming pool.

If you thought Hermès was about horsey scarves and little else, a visit to the new rue de Sèvres shop (see p138) should dispel the equestrian rumours forever. Designed by Denis Montel, the concept store is set in the Hôtel Lutetia's former indoor pool. The sensitive renovations have produced one of the best-looking retail spaces on the Left Bank.

The first thing that strikes as you enter is the gorgeous smell from the flower shop tucked just inside the entrance, featuring arrangements by swanky Paris florist Baptiste Pitou. Beyond the blooms, the space opens up into the main old pool hall, with iron balconies around the top and a main floor awash with original mosaic tiles from the building's watery past. Dominating the main room are three vast latticed ash wood huts, which break up the floor into manageable sections.

While the trademark scarves and ties are all present and correct, the three-floor store also focuses strongly on homewares, from wallpaper and carpets to sumptuous reproductions of 1930s-era furniture by renowned designer Jean-Michel Frank.

And if you need to sit down after shelling out on a sofa or scarf, there is a tea room on the balcony called Le Plongeoir (diving board). Unsurprisingly, it's not your usual pool café grub – tea is served in Hermès china rather than polystyrene cups, although at €14 a pot you wouldn't expect anything less.

suckling pig. But for the same price you could also enjoy the marvellous four-course *menu dégustation* or, even better, the *menu surprise*. Highlights have included smoked Somme eel with horse-radish and lime.

Le Rostand

6 pl Edmond-Rostand, 6th (01.43.54. 61.58). RER Luxembourg. **Open** 8am-2am daily. **Bar**. **Map** p131 C3 ㉑
Le Rostand has a truly wonderful view of the Jardin du Luxembourg from its classy interior, decked out with oriental paintings, a mahogany bar and wall-length mirrors. Perfect for a civilised drink after a stroll round the gardens.

Le Timbre

3 rue Ste-Beuve, 6th (01.45.49.10.40, www.restaurantletimbre.com). Mº Vavin. **Open** noon-2pm, 7.30-10.30pm Tue-Sat. Closed Aug & 1wk Dec. **€€**. **Bistro**. **Map** p131 B4 ㉒
Chris Wright's restaurant, open kitchen included, might be the size of the average student garret, but this Mancunian aims high. Typical of his cooking is a plate of fresh asparagus elegantly cut in half lengthways and served with dabs of anise-spiked sauce and balsamic vinegar, and a little crumbled parmesan. Mains are also pure in presentation and flavour – a thick slab of pork, pan-fried, comes with petals of red onion.

Shopping

APC

38 rue Madame, 6th (01.42.22.12.77, www.apc.fr). Mº St-Placide. **Open** 11am-7.30pm Mon-Sat. **Map** p131 B4 ㉓
The look is simple but stylish: think perfectly cut basics in muted tones. Hip without trying too hard, its jeans are a big hit.

L'Artisan Parfumeur

24 bd Raspail, 7th (01.42.22.23.32, www.artisanparfumeur.com). Mº Rue du Bac. **Open** 10.30am-7.30pm Mon-Sat. **Map** p131 A2 ㉔

Germain p135

Among the scented candles, potpourri and charms, you'll find the best vanilla perfume that Paris can offer – Mûres et Musc, a bestseller for two decades.

Arty Dandy

1 rue de Furstemberg, 6th (01.43.54. 00.36, www.artydandy.com). M° Mabillon. **Open** 10am-7pm Mon-Sat. **Map** p131 C2 ㉕

Arty Dandy is a concept shop that embraces the surreal, the tongue-in-cheek and the poetic – an R.MUTT sticker to create your own Duchampian loo, and the 'Karl who?' bag (which KL himself has been carrying) are instant pleasers. More sublime offerings include Jaime Hayon's 'Lover' figurines.

Le Bon Marché

24 rue de Sèvres, 7th (01.44.39.80.00, www.bonmarche.fr). M° Sèvres Babylone. **Open** 10am-8pm Mon-Wed, Sat; 10am-9pm Thur, Fri. **Map** p131 A3 ㉖

Luxury boutiques take pride of place on the ground floor; escalators designed by Andrée Putman take you up to the fashion floor, which has an excellent selection of designer labels. Designer names also abound in Balthazar, the men's section. For top-notch nibbles, try the Grande Epicerie.

Bruno Frisoni

34 rue de Grenelle, 6th (01.42.84. 12.30, www.brunofrisoni.fr). M° Rue du Bac. **Open** 10.30am-7pm Tue-Sat. **Map** p131 B2 ㉗

Innovative Frisoni's shoes have a cinematic, pop edge: modern theatrics for the unconventional.

Christian Constant

37 rue d'Assas, 6th (01.53.63.15.15, www.christianconstant.fr). M° Rennes or St-Placide. **Open** 9.30am-8.30pm Mon-Fri; 9am-8pm Sat, Sun. **Map** p131 B4 ㉘

A master chocolate-maker and *traiteur*, Constant scours the globe for ideas. His *ganaches* are subtly flavoured with verbena, jasmine or cardamom.

Deyrolle

46 rue du Bac, 7th (01.42.22.30.07, www.deyrolle.com). M° Rue du Bac. **Open** 10am-1pm, 2-7pm Mon; 10am-7pm Tue-Sat. **Map** p131 A2 ㉙

Famous taxidermy shop Deyrolle has a bizarre menagerie of lions, giraffes, polar bears, butterflies and bugs of all shapes and sizes, set in the confines of an authentic 19th-century *hôtel particulier*. It remains a great place to escape the city, buy a tiger for the living room, purchase a few creepy crawlies to scare friends and family, or simply to fire your children's imagination.

Gérard Mulot

76 rue de Seine, 6th (01.43.26.85.77, www.gerard-mulot.com). M° Odéon. **Open** 6.45am-8pm Mon, Tue, Thur-Sun. Closed Easter & Aug. **Map** p131 C3 ㉚

Gérard Mulot rustles up stunning pastries. Try the *mabillon*: caramel mousse with apricot marmalade.

Hermès

17 rue de Sèvres, 6th (01.42.22. 80.83). M° Sèvres Babylone. **Open** 10.30am-7pm Mon-Sat. **Map** p131 A3 ㉛

See box p136.

Hervé Chapelier

1bis rue du Vieux-Colombier, 6th (01.44.07.06.50, www.hervechapelier.fr). M° St-Germain-des-Prés or St-Sulpice. **Open** 10.15am-7pm Mon-Sat. **Map** p131 B3 ㉜

Pick up a classic bicoloured bag. Prices range from a dinky purse at €22 to a weekend bag at €130.

Huilerie Artisanale Leblanc

6 rue Jacob, 6th (01.46.34.61.55, www.huile-leblanc.com). M° St-Germain-des-Prés. **Open** noon-7pm Tue-Fri; 10am-7pm Sat. Closed 2wks Aug. No credit cards. **Map** p131 C2 ㉝

The Leblanc family started making walnut oil before branching out to press pure oils from hazelnuts, almonds, pine nuts, grilled peanuts and olives.

La Hune

170 bd St-Germain, 6th (01.45.48. 35.85). Mº St-Germain-des-Prés. **Open** 10am-11.45pm Mon-Sat; 11am-7.45pm Sun. **Map** p131 B2 ③④

This Left Bank institution boasts a global selection of art and design books, and a truly magnificent collection of French literature and theory.

Jean-Paul Hévin

3 rue Vavin, 6th (01.43.54.09.85, www.jphevin.com). Mº Notre-Dame-des-Champs or Vavin. **Open** 10am-7pm Tue-Sat. Closed Aug. **Map** p131 B4 ③⑤

Hévin specialises in the beguiling combination of chocolate with potent cheese fillings, which loyal customers serve with wine as an aperitif.

Lefranc.ferrant

22 rue de l'Echaudé, 6th (01.44.07. 37.96, www.lefranc-ferrant.fr). Mº St-Germain-des-Prés. **Open** 11am-7pm Tue-Sat and by appointment. **Map** p131 C2 ③⑥

Béatrice Ferrant and Mario Lefranc have a surreal approach to tailoring, as in a strapless yellow evening gown made like a pair of men's trousers – complete with flies. Prices are in the €1,000 range.

Marie-Hélène de Taillac

8 rue de Tournon, 6th (01.44.27. 07.07, www.mariehelenedetaillac.com). Mº Mabillon. **Open** 11am-7pm Mon-Sat. **Map** p131 C3 ③⑦

Marie-Hélène de Taillac is a fine jeweller, using diamonds and emeralds in simple settings. This combination of precious stones and modern styling has made her very popular with the fashion elite. They also adore her Left Bank shop.

Marie Mercié

23 rue St-Sulpice, 6th (01.43.26.45.83). Mº Odéon. **Open** 11am-7pm Mon-Sat. **Map** p131 C3 ③⑧

Mercié's creations make you wish you lived in an era when hats were de rigueur. Step out in one shaped like curved fingers (with shocking-pink nail varnish and pink diamond ring) or a beret like a face with red lips and turquoise eyes. Ready-to-wear starts at €30; *sur mesure* takes ten days.

Papillon pour Bonton

84 rue de Grenelle, 7th (01.42.84.42.43, www.bonton.fr). Mº Rue du Bac. **Open** 10am-7pm Mon-Sat. **Map** p131 A2 ③⑨

Bonton's new venture is all about nostalgia, with hand-knits, cashmere and alpaca, dinky stripes and Liberty prints, displayed in an old perfume shop amid flowery wallpaper and hunting trophies. Pure *Bagpuss*.

Patrick Roger

108 bd St-Germain, 6th (01.43.29. 38.42, www.patrickroger.com). Mº Odéon. **Open** 10.30am-7.30pm Mon-Sat. **Map** p131 B2 ④⓪

Roger is shaking up the art of chocolate-making. Whereas other *chocolatiers* aim for gloss, Roger may create a brushed effect on hens so realistic you almost expect them to lay (chocolate) eggs.

Paul & Joe

64 rue des Sts-Pères, 7th (01.42.22. 47.01, www.paulandjoe.com). Mº Rue du Bac or St-Germain-des-Prés. **Open** 10am-7pm Mon-Sat. **Map** p131 B2 ④①

Paul & Joe dresses leggy young things in a range of winter shorts, colourful mini dresses and voluminous trousers, with their intellectual paramours in slouchy woollens and chunky boots.

Peggy Huyn Kinh

9-11 rue Coëtlogon, 6th (01.42.84. 83.82, www.phk.fr). Mº St-Sulpice. **Open** 11am-7pm Mon-Sat. **Map** p131 B3 ④②

Once creative director at Cartier, Peggy Huyn Kinh now makes bags of boar skin and python, plus silver jewellery.

Pierre Hermé

72 rue Bonaparte, 6th (01.43.54.47.77). Mº Mabillon, St-Germain-des-Prés or St-Sulpice. **Open** 10am-7pm Tue-Fri, Sun; 10am-7.30pm Sat. Closed 1st 3wks Aug. **Map** p131 B3 ④③

Pastry superstar Hermé attracts connoisseurs from near and far with his seasonal collections.

Poilâne

8 rue du Cherche-Midi, 6th (01.45.48. 42.59, www.poilane.com). Mº Sèvres Babylone or St-Sulpice. **Open** 7.15am-8.15pm Mon-Sat. **Map** p131 B3 ㊹
Apollonia Poilâne runs the family shop, where locals queue for fresh country *miches*, flaky-crusted apple tarts and shortbread biscuits.

Richart

258 bd St-Germain, 7th (01.45.55.66.00, www.richart.com). Mº Solférino. **Open** 10am-7pm Mon-Sat. **Map** p131 A1 ㊺
Each chocolate *ganache* has an intricate design, packages look like jewel boxes, and each purchase comes with a tract on how best to savour the stuff.

Ryst Dupeyron

79 rue du Bac, 7th (01.45.48.80.93, www.vintageandco.com). Mº Rue du Bac. **Open** 12.30-7.30pm Mon; 10.30am-7.30pm Tue-Sat. Closed 2wks Aug. **Map** p131 A2 ㊻
The Dupeyrons have been selling armagnac for four generations, and still have bottles from 1868. Treasures here include 200 fine Bordeaux wines.

Sonia Rykiel

175 bd St-Germain, 6th (01.49.54. 60.60, www.soniarykiel.com). Mº St-Germain-des-Prés or Sèvres Babylone. **Open** 10.30am-7pm Mon-Sat. **Map** p131 B2 ㊼
The queen of St-Germain's flagship store features a glamorous black and smoked glass look, perfect for narcissists. Menswear is located across the street, and two newer boutiques stock the Sonia by Sonia Rykiel range.

Vanessa Bruno

25 rue St-Sulpice, 6th (01.43.54.41.04, www.vanessabruno.com). Mº Odéon. **Open** 10.30am-7.30pm Mon-Sat. **Map** p131 C3 ㊽

Bruno's mercerised cotton tanks, flattering trousers and tops have a Zen-like quality. She also makes great bags.

Yves Saint Laurent

6 pl St-Sulpice, 6th (01.43.29.43.00, www.ysl.com). Mº St-Sulpice. **Open** 11am-7pm Mon; 10.30am-7pm Tue-Sat. **Map** p131 C3 ㊾
The memory of the founding designer, who died in 2008, lives on in this wonderfully elegant boutique, which was splendidly refitted in red in the same year. You'll find the menswear collection at 32 rue du Fbg-St-Honoré (8th).

Nightlife

Wagg

62 rue Mazarine, 6th (01.55.42.22.01, www.wagg.fr). Mº Odéon. **Open** 11.30pm-6am Fri, Sat; 3.30pm-2am Sun. **Admission** €12 Fri, Sat; €12 Sun (incl 1 drink). **Map** p131 C2 ㊿
Wagg hosts a well-to-do Left Bank crowd. Expect funk, house and disco.

Arts & leisure

Le Lucernaire

53 rue Notre-Dame-des-Champs, 6th (01.42.22.26.50, www.lucernaire.fr). Mº Notre-Dame-des-Champs or Vavin. **Box office** 10am-7pm daily. **Admission** €10-€30. **Map** p131 B4 ㉑
Three theatres, three cinemas, a restaurant and a bar make up this versatile cultural centre. Molière and other classic playwrights get a good thrashing.

Odéon, Théâtre de L'Europe

Pl de l'Odéon, 6th (01.44.85.40.00, bookings 01.44.85.40.40, www.theatre-odeon.fr). Mº Odéon. **Box office** 11am-6.30pm Mon-Sat. **Admission** €6-€32. **Map** p131 C3 ㉒
Highlights in 2012 included *Prometheus Bound*, directed by Oliver Pry, and *Measure for Measure* in German, plus the Impatience festival for young theatre companies.

Le Panthéon p146

The Latin Quarter & the 13th

The Latin Quarter

To many first-time visitors – especially those from the States – the Latin Quarter can be a big disappointment. Countless books have led them to believe that the area is somehow the quintessence of Paris, and they come with their heads stuffed with expat writers – Orwell, Hemingway, Henry Miller – only to find a touristy jam of bad restaurants and uninspiring shops. Granted, many of the narrow, crooked streets (like the Marais, the Latin Quarter was another part of Paris largely untouched by Haussmann) are charming, and there are some real architectural glories, especially ecclesiastical ones; but the crowds can make the experience of seeing them rather dispiriting.

The 'Latin' in the area's name probably derives from the fact that it has been the university quarter since medieval times, when Latin was the language of instruction. The district's long association with learning began in about 1100, when a number of renowned scholars, including Pierre Abélard, began to live and teach on Montagne Ste-Geneviève, independent of the established cathedral school of Notre-Dame. This loose association of scholars came to be referred to as a 'university'. The Paris schools attracted students from all over Europe and the 'colleges' multiplied, until the University of Paris was given official recognition with a charter from Pope Innocent III in 1215.

Sights & museums

Arènes de Lutèce

Rue Monge, rue de Navarre or rue des Arènes, 5th. M° Cardinal Lemoine or Place Monge. **Open** *Summer* 9am-

PARIS BY AREA

9.30pm daily. *Winter* 8am-5.30pm
daily. **Admission** free. **Map**
p143 B4 ❶
This Roman arena, where wild beasts
and gladiators fought, could seat 10,000
people. It was still visible during the
reign of Philippe-Auguste in the 12th
century, then disappeared under rubble.
The site now attracts skateboarders,
footballers and boules players.

Eglise St-Etienne-du-Mont

*Pl Ste-Geneviève, 5th (01.43.54.11.79,
www.saintetiennedumont.fr). Mº
Cardinal Lemoine/RER Luxembourg.*
Open *Sept-May* 8.45am-7.30pm
Tue-Fri; 8.45am-noon, 2-7.45pm Sat;
8.45am-12.15pm, 2.30-7.45pm Sun. *July,
Aug* 10am-noon, 4-7.15pm Tue-Sun.
Map p143 B4 ❷
Geneviève, patron saint of Paris, is cred-
ited with having miraculously saved
the city from the ravages of Attila the
Hun in 451, and her shrine has been a
site of pilgrimage ever since. The present church was built in an amalgam of
Gothic and Renaissance styles between
1492 and 1626, and the interior is wonderfully tall and light, with soaring
columns and a classical balustrade. The
stunning Renaissance rood screen, with
its double spiral staircase and ornate
stone strapwork, is the only surviving
one in Paris. At the back of the church
(reached through the sacristy), the cat-
echism chapel constructed by Baltard
in the 1860s has a cycle of paintings
relating the saint's life story.

Eglise St-Séverin

*3 rue des Prêtres-St-Séverin, 5th
(01.42.34.93.50, www.saint-severin.
com). Mº Cluny La Sorbonne or St-
Michel.* **Open** 11am-7.30pm Mon-Sat;
9am-8.30pm Sun. **Map** p143 A3 ❸
Built on the site of the chapel of the
hermit Séverin, itself set on a much
earlier Merovingian burial ground, this
lovely Flamboyant Gothic edifice
was long the parish church of the Left
Bank. The church dates from the 15th
century, though the doorway, carved

with foliage, was added in 1837 from
the demolished Eglise St-Pierre-aux-
Boeufs on Ile de la Cité. The double
ambulatory is famed for its forest of
'palm tree' vaulting, which meets at the
end in a unique spiral column that
inspired a series of paintings by Robert
Delaunay. The bell tower, a survivor
from one of the earlier churches on the
site, has the oldest bell in Paris (1412).

Eglise du Val-de-Grâce

*Pl Alphonse-Laveran, 5th (01.40.51.
51.92). RER Luxembourg or Port-Royal.*
Open noon-6pm Tue, Wed, Sat, Sun.
Admission €5; free-€2.50 reductions.
No credit cards. **Map** p143 A5 ❹
Anne of Austria, the wife of Louis XIII,
vowed to erect 'a magnificent temple'
if God blessed her with a son. She
got two. The resulting church and
surrounding Benedictine monastery –
these days a military hospital and the
Musée du Service de Santé des Armées
– were built by François Mansart and
Jacques Lemercier. This is the most
luxuriously baroque of the city's 17th-
century domed churches. In contrast,
the surrounding monastery offers the
perfect example of François Mansart's
classical restraint. Phone in advance if
you're after a guided visit.

Grande Galerie
de l'Evolution

*36 rue Geoffroy-St-Hilaire,
2 rue Bouffon or pl Valhubert, 5th
(01.40.79.56.01). Mº Gare d'Austerlitz
or Jussieu.* **Open** *Grande Galerie* 10am-
6pm Mon, Wed-Sun. *Other galleries*
10am-5pm Mon, Wed-Fri; 10am-6pm
Sat, Sun. **Admission** *Grande Galerie*
€7; free-€5 reductions. *Other galleries*
(each) €7; free-€5 reductions. No credit
cards. **Map** p143 C5 ❺
One of the city's most child-friendly
attractions, this is guaranteed to bowl
adults over too. Located within the
Jardin des Plantes, this 19th-century
iron-framed, glass-roofed structure
has been modernised with lifts, galleries and false floors, and filled with

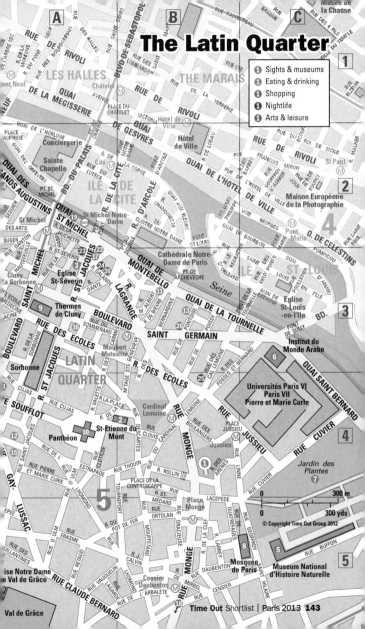

The Latin Quarter

Legend:
1 Sights & museums
1 Eating & drinking
1 Shopping
1 Nightlife
1 Arts & leisure

© Copyright Time Out Group 2012

life-size models of tentacle-waving squid, open-mawed sharks and monkeys swarming down from the ceiling. The centrepiece is a procession of African wildlife across the first floor that resembles the procession into Noah's Ark. Glass-sided lifts take you up through suspended birds to the second floor, which deals with man's impact on nature (crocodile into handbag). The third floor focuses on endangered species.

Institut du Monde Arabe

1 rue des Fossés-St-Bernard, 5th (01.40.51.38.38, www.imarabe.org). M° Jussieu. **Open** Museum 10am-6pm Tue-Sun. *Library* 1-8pm Tue-Sat. *Café* noon-6pm Tue-Sun. *Tours* 3pm Tue-Fri; 3pm & 4.30pm Sat, Sun. **Admission** Museum €6; free-€4 reductions. *Roof terrace, library* free. *Exhibitions* varies. *Tours* €8. **Map** p143 C3 ⑥

See box right.

Jardin des Plantes

36 rue Geoffroy-St-Hilaire, 2 rue Bouffon, pl Valhubert or 57 rue Cuvier, 5th. M° Gare d'Austerlitz, Jussieu or Place Monge (01.40.79.56.01, www.jardindesplantes.net). **Open** Main garden Winter 8am-5.30pm daily. Summer 7.30am-7.45pm daily. *Alpine garden* Apr-Oct 8am-4.40pm Mon-Fri; 1.30-6pm Sat; 1.30-6.30pm Sun. Closed Nov-Mar. *Ménagerie* 9am-6pm daily. **Admission** Alpine Garden free Mon-Fri; €2 Sat, Sun. *Jardin des Plantes* free. *Ménagerie* €9; free-€7 reductions. **Map** p143 C4 ⑦

The Paris botanical garden – which contains more than 10,000 species and includes tropical greenhouses and rose, winter and Alpine gardens – is an enchanting place. Begun by Louis XIII's doctor as the royal medicinal plant garden in 1626, it opened to the public in 1640. The formal garden, which runs between two avenues of trees, is like something out of *Alice in Wonderland*. There's also a small zoo and the terrific Grande Galerie de

l'Evolution. Ancient trees on view include a false acacia planted in 1636. A plaque on the old laboratory declares that this is the spot where Henri Becquerel discovered radioactivity in 1896.

La Mosquée de Paris

2 pl du Puits-de-l'Ermite, 5th (01.45. 35.97.33, tearoom 01.43.31.38.20, baths 01.43.31.18.14, www.mosquee-de-paris.net). M° Monge. **Open** Tours 9am-noon, 2-6pm Mon-Thur, Sat, Sun (closed Muslim hols). *Tearoom* 9am-midnight daily. *Restaurant* noon-2.30pm, 7.30-midnight daily. *Baths* (women) 10am-9pm Mon, Wed, Thur, Sat; 2-9pm Fri; (men) 2-9pm Tue; 10am-9pm Sun. **Admission** €3; free-€2 reductions. *Tearoom* free. *Baths* €15. **Map** p143 C5 ⑧

This vast Hispano-Moorish construct is the spiritual heart of France's Algerian-dominated Muslim population. In plan and function it divides into three sections: religious (grand patio, prayer room and minaret, all for worshippers and not curious tourists); scholarly (Islamic school and library); and, via rue Geoffroy-St-Hilaire, commercial (café and domed hammam). La Mosquée café is delightful – a courtyard shaded beneath green foliage and scented with the sweet smell of sheesha smoke.

Musée National du Moyen Age – Thermes de Cluny

6 pl Paul-Painlevé, 5th (01.53.73.78.00, www.musee-moyenage.fr). M° Cluny La Sorbonne. **Open** 9.15am-5.45pm Mon, Wed-Sun. **Admission** €8; free-€6 reductions. **Map** p143 A3 ⑨

The national museum of medieval art is best known for the beautiful, allegorical *Lady and the Unicorn* tapestry cycle, but it also has important collections of medieval sculpture and enamels. The building itself, commonly known as Cluny, is also a rare example of 15th-century secular Gothic architecture, with its foliate Gothic doorways,

Brave new world

The Institute of the Arab World marked its 25th year in style.

One of Paris's most innovative museums reopened to the public in spring 2012, after a three-year, €5 million revamp. The beautiful museum of the **Institut du Monde Arabe** (see left), dedicated to the development of Islamic art and the history and culture of the Arab world, has been transformed, and reopened in time to mark its 25th anniversary. Collections from the 22 Arab countries that co-founded the museum can now be enjoyed once again, in an exciting and dynamic new interior.

A clever blend of high-tech and Arab influences, this Seine-side *grand projet* was constructed between 1980 and 1987 to a design by Jean Nouvel, who sought to build a modern interpretation of a Moorish palace.

Some 600 items are on display, from places as diverse as Damascus, Aleppo, Latakia, Amman, Kairouan and Manama, as well as the Louvre, the Musée du Quai Branly and the Bibliothèque Nationale de France. And where before the collection was limited to art, the new museum has widened its scope (as well as its physical space), showcasing the Arab world in thematic ways, covering its ethno-linguistic, historical, cultural, anthropological and geographical diversity. Museographer Roberto Ostinelli's subtle but dynamic staging – conceived as a pathway dotted with bridges between past and present – works on both an emotional and intellectual level.

What's more, there's a lively programme of events (exhibitions, film screenings, music and dance) and an excellent Middle East bookshop on the ground floor, and the views from the roof terrace (to which access is free) are fabulous.

And if your thirst for Arab culture is still unquenched after a visit here, head to the Louvre to check out its new Islamic arts wing.

PARIS BY AREA

hexagonal staircase jutting out of the façade and vaulted chapel. It was built from 1485 to 1498 – on top of a Gallo-Roman baths complex. The baths, built in characteristic Roman bands of stone and brick masonry, are the finest Roman remains in Paris. The vaulted *frigidarium* (cold bath), *tepidarium* (warm bath), *caldarium* (hot bath) and part of the hypocaust heating system are all still visible. A themed garden fronts the whole complex.

Le Panthéon

Pl du Panthéon, 5th (01.44.32.18.00).
Mº Cardinal Lemoine/RER Luxembourg.
Open 10am-6pm (until 6.30pm summer) daily. **Admission** €8; free-€5 reductions. **Map** p143 A4 ⑩
Soufflot's neo-classical megastructure was the architectural *grand projet* of its day, commissioned by a grateful Louis XV to thank Sainte Geneviève for his recovery from illness. But by the time it was ready in 1790, a lot had changed; during the Revolution, the Panthéon was rededicated as a 'temple of reason' and the resting place of the nation's great men. The barrel-vaulted crypt now houses Voltaire, Rousseau, Hugo and Zola. New heroes are installed but rarely: Pierre and Marie Curie's remains were transferred here in 1995; Alexandre Dumas in 2002. Mount the steep spiral stairs to the colonnade encircling the dome for superb views.

Eating & drinking

Atelier Maître Albert

1 rue Maître-Albert, 5th (01.56.81. 30.01, www.ateliermaitrealbert.com). Mº Maubert Mutualité or St-Michel.
Open noon-2.30pm, 6.30-11pm Mon-Wed; noon-2.30pm, 6.30pm-1am Thur, Fri; 6.30pm-1am Sat; 6.30-11.30pm Sun. €€. **Bistro. Map** p143 B3 ⑪
This Guy Savoy outpost in the fifth has slick decor by Jean-Michel Wilmotte. The indigo-painted, grey marble-floored dining room with open kitchen

and rôtisseries on view is attractive but very noisy at night. The short menu lets you have a Savoy classic or two to start with, including oysters in seawater *gelée* or more inventive dishes such as the ballotine of chicken, foie gras and celery root in a chicken-liver sauce. Next up, perhaps, tuna served with tiny iron casseroles of dauphinois potatoes, and cauliflower in béchamel sauce.

Le Crocodile

6 rue Royer-Collard, 5th (01.43.54. 32.37). RER Luxembourg. **Open** 10pm-4am Mon-Sat. Closed Aug.
Bar. Map p143 A4 ⑫
Ignore the apparently boarded-up windows at Le Crocodile; if you're here late, then it's open. Friendly young regulars line the sides of this small, narrow bar and try to decide what to drink – not easy, given the length of the cocktail list: at last count there were 317 varieties. The generous €6-per-cocktail happy hour (Monday to Thursday before midnight) will allow you to start with a champagne *accroche-coeur*, followed up with a Goldschläger (served with gold leaf) before moving on to one of the other 316.

Itinéraires

5 rue de Pontoise, 5th (01.46.33.60.11). Mº Maubert Mutualité. **Open** noon-2pm, 8-10.30pm Tue-Thur; 8-11pm Fri, Sat. €€. **Bistro. Map** p143 B3 ⑬
Chef Sylvain Sendra played to a full and appreciative house every night at his little bistro Le Temps au Temps near the Bastille before upping sticks and moving on to this larger space near Notre Dame. The sleek space brings together all the elements that make for a successful bistro today: a long *table d'hôte*, a bar for solo meals or quick bites, and a reasonably priced, market-inspired menu. Not everything is a wild success, but it's hard to fault a chef who so often hits the mark, in dishes such as squid-ink risotto with clams, *botargo* (dried mullet roe) and tomato.

Lapérouse

*51 quai des Grands-Augustins, 6th
(01.56.79.24.31, www.laperouse.fr).
M° St-Michel.* **Open** noon-2.30pm,
7.30-11pm Mon-Fri; 7.30-11pm Sat.
Closed 1wk Jan & Aug. €€€€.
Brasserie. **Map** p143 A2 ⑭

Lapérouse was formerly a clandestine
rendezvous for French politicians and
their mistresses; the tiny private dining
rooms upstairs used to lock from the
inside. Chef Alain Hacquard does a reasonable take on classic French cooking:
his beef fillet is smoked for a more complex flavour; a tender saddle of rabbit
is cooked in a clay crust, flavoured with
lavender and rosemary and served with
ravioli of onions. The only snag is the
cost, especially of the wine – a half-bot-
tle of Pouilly-Fuissé will set you back
around €35.

Le Pantalon

*7 rue Royer-Collard, 5th (no phone).
RER Luxembourg.* **Open** 5.30pm-2am
Mon-Sat. No credit cards. €. **Café**.
Map p143 A4 ⑮

Le Pantalon is a local café that seems
familiar yet is utterly surreal. It has
the standard fixtures, including the
old soaks at the bar – but the regulars
and staff are enough to tip the balance
into eccentricity. Friendly and funny
French grown-ups and foreign students chat in a mishmash of languages; drinks are cheap enough to
make you tipsy without the worry of
a cash hangover.

Le Pré Verre

*8 rue Thénard, 5th (01.43.54.59.47,
www.lepreverre.com). M° Maubert
Mutualité.* **Open** noon-2pm, 7.30-
10.30pm Tue-Sat. Closed 3wks Aug &
2wks Dec. €€. **Bistro**. **Map** p143 A3 ⑯

Philippe Delacourcelle knows how to
handle spices like few other French
chefs. Salt cod with cassia bark and
smoked potato purée is a classic: what
the fish lacks in size it makes up for in
rich, cinnamon-like flavour and
crunchy texture, and smooth potato

cooked in a smoker makes a startling
accompaniment. Spices have a way of
making desserts seem esoteric rather
than decadent, but the roast figs with
olives are an exception to the rule.

Ribouldingue

*10 rue St-Julien-le-Pauvre, 5th
(01.46.33.98.80, www.restaurant-
ribouldingue.com). M° St-Michel.*
Open noon-2pm, 7-11pm Mon-Sat.
€€. **Bistro**. **Map** p143 A3 ⑰

This bistro facing St-Julien-le-Pauvre
church is the creation of Nadège
Varigny, who spent ten years working
with Yves Camdeborde before opening
a restaurant inspired by the food of her
childhood in Grenoble. It's full of
people, including critics and chefs, who
love simple, honest bistro fare, such as
daube de boeuf or seared tuna on a bed
of melting aubergine. If you have an
appetite for offal, then you might want
to opt for the gently sautéed brains
with new potatoes or veal kidneys with
a perfectly prepared potato gratin.
For dessert, try the fresh ewe's cheese
with bitter honey.

Shopping

Le Boulanger de Monge

*123 rue Monge, 5th (01.43.37.54.20,
www.leboulangerdemonge.com).
M° Censier Daubenton.* **Open** 7am-
8.30pm Tue-Sun. **Map** p143 B5 ⑱

Dominique Saibron uses spices to
give wonderful flavour to his organic
sourdough *boule*. Every day about
2,000 bread-lovers visit this boutique,
which also produces one of the city's
best baguettes.

Bouquinistes

*Along the quais, especially quai de
Montebello & quai St-Michel, 5th.
M° St-Michel.* **Open** times vary from
stall to stall, generally Tue-Sun.
No credit cards. **Map** p143 A2 ⑲

The green, open-air boxes along the
quais are one of the city's institutions.
As well as the inevitable postcards and

tourist tat, most sell a good selection of second-hand books – rummage through boxes packed with ancient paperbacks for something existential.

Diptyque

34 bd St-Germain, 5th (01.43.26.77.44, www.diptyqueparis.com). Mº Maubert Mutualité. **Open** 10am-7pm Mon-Sat. **Map** p143 B3 ⑳

Diptyque's divinely scented candles are the quintessential gift from Paris. They come in 48 varieties and are probably the best you'll ever find. Prices aren't cheap, but with 50 to 60 hours' burn time, they're worth every euro.

Princesse Tam-Tam

52 bd St-Michel, 6th (01.40.51.72.99, www.princessetamtam.com). Mº Cluny La Sorbonne. **Open** 1.30-7pm Mon; 10am-7pm Tue, Thur-Sat; 10am-1.30pm, 2-7pm Wed. **Map** p143 A4 ㉑

This fun, inexpensive underwear and swimwear brand has traffic-stopping promotions. Bright colours and sexily transparent gear rule.

Shakespeare & Company

37 rue de la Bûcherie, 5th (01.43.25. 40.93, www.shakespeareandcompany. com). Mº St-Michel. **Open** 10am-11pm Mon-Fri; 11am-11pm Sat, Sun. **Map** p143 A3 ㉒

Unequivocably the best bookshop in Paris, the ramshackle Shakespeare & Co is always packed to the rafters with expat and tourist book lovers. There is a large second-hand section, antiquarian books next door, and just about anything you could ask for new.

Nightlife

Caveau de la Huchette

5 rue de la Huchette, 5th (01.43.26. 65.05, www.caveaudelahuchette.fr). Mº St-Michel. **Open** *Concerts* 10.15pm-2.30am Mon-Wed, Sun; 10.15pm-6am Thur-Sat. **Admission** €12 Mon-Thur, Sun; €14 Fri, Sat; €10 reductions. **Map** p143 A2 ㉓

This medieval cellar has been a mainstay for 60 years. The jazz shows are followed by early-hours performances in a swing, rock, soul or disco vein.

Caveau des Oubliettes

52 rue Galande, 5th (01.46.34.23.09, www.caveaudesoubliettes.fr). Mº St-Michel. **Open** 5pm-4am daily. *Concerts* 10pm daily. **Admission** free. **Map** p143 A3 ㉔

Atmosphere abounds in this former dungeon, a tiny space complete with instruments of torture and underground passages. There are various jam sessions in the week, and on Sundays.

Paradis Latin

28 rue Cardinal Lemoine, 5th (01.43. 25.28.28, www.paradislatin.com). Mº Cardinal Lemoine. **Dinner** 8pm. **Show** 9.30pm daily. **Admission** *9.30pm show* (incl champagne) €85. *Dinner & show* €123-€179. **Map** p143 B4 ㉕

This is the most authentic of the cabarets, not only because it's family-run (the men run the cabaret, the daughter does the costumes), but also because the clientele is mostly French, something which has a direct effect on the prices (this is the cheapest revue) and the cuisine, which tends to be high quality. Show-wise you can expect the usual fare: generous doses of glitter, live singing and cheesy *entr'acte* acts performed in a stunning belle époque room. There's also a twice-monthly matinée: lunch and show €100.

Arts & leisure

Studio Galande

42 rue Galande, 5th (01.43.54.72.71, www.studiogalande.fr). Mº Cluny La Sorbonne or St-Michel. **Admission** €8; €6 reductions. No credit cards. **Map** p143 A3 ㉖

Some 20 different films are screened in subtitled versions at this venerable Latin Quarter venue every week: international arthouse fare, combined with the occasional instalment from the

Matrix series. On Friday and Saturday nights, dedicated fans of *The Rocky Horror Picture Show* turn up in drag, equipped with rice and water pistols.

The 13th

The construction in the mid-1990s of the **Bibliothèque Nationale de France** breathed life into the desolate area, now known as the ZAC Rive Gauche, between Gare d'Austerlitz and the Périphérique. The ambitious, long-term ZAC project includes a new university quarter, new housing projects and a tramway providing links to the suburbs. This is one of the city's fastest rising quarters.

Sights & museums

Bibliothèque Nationale de France François Mitterrand

10 quai François-Mauriac, 13th (01.53.79.59.59, www.bnf.fr). M° Bibliothèque François Mitterrand. **Open** 2-7pm Mon; 9am-7pm Tue-Sat; 1-7pm Sun. **Admission** *1 day* €3.50. *1 year* €38; €20 reductions. **Map** p151 E2 ㉗
Opened in 1996, the new national library was the last and costliest of Mitterrand's *grands projets*. Its architect, Dominique Perrault, was criticised for his curiously dated design. He also forgot to specify blinds to protect books from sunlight; they had to be added afterwards. The library houses over ten million volumes. Much of the library is open to the public: books, newspapers and periodicals are accessible to anyone over 18, and you can browse through photographic, film and sound archives in the audio-visual section.

Chapelle St-Louis-de-la-Salpêtrière

47 bd de l'Hôpital, 13th (01.42.16. 04.24). M° Gare d'Austerlitz. **Open** 8.30am-6pm Mon-Fri, Sun; 11am-6pm Sat. **Admission** free. **Map** p151 C2 ㉘

This austerely beautiful chapel, designed by Bruand and completed in 1677, features an octagonal dome in the centre and eight naves in which the sick were separated from the insane, the destitute from the debauched. Around the chapel sprawls the vast Hôpital de la Pitié-Salpêtrière, which became a centre for research into insanity in the 1790s, when renowned doctor Philippe Pinel began to treat some of the inmates as sick rather than criminal; Charcot later pioneered neuropsychology here. Salpêtrière is one of the city's main teaching hospitals.

Manufacture Nationale des Gobelins

42 av des Gobelins, 13th (tours 01.44. 08.53.59). M° Les Gobelins. **Open** 11am-6pm Tue-Sun. **Admission** €6; free-€4 reductions. No credit cards. **Map** p151 B2 ㉙
The royal tapestry factory, founded by Colbert, is named after Jean Gobelin, a dyer who owned the site. Tapestries are still made here (mainly for French embassies), and visitors can watch weavers at work. The tour (in French; €7.50-€10) through the 1912 factory takes in the 18th-century chapel and the Beauvais workshops. Arrive 30 minutes before the tour starts.

Eating & drinking

L'Avant-Goût

26 rue Bobillot, 13th (01.53.80.24.00, www.lavantgout.com). M° Place d'Italie. **Open** noon-2pm, 7.45-10.45pm Tue-Sat. Closed 3wks Aug. **€**. **Bistro**. **Map** p151 B3 ㉚
Self-taught chef Christophe Beaufront has turned this nondescript street on the edge of the villagey Butte-aux-Cailles into a foodie destination. Typical of Beaufront's cooking is his *pot-au-feu de cochon aux épices*, a much-written-about dish that has been on his menu for years. It's good, if not earth-shaking; however, a starter of piquillo pepper stuffed with smoked haddock rillettes

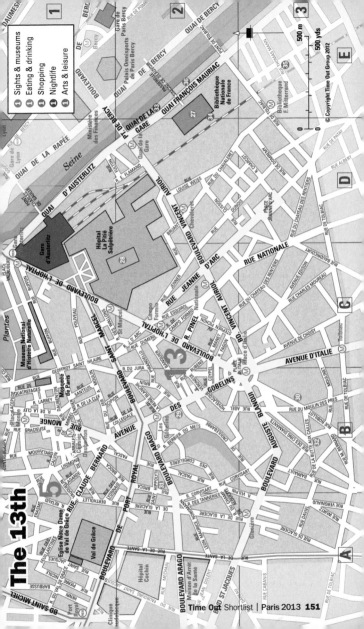

The 13th

Sights & museums
Eating & drinking
Shopping
Nightlife
Arts & leisure

Bibliothèque
Nationale
de France

Bibliothèque
F. Mitterrand

Hôpital
La Pitié
Salpêtrière

Museum National
d'Histoire Naturelle

Mosquée
de Paris

AVENUE D'ITALIE

GOBELINS

Église Notre Dame de
de Val de Grâce

Val de Grâce

Hôpital
Cochin

Maison d'Arrêt
de la Santé

© Copyright Time Out Group 2012

does illustrate his talent. Beaufront's food is available to take away at the *épicerie* across the street.

L'Ourcine

92 rue Broca, 13th (01.47.07.13.65). Mº Glacière or Les Gobelins. **Open** noon-2pm, 7-10.30pm Tue-Thur; noon-2.30pm, 7-11pm Fri, Sat. Closed Aug. **€. Bistro. Map** p151 B2 ③

This restaurant near Gobelins is a wonderful bistro stop. Start with *pipérade*, succulent chorizo or a spread of sliced beef tongue with piquillo peppers; then try the sautéed baby squid with parsley, garlic and Espelette peppers, or the *piquillos* stuffed with puréed cod and potato. An appealing atmosphere is generated by a growing band of regulars.

Sputnik

14 rue de la Butte aux Cailles, 13th (01.45.65.19.82, www.sputnik.fr). Mº Place d'Italie. **Open** 2pm-2am Mon-Sat; 4pm-midnight Sun. **Café. Map** p151 B3 ③

A hip young crowd gathers in this rock-oriented bar, which doubles as a sports bar during important football and rugby fixtures, and trebles as an internet café at other times. Ever-changing art exhibitions add interest to the walls, and bands once a month draw an indie crowd.

Nightlife

Batofar

Opposite 11 quai François-Mauriac, 13th (09.71.25.50.61, www.batofar. org). Mº Quai de la Gare. **Open** 11pm-6am Mon-Sat; 6am-noon 1st Sun of mth. **Admission** free-€12. **Map** p151 E2 ③

In recent years, the Batofar has gone through a rapid succession of management teams. The current managers have helped revive the venue's tradition of playing cutting-edge music, including electro, dub step, techno and dancehall nights featuring international acts. It's also a destination for early morning clubbers determined to shun their beds.

Arts & leisure

MK2 Bibliothèque

128-162 av de France, 13th (08.92.69. 84.84, www.mk2.com). Mº Bibliothèque François Mitterrand or Quai de la Gare. **Admission** €10.50; €5-€7 reductions; €19.80 monthly pass. **Map** p151 E2 ③

The MK2 chain's flagship offers 14 screens, three restaurants and a bar open until 5am at weekends. A paragon of imaginative programming, MK2 is growing all the time; it has added ten more venues in town, including two situated along the Bassin de la Villette.

Musée National du Sport

93 av de France, 13th (01.45.83.15.80, www.museedusport.fr). Mº Bibliothèque François Mitterrand. **Open** 10am-6pm Tue-Fri; 2-6pm Sat & 1st Sun of mth. **Admission** €2; free reductions. **Map** p151 E3 ③

The Musée National du Sport traces the history of sport via a small selection of the 100,000 artefacts in its collection. Even if the thrust of the collection is French sports and heroes, many of the exhibits will be familiar to an international audience: a clutch of Olympic medals from the 1992 Winter Games in Albertville; an autographed ball used in France's triumphant 1998 World Cup victory; and Alain Prost's protective bodysuit.

Piscine Josephine-Baker

Quai François-Mauriac, 13th (01.56. 61.96.50). Mº Quai de la Gare. **Open** 7-8.30am, 1-9pm Mon; 1-11pm Tue, Thur; 7-8.30am, 1-9pm Wed, Fri; 11am-8pm Sat; 10am-8pm Sun. **Admission** €3; €1.70 reductions. **Map** p151 E2 ③

Moored on the River Seine by the Bibliothèque Nationale, the Piscine Josephine-Baker complex boasts a 25m main pool (with sliding glass roof), a paddling pool and café, and a busy schedule of exercise classes.

View from the Tour Montparnasse p155

Montparnasse

Yet another artists' quarter that has long since lost the character – and the characters – that made its name, Montparnasse is now conspicuously lacking in charm. Between the two world wars, it was the emblematic 'gay Paree' district of after-dark merriment and fruitful artistic exchange – and it was also remarkably cosmopolitan.

A great number of its most prominent figures were expats (including its best chronicler, the Hungarian photographer Brassaï), and the late-night bars and artists' studios formed a bubble of cordial international relations that was irreparably popped in 1939. The local atmosphere soured further with the completion of the much-loathed **Tour Montparnasse** in the early 1970s. Granted, it's rich territory for art museums – but with the exception of the **Fondation Cartier**, they're all about past glories.

The old Montparnasse station witnessed two events of historical significance. In 1898, a runaway train burst through its façade; and on 25 August 1944, the German forces surrendered Paris here. The station was rebuilt in the 1970s, a grey affair above which can be found the Jardin Atlantique, a modest oasis of granite paths, trees and bamboo spread over a roof, the Mémorial du Maréchal Leclerc and the Musée Jean Moulin.

Sights & museums

Les Catacombes
1 av Colonel Henri-Rol-Tanguy, 14th (01.43.22.47.63, www.catacombes-de-paris.fr). Mº/RER Denfert Rochereau. **Open** 10am-5pm Tue-Sun. **Admission** €8; free-€6 reductions. **Map** p155 C3 ❶ This is the official entrance to the 3,000km (1,864-mile) tunnel network that runs under much of the city. With public burial pits overflowing in the era

of the Revolutionary Terror, the bones of six million people were transferred to the *catacombes*. The bones of Marat, Robespierre and their cronies are packed in with wall upon wall of their fellow citizens. A damp, cramped tunnel takes you through a series of galleries before you reach the ossuary, the entrance to which is announced by a sign engraved in the stone: 'Stop! This is the empire of death.' The tour lasts approximately 45 minutes.

Cimetière du Montparnasse

3 bd Edgar-Quinet, 14th (01.44.10. 86.50). Mº Edgar Quinet or Raspail. **Open** *16 Mar-5 Nov* 8am-6pm Mon-Fri; 8.30am-6pm Sat; 9am-6pm Sun. *6 Nov-15 Mar* 8am-5.30pm Mon-Fri; 8.30am-5.30pm Sat; 9am-5.30pm Sun. **Admission** free. **Map** p155 B2 ❷
This huge cemetery was formed by commandeering three farms (you can still see the ruins of a windmill in rue Froidevaux) in 1824. As with much of the Left Bank, the boneyard has literary clout: Beckett, Baudelaire, Sartre, de Beauvoir, Maupassant, Ionesco and Tristan Tzara all rest here. There are also artists, including Brancusi, Henri Laurens, Frédéric Bartholdi (sculptor of the Statue of Liberty) and Man Ray. The celebrity roll-call continues with Serge Gainsbourg, André Citroën, Coluche and Jean Seberg.

Fondation Cartier pour l'Art Contemporain

261 bd Raspail, 14th (01.42.18.56.50, www.fondation.cartier.fr). Mº Denfert-Rochereau or Raspail. **Open** 11am-10pm Tue; 11am-8pm Wed-Sun. **Admission** €9.50; free-€6.50 reductions. **Map** p155 C2 ❸
Jean Nouvel's glass and steel building, an exhibition centre with Cartier's offices above, is as much a work of art as the installations inside. Shows by artists and photographers have wide-ranging themes. Live events around the shows are called Nuits Nomades.

Fondation Henri Cartier-Bresson

2 impasse Lebouis, 14th (01.56.80. 27.00, www.henricartierbresson.org). Mº Gaîté. **Open** 1-6.30pm Tue, Thur, Fri, Sun; 1-8.30pm Wed; 11am-6.45pm Sat. Closed Aug & between exhibitions. **Admission** €6; €3 reductions. No credit cards. **Map** p155 A2 ❹
This two-floor gallery is dedicated to the work of acclaimed French photographer Henri Cartier-Bresson. It consists of a tall, narrow *atelier* in a 1913 building, with a minutely catalogued archive, open to researchers, and a lounge on the fourth floor screening films. In the spirit of Cartier-Bresson, who assisted on three Jean Renoir films and drew and painted all his life (some drawings are also found on the fourth floor), the Fondation opens its doors to other disciplines with three annual shows.

Musée Bourdelle

16-18 rue Antoine-Bourdelle, 15th (01.49.54.73.73, www.bourdelle. paris.fr). Mº Falguière or Montparnasse Bienvenüe. **Open** 10am-6pm Tue-Sun. **Admission** free. *Exhibitions* prices vary. **Map** p155 A1 ❺
The sculptor Antoine Bourdelle (1861-1929), a pupil of Rodin, produced a number of monumental works, including the modernist relief friezes at the Théâtre des Champs-Elysées. Set around a small garden, the museum includes the artist's apartment and studios. A 1950s extension tracks the evolution of Bourdelle's equestrian monument to General Alvear in Buenos Aires, Argentina, and his masterful *Hercules the Archer*. A new wing houses bronzes.

Musée du Montparnasse

21 av du Maine, 15th (01.42.22.91.96, www.museedumontparnasse.net). Mº Montparnasse Bienvenüe. **Open** 12.30-7pm Tue-Sun. **Admission** €6; free-€5 reductions. No credit cards. **Map** p155 A1 ❻

Set in one of the last surviving alleys of studios, this was home to Marie Vassilieff, whose own academy and cheap canteen welcomed poor artists Picasso, Cocteau and Matisse. Shows focus on present-day artists and the area's creative past.

Tour Montparnasse

33 av du Maine, 15th (01.45.38.52.56, www.tourmontparnasse56.com). Mº Montparnasse Bienvenüe. **Open** *Oct-Mar* 9.30am-10.30pm Mon-Thur, Sun; 9.30am-11pm Fri, Sat. *Apr-Sept* 9.30am-11.30pm daily. **Admission** €11.50; free-€8.50 reductions. **Map** p155 A1 ⑦
Built in 1974 on the site of the old station, this 209m (686ft) steel-and-glass monolith is shorter than the Eiffel Tower, but better placed for fabulous views of the city. A lift whisks you up in 38 seconds to the 56th floor, where you'll find a display of aerial scenes of Paris, an upgraded café-lounge, a souvenir shop – and lots and lots of sky.

Eating & drinking

La Cerisaie

70 bd Edgar Quinet, 14th (01.43. 20.98.98). Mº Edgar Quinet or Montparnasse. **Open** noon-2pm, 7-10pm Mon-Fri. Closed Aug & 1wk Dec. **€€**. **Bistro**. **Map** p155 A1 ⑧
Nothing about La Cerisaie's unprepossessing red façade hints at the talent that lurks inside. On the daily changing blackboard menu you might find *bourride de maquereau*, a thrifty take on the garlicky French fish stew, or *cochon noir de Bigorre*, an ancient breed of pig that puts ordinary pork to shame. *Baba à l'armagnac*, a variation on the usual rum cake, comes with great chantilly.

La Coupole

102 bd du Montparnasse, 14th (01.43.20.14.20, www.flobrasseries. com/coupoleparis). Mº Vavin. **Open** 8.30am-midnight daily. **€€**. **Brasserie**. **Map** p155 B1 ⑨

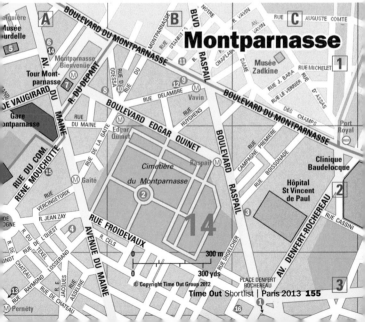

Museée Bourdelle p154

La Coupole still glows with some of the old glamour. The people-watching remains superb, inside and out, and the long ranks of linen-covered tables, 32 art deco columns, mosaic floor and sheer scale of the operation still make coming here an event. The set menu offers steaks, foie gras, fish and autumn game stews, but the real treat is the shellfish, which is displayed along a massive counter. Take your pick from *claires*, *spéciales* and *belons*, or go for a platter with crabs, oysters, prawns, periwinkles and clams.

Josselin

67 rue du Montparnasse, 14th (01.43.20.93.50). M° Edgar Quinet. **Open** noon-11pm Tue-Sun. **€**. No credit cards. **Crêperie**. **Map** p155 B1 ⑩
Josselin is the star crêperie of the area, and the one with the longest queues. The speciality is the Couple – two layers of galette with the filling in the middle. Wash it all down with bowls of cider, of which the brut is best.

Le Select

99 bd du Montparnasse, 6th (01.45.48.38.24). M° Vavin. **Open** 7am-2am Mon-Thur, Sun; 7am-4am Fri, Sat. **€**. **Café**. **Map** p155 B1 ⑪
For a decade between the wars, the junction of boulevards Raspail and du Montparnasse was where Man Ray, Cocteau and Lost Generation Americans hung out in the vast, glass-fronted cafés. Eight decades on, Le Select is the best of these inevitable tourist haunts, managing to hold on to its heyday with dignity.

Shopping

Storie

20 rue Delambre, 14th (01.83.56.01.98, www.storieblog.com). M° Vavin. **Open** 11am-2pm, 3-8pm Tue-Sat; 5-8pm Sun. **Map** p155 B1 ⑫
A magical new shop selling an eclectic mix of objects from around the world – from Korean coffee cups to wooden deer heads.

Nightlife

Au Magique

42 rue de Gergovie, 14th (01.45.42.26.10, www.aumagique.com). M° Pernety. **Open** 8pm-2am Wed-Sun. **Admission** prices vary. **Map** p155 A3 (off map) ⑬
Artist-in-residence Marc Havet serenades punters with politically incorrect *chanson* at weekends; you can also expect spoken word events.

Mix Club

24 rue de l'Arrivée, 15th (01.56.80.37.37, www.mixclub.fr). M° Montparnasse Bienvenüe. **Open** 11pm-6am Thur-Sat. **Admission** free-€20. **Map** p155 A1 ⑭
The Mix Club has one of the city's biggest dancefloors. Regular visitors include Erick Morillo's Subliminal and Ministry of Sound parties, plus just about everyone else who's big in France – or anywhere else in the world.

Le Petit Journal Montparnasse

13 rue du Commandant-René-Mouchotte, 14th (01.43.21.56.70, www.petitjournalmontparnasse.com). M° Gaîté or Montparnasse-Bienvenüe. **Open** 8pm-2am daily. *Concerts* 10pm Mon-Sat. **Admission** (incl 1 drink) €25; €15 reductions. **Map** p155 A2 ⑮
Two-level jazz brasserie in the shadow of the Tour Montparnasse with Latin sounds, R&B and soul-gospel.

Arts & leisure

Le Denfert

24 pl Denfert-Rochereau, 14th (01.43.21.41.01, www.allocine.fr). M° Denfert Rochereau/RER Denfert Rochereau. **Admission** €7.50; €5.50-€6 reductions. No credit cards. **Map** p155 C3 ⑯
This charming little cinema offers a nicely eclectic repertory selection that ranges from François Ozon and Hayao Miyazaki to shorts and animation.

Worth the Trip

North

Basilique St-Denis

*1 rue de la Légion-d'Honneur, 93200
St-Denis (01.48.09.83.54). M° St-Denis
Basilique/tram 1.* **Open** *Apr-Sept*
10am-6.15pm Mon-Sat; noon-6.15pm
Sun. *Oct-Mar* 10am-5.15pm Mon-Sat;
noon-5.15pm Sun. **Tours** 10.30am,
3pm Mon-Sat; 12.15pm, 3pm Sun.
Admission €7; free-€4.50 reductions.
Legend has it that when St Denis was
beheaded, he picked up his noggin and
walked with it to Vicus Catulliacus
(now St-Denis) to be buried. The first
church, parts of which can be seen in
the crypt, was built over his tomb in
around 475. The present edifice was
begun in the 1130s. It is considered to
be the first example of Gothic architecture. In the 13th century, mason Pierre
de Montreuil erected the spire and
rebuilt the choir nave and transept. St-
Denis was the burial place for all but
three French monarchs between 996
and the end of the *ancien régime*, so the
ambulatory is a museum of French
funerary sculpture. It includes a fanci-
ful Gothic tomb for Dagobert, the aus-
tere effigy of Charles V, and the
Renaissance tomb of Louis XII and his
wife Anne de Bretagne. In 1792, these
tombs were desecrated, and the royal
remains thrown into a pit.

Musée de l'Air et de l'Espace

*Aéroport de Paris-Le Bourget, 93352
Le Bourget Cedex (01.49.92.70.00,
www.mae.org). M° Gare du Nord, then
bus 350/RER Le Bourget, then bus
152.* **Open** *Apr-Sept* 10am-6pm Tue-
Sun. *Oct-Mar* 10am-5pm Tue-Sun.
Admission free. *With Concorde &
Boeing 747* €7; free-€5 reductions.
The impressive air and space museum
is set in the former passenger terminal
at Le Bourget airport. The collection
begins with the pioneers, including
fragile-looking biplanes and the com-
mand cabin of a Zeppelin airship. On
the runway are Mirage fighters, a US

Thunderchief, and Ariane launchers 1 and 5. A hangar houses the prototype Concorde 001 and wartime survivors. A scale models gallery opened in 2008.

East

104

104 rue d'Aubervilliers, 19th (01.53.35. 50.00, www.104.fr). Mº Riquet. **Open** noon-8pm Tue-Fri; 11am-8pm Sat, Sun. **Admission** free. *Exhibitions* €5; free-€3 reductions.

It's more than a century since tourist-choked Montmartre was the centre of artistic activity in Paris. But now the north-east of Paris is again where the action is, in a previously neglected area of bleak railway goods yards and dilapidated social housing. 104, described as a 'space for artistic creation', occupies a vast 19th-century building on the rue d'Aubervilliers that used to house Paris's municipal undertakers. There aren't any constraints on the kind of work the resident artists do – 104 is open to 'all the arts' – but they're expected to show finished pieces in one of four annual 'festivals'.

La Cité des Sciences et de l'Industrie

La Villette, 30 av Corentin-Cariou, 19th (01.40.05.70.00, www.cite-sciences.fr). Mº Porte de la Villette. **Open** 10am-6pm Tue-Sat; 10am-7pm Sun. **Admission** €8; free-€6 reductions.

This ultra-modern science museum pulls in five million visitors a year. Explora, the permanent show, occupies the upper two floors, whisking visitors through 30,000sq m (320,000sq ft) of space, life, matter and communication: scale models of satellites including the Ariane space shuttle, planes and robots, plus the chance to experience weightlessness, make for an exciting trip. In the Espace Images, try the delayed camera and other optical illusions, draw 3D images on a computer or lend your voice to the *Mona Lisa*. The hothouse garden investigates developments in agriculture and bio-technology. The Cité des Enfants runs workshops for younger children.

Disneyland Paris/Walt Disney Studios Park

Marne-la-Vallée (08.25.30.60.30, from UK 0870 503 0303, www.disneyland paris.com). 32km E of Paris. RER A or TGV Marne-la-Vallée-Chessy. By car, A4 exit 14. **Open** Times vary, see website for details. **Admission** *1 park* €57; free-€51 reductions. *1-day hopper* (both parks) €69; free-€62 reductions. Young ones will get a real kick out of Fantasyland, with its Alice maze, Sleeping Beauty's castle and teacup rides. Walt Disney Studios focuses on special effects and the tricks of the animation trade. Disney's newest adrenaline ride, the Twilight Zone Tower of Terror, sends daredevils plummeting down a 13-storey lift shaft.

South

Maison de Jean Cocteau

15 rue du Lau, 91490 Milly-la-Forêt (01.64.98.11.50, www.jeancocteau. net). 60km S of Paris. RER D Maisse, then 7km taxi ride. By car, A6 exit 13. **Open** *Mar-Oct* 2-7pm Wed-Sun. *Early Jan, Nov-Dec* 2-6pm Wed-Sun. Closed mid Jan-Feb. **Admission** €7; free-€4.50 reductions.

Thanks to the hefty financial input of Pierre Bergé (partner of the late Yves Saint Laurent) and five years of refurbishment, Cocteau's old country house has been transformed into a fascinating museum. The living room is wonderfully flamboyant, with antique furniture and gold palm trees framing a Bérard painting of Oedipus. The bedroom, meanwhile, with its four-poster bed and a mural of a castle, boasts a fairytale quality reminiscent of Cocteau's romantic fantasy *La Belle et la Bête*. Finally the study, with its leopard print walls and erotic memorabilia, offers the most intimate glimpse into the artist's creative process, by turns both inspiring and provocative. The rest of the house has been converted into exhibition space with two galleries: one a collection of portraits of Cocteau by artists such as Picasso, Warhol and Modigliani; the other dedicated to temporary collections. Cocteau's body rests nearby, in the Chapelle Saint-Blaise-des-Simples (rue de l'Amiral de Graville, Milly-la-Forêt, 01.64.98.84.94, open 10am-12.30pm, 2-6pm Wed-Sun).

Musée Fragonard

7 av du Général de Gaulle, 94704 Maisons-Alfort (01.43.96.71.72, http://musee.vet-alfort.fr). M° Ecole Vétérinaire de Maisons-Alfort. **Open** 2-6pm Wed, Thur; 1-6pm Sat, Sun. Closed Aug.
Admission €7; free reductions.
In 18th-century French medical schools, study aids were produced in one of two ways. They were either painstakingly sculpted in coloured wax or made from the real things – organs, limbs, tangled vascular systems – dried or preserved in formaldehyde. Veterinary surgeon Honoré Fragonard (cousin of the famous rococo painter) was a master of the second method, and many of his most striking works are now on display here. *Homme à la mandibule* is a flayed, grimacing man holding a jawbone in his right hand – an allusion to the story of Samson slaying the Philistines. *Tête humaine injectée* is a rather more sober human head whose blood vessels were injected with coloured wax, red for arteries and blue for veins. And, most grandiose of all, *Cavalier de l'apocalypse* is a flayed man on the back of a flayed horse, inspired, according to the museum notes, by a painting by Dürer.

Parc André Citroën

Rue Balard, rue St-Charles or quai Citroën, 15th. M° Balard or Javel. **Open** 8am-dusk Mon-Fri; 9am-dusk Sat, Sun, public hols.
This park is a fun, postmodern version of a French formal garden, designed by Gilles Clément and Alain Prévost. It comprises glasshouses, computerised fountains, waterfalls, a wilderness and themed gardens with different coloured plants and even sounds. The tethered Eutelsat helium balloon takes visitors up for panoramic views. If the weather looks unreliable, call 01.44.26.20.00.

West

Bois de Boulogne

16th. M° Les Sablons or Porte Dauphine. **Admission** free.
Covering 865 hectares, the Bois was once the Forêt de Rouvray hunting grounds. It was landscaped in the 1860s, when artificial grottoes and waterfalls were created around the Lac Inférieur. The Jardin de Bagatelle is famous for its roses, daffodils and water lilies. The Jardin d'Acclimation is a children's amusement park, complete with miniature train, farm, rollercoaster and boat rides.

Musée Belmondo

14 rue de L'Abreuvoir, 92100 Boulogne-Billancourt (01.55.18.69.01, www.musee paulbelmondo.fr). M° Boulogne Jean Jaurès, then bus 123. **Open** 2-6pm Tue-Fri, 11am-6pm Sat, Sun. **Admission** €5; free-€3.70 reductions.
See box right.

Musée Marmottan – Claude Monet

2 rue Louis-Boilly, 16th (01.44.96.50.33, www.marmottan.com). M° La Muette. **Open** 10am-6pm Tue, Wed, Fri-Sun; 10am-8pm Thur. **Admission** €10; free-€5 reductions.
This old hunting pavilion has become a famed holder of Impressionist art thanks to two bequests: the first by the daughter of the doctor of Manet, Monet, Pissarro, Sisley and Renoir; the second by Monet's son Michel. Its Monet collection, the largest in the world, numbers 165 works, plus sketchbooks, palette and photos. Upstairs are works by Renoir, Manet, Gauguin, Caillebotte and Berthe Morisot, a Sèvres clock and a collection of First Empire furniture.

Belmondo rediscovered

Jean-Paul's dad was also one of France's finest sculptors.

For most people in France, the name Belmondo is associated with Nouvelle Vague actor Jean-Paul, who shot to fame in 1960s films such as Jean-Luc Godard's *A Bout de Souffle*. What most of us don't know is that the actor's father, Paul (1898-1982), was one of France's most important 20th-century sculptors, and one of the last to use neo-classical, academic techniques.

Many of his works (characterised by harmonious forms and unfussy lines) epitomise the 1930s style, particularly the gracious proportions of *La Danse*, in the Théâtre de Chaillot, which was commissioned for Paris's Universal Exposition in 1937; and two statues in the Jardin de Tuileries (a well-hung *Apollo* and an elegant *Jeanette*). Since the war, Paul Belmondo's talents have mysteriously remained unknown to most, but the new **Musée Belmondo** (see left), set inside in the 18th-century, neo-classical Château Buchillot, looks set to

thrust his works back into the limelight. The space, revamped by architects Chartier-Corbasson, is an interior designer's dream – the mix of stark white, black and timber materials lends a different mood to each section. Several rooms harbour niches and alcoves in which Belmondo's sculptures sit enticingly, as if in a workshop; and numerous artificial backdrops, along with raised floors and frames, create multiple sightlines. Clever use of natural and artificial lighting highlights the detail on each sculpture, and a special 'replica' room on the first floor encourages visitors to feel the works' grooves and textures.

The visit ends in the château gardens, where works created by Belmondo's contemporaries – Raoul Lamourdedieu, Pierre Traverse, Léon Séverac, Karl-Jean Longuet, Henri Le Pecq, Marcel Chauvenet-Delclos and Marguerite Cossaceanu-Lavrillier – pepper the lawns in 1930s glory. A real treat on a sunny day.

PARIS BY AREA

Centuries of makeovers have made Versailles the most sumptuously clad château in the world. Architect Louis Le Vau first embellished the original building – a hunting lodge built during Louis XIII's reign – after Louis XIV saw Vaux-le-Vicomte, the impressive residence of his finance minister, Nicolas Fouquet. After Le Vau's death in 1670, Jules Hardouin-Mansart took over as principal architect, transforming Versailles into the château we know today.

The gardens are works of art in themselves, their ponds and statues once again embellished by a fully working fountain system.

Château de Versailles

78000 Versailles (01.30.83.78.00, advance tickets 08.92.68.46.94, www.chateauversailles.fr). **Open** *Apr-Oct* 9am-6.30pm Tue-Sun. *Nov-Mar* 9am-5.30pm Tue-Sun. **Admission** €15; free-€13 reductions.
Versailles is a masterpiece – and it's almost always packed with visitors. Allow yourself a whole day to appreciate the sumptuous State Apartments and the Hall of Mirrors, the highlights of any visit and most accessible with a day ticket. The Grand Appartement, where Louis XIV held court, consists of six gilded salons (Venus, Mercury, Apollo and so on). No less luxurious, the Queen's Apartment includes her bedroom, where royal births took place in full view of the court. Hardouin-Mansart's showpiece, the Hall of Mirrors, where a united Germany was proclaimed in 1871 and the Treaty of Versailles was signed in 1919, is flooded with light from its 17 windows.

Domaine de Versailles

Gardens **Open** *Apr-Oct* 7am-dusk daily. *Nov-Mar* 8am-dusk daily. **Admission** *Winter* free (statues covered over). *Summer* €3; free-€1.50 reductions.

Grandes Eaux Musicales (01.30.83.78.88). **Open** *Apr-Sept* Sat, Sun. **Admission** €8; free-€6 reductions. *Park* **Open** dawn-dusk daily. **Admission** free.
Sprawling across eight square kilometres (three square miles), the gardens consist of formal parterres, ponds, elaborate statues and a spectacular series of fountains. On weekend afternoons in spring and autumn, the fountains are set to music: Grandes Eaux Musicales.

Grand Trianon/Petit Trianon/Domaine de Marie-Antoinette

Open *Apr-Oct* noon-6.30pm daily. *Nov-Mar* noon-5.30pm daily. **Admission** *Summer* €10; €6 after 4pm; free under-18s. *Winter* €6; free under-18s.
In 1687, Hardouin-Mansart built the pink marble Grand Trianon in the north of the park. Here Louis XIV and his children's governess and secret second wife, Madame de Maintenon, could admire the intimate gardens from the colonnaded portico. It retains the Empire decor of Napoleon, who stayed here with his second Empress, Marie-Louise. The Petit Trianon, built for Louis XV's mistress Madame de Pompadour, is a wonderful example of neo-classicism. It later became part of the Domaine de Marie-Antoinette, an exclusive hideaway located beyond the canal in the wooded parkland. Given to Marie-Antoinette as a wedding gift by her husband Louis XVI in 1774, the domain also includes the chapel adjoining the Petit Trianon, plus a theatre, a neo-classical 'Temple d'Amour', and Marie-Antoinette's fairy-tale farm and dairy.

Getting there

By car

20km (12.5 miles) from Paris by the A13 or D10.

By train

For the station nearest the château, take the RER C5 (VICK or VERO trains) to Versailles-Rive Gauche.

Essentials

Hôtel Jules et Jim p175

Hotels

Paris's luxury palaces continue to offer the ultimate dream hotel experience, and the last couple of years have brought even more competition to the luxury sector with the completion of the new **Hôtel W Paris-Opéra**, the **Shangri-La** in the 16th and the complete makeover of the **Royal Monceau** on avenue Hoche by Philippe Starck. The **Peninsula Paris** is also due to open in 2013.

Better value for money can be found at Paris's boutique hotels. For several hundred euros less a night than a palace, you can be soothed by fine linen, marble baths and a dreamy pool and hammam at **Le Metropolitan**, walk through silk taffeta curtains to your own terrace at **Le Petit Paris**, fall into a deep sleep at the pure white marvel that is the **Hôtel Gabriel**, and fraternise at the trendy cava bar of the Spanish-owned **Banke**.

For those who like a bit more glitz, the sparkly **Opéra Diamond** and sexy **Sublim Eiffel** use fibre optics to create a starry galaxy.

Further down the scale, there is a wide choice of moderately priced and even budget design hotels, especially in the trendy east and north-east of the city, such as the Starck-designed **Mama Shelter**, **Standard Design Hotel**, **Le Quartier Bastille** and **20 Prieuré**, along with sustainable sleeps at the **Solarhôtel**.

Classification

We've divided the hotels by area, then listed them in four categories, according to the standard prices (not including seasonal offers or discounts) for one night in a double room with en suite shower/bath. For deluxe hotels (€€€€), you can expect to pay more than €350; for properties in the expensive bracket

(€€€), €220-€350; for moderate properties (€€), allow €130-€219; while budget rooms (€) go for less than €130.

In the know

All hotels in France charge a room tax (*taxe de séjour*) of around €1 per person per night, although this is sometimes included in the rate.

Champs-Elysées & Western Paris

Four Seasons George V

31 av George V, 8th (01.49.52.70.00, www.fourseasons.com/paris). M° Alma Marceau or George V. €€€€.
There's no denying that the George V is serious about luxury: chandeliers, marble and tapestries, over-attentive staff, glorious flower arrangements, divine bathrooms, and ludicrously comfortable beds in some of the largest rooms in Paris. The spa area includes whirlpools, saunas and treatments; non-guests can reserve appointments.

Hôtel le Bristol

112 rue du Fbg-St-Honoré, 8th (01.53. 43.43.00, www.hotel-bristol.com). M° Champs-Elysées Clémenceau. €€€€.
Set on the exclusive rue du Faubourg St-Honoré, near luxury boutiques such as Christian Lacroix, Azzaro, Salvatore Ferragamo, Givenchy and Dolce & Gabbana, the Bristol is a luxurious 'palace' hotel with a loyal following of fashionistas and millionaires drawn by the location, impeccable service, larger than average rooms and a three Michelin-starred restaurant with Eric Fréchon at the helm. The Bristol's seven-storey wing opened in late 2009.

Hôtel Daniel

8 rue Frédéric-Bastiat, 8th (01.42.56. 17.00, www.hoteldanielparis.com). M° Franklin D. Roosevelt or St-Philippe-du-Roule. €€€€.

SHORTLIST

Best newcomers
- Hôtel Jules et Jim (see p175)
- Hôtel W Paris-Opéra (see p171)
- Royal Monceau (see p168)
- Shangri-La Paris (see p168)

Best spa splurge
- Four Seasons George V (see p165)
- Hôtel Fouquet's Barrière (see p167)
- Le Meurice (see p172)

Best alfresco breakfast
- Hôtel de l'Abbaye Saint-Germain (see p179)
- Mama Shelter (see p173)

Best bars
- Hôtel Plaza Athénée (see p167)
- Royal Monceau (see p168)

Best for fashion week
- L'Hôtel (see p179)
- Le Montalembert (see p177)

Best bathrooms
- Four Seasons George V (see p165)
- Renaissance Paris Arc de Triomphe (see p168)

Best bargain beds
- Solarhôtel (see p181)
- Mama Shelter (see p173)
- St Christopher's Inn (see p173)

Chic sleeps
- Hôtel La Belle Juliette (see p179)
- Hôtel Amour (see p172)

Lap of luxury
- Hôtel le Bristol (see p165)
- Hôtel Ritz (see p171)

ESSENTIALS

This romantic hideaway close to the Champs-Elysées is decorated in chinoiserie and a palette of rich colours, with 26 rooms (free Wi-Fi) cosily appointed in *toile de Jouy* and an intricately hand-painted restaurant that feels like a courtyard. At about €50 a head, the gastronomic restaurant Le Lounge, run by chef Denis Fetisson, is a good deal for this neighbourhood.

Hôtel Fouquet's Barrière

46 av George V, 8th (01.40.69.
60.00, www.fouquets-barriere.com).
M° George V. €€€€.
This grandiose five-star is built around the fin-de-siècle brasserie Le Fouquet's. Five buildings form the hotel complex, with 107 rooms (including 40 suites), upmarket restaurant Le Diane, the Sparis spa, indoor pool and a rooftop terrace for hire. Jacques Garcia, of Hôtel Costes and Westin fame, was responsible for the interior design, which retains the Empire style of the exterior while incorporating luxurious touches inside – flat-screen TVs and mist-free mirrors in the marble bathrooms. And, of course, it's unbeatable for location – right at the junction of avenue George V and the Champs-Elysées.

Hôtel Plaza Athénée

25 av Montaigne, 8th (01.53.67.
66.65, www.plaza-athenee-paris.com).
M° Alma Marceau. €€€€.
This palace is ideally placed for power shopping at Chanel, Louis Vuitton, Dior and other avenue Montaigne boutiques. Material girls and boys will enjoy the high-tech room amenities, such as remote-controlled air con, internet and video-game access on the TV via infrared keyboard, and mini hi-fi. Make time for a drink in the Bar du Plaza, a cocktail bunny's most *outré* fantasy.

Hôtel Square

3 rue de Boulainvilliers, 16th (01.44.
14.91.90, www.hotelsquare.com). M°
Passy/RER Avenue du Pdt Kennedy).
€€€€.

Located in the upmarket 16th, this courageously modern hotel has a dramatic yet welcoming interior, and attentive service that comes from having to look after only 22 rooms. They're decorated in amber, brick or slate colours, with exotic woods, quality fabrics and bathrooms seemingly cut from one huge chunk of Carrara marble. View exhibitions in the atrium gallery or mingle with media types at the hip Zebra Square restaurant and DJ bar.

Les Jardins de la Villa

5 rue Bélidor, 17th (01.53.81.01.10,
www.jardinsdelavilla.com). M° Porte
Maillot. €€€.
Behind a sober frontage, the 33-room Jardins de la Villa is an unexpectedly playful affair, with a couture theme and a penchant for fuchsia pink. It's dotted with surreal touches – not least the high heel-shaped couch in reception. Beautifully appointed rooms pair modern luxuries (Nespresso machines, free Wi-Fi, sleek flatscreen TVs) with old-fashioned attention to detail. The location is off the tourist trail, though close to the métro; not one to pick if you like being in the thick of things, perhaps, but perfect for a little peace and quiet.

Jays Paris

6 rue Copernic, 16th (01.47.04.16.16,
www.jays-paris.com). M° Kléber or
Victor Hugo. €€€€.
Jays is a luxurious *boutique-apart* hotel that trades on a clever blend of antique furniture, modern design and high-tech equipment. The marble staircase, lit entirely by natural light filtered through the glass atrium overhead, gives an instant feeling of grandeur, and leads to five suites, each with a fully equipped kitchenette and free Wi-Fi. A cosy salon is available to welcome in-house guests and their visitors.

Le Metropolitan

10 pl de Mexico, 16th (01.56.90.
40.04, www.radissonblu.com).
M° Trocadero. €€€.

This 40-room offering from Radisson Blu is supremely sleek. The discreet entrance is only a few metres wide, but once inside the triangular structure opens out into a surprisingly large area, with a monumental art deco-style fireplace, and cream leather and black granite reminiscent of New York in the 1930s. The first floor contains a swank insiders' cocktail bar, but the biggest surprise of all is the breathtaking view of the Eiffel Tower from the front façade, best enjoyed through the huge oval window while lying on the four-poster bed of the sixth floor suite. All rooms exude *luxe, calme et volonté* with solid oak floors, linen curtains and baths or showers carved from black or cream marble. And below ground is a sublime swimming pool and hammam reserved for guests.

Opéra Diamond

4 rue de la Pépinière, 8th (01.44.70. 02.00, www.paris-hotel-diamond.com). Mº St-Lazare. €€.
This sparkling newcomer lives up to its name with a night-sky decor made up of black granite resin punctuated with crystals and LEDs. The 30 rooms are equally splendid, with Swarovski crystal touches to the furniture, black bathrooms and satin curtains that close to become a photomontage of a female nude crossed with architectural imagery. The Executive rooms have iPod stations, Nespresso machines, and speakers in the bathrooms. A courtyard with a fountain adds to the appeal.

Renaissance Paris Arc de Triomphe

39 av de Wagram, 17th (01.55.37. 55.37, www.marriott.com). Mº Ternes. €€€.
You can't miss it. This six-storey undulating glass façade on avenue de Wagram is like no other part of the neighbourhood. All rooms are stylishly done out in pale greys, charcoals and dark wood, with Eames-style furniture. Nice high-tech touches include an iPod

dock on the bedside radio and a large flat-screen TV with Wi-Fi keyboard. Bathrooms are a glory of polished metal, tasteful tiles and gleaming glass. The Makassar restaurant serves delicate and delicious Franco-Asian fusion food.

Royal Monceau

37 av Hoche, 8th (01.42.99.88.00, www.leroyalmonceau.com). Mº Charles de Gaulle Etoile. €€€€.
The recently renovated Royal Monceau is a supremely classy retreat. This is a hotel that takes its art appreciation seriously, with its own art agenda blog and a special art concierge. Philippe Starck was in charge of the refit, and his cheeky touches are everywhere. The bedrooms are a studied jumble, with beds in the middle of the room, pictures leaned up against the wall, a guitar waiting to be strummed and a lampshade decked with scribbled notes. But beyond all this designer frippery there lie some gorgeous treats, including vast walk-in wardrobes, spacious bathrooms with twin sinks and walk-in showers, and huge mirrors that magically transform into a TVs. Breakfast is a lavish affair.

Le Sezz

6 av Frémiet, 16th (01.56.75.26.26, www.hotelsezz.com). Mº Passy. €€€.
Le Sezz has 27 sleek, luxurious rooms and suites. The understated decor represents a refreshingly modern take on luxury, with black parquet flooring, rough-hewn stone walls and bathrooms partitioned off with sweeping glass façades. The bar and public areas are equally sleek and chic. Free Wi-Fi.

Shangri-La Paris

10 av d'Iéna, 16th (01.53.67.19.98, www.shangri-la.com). Mº Iéna. €€€€.
Pierre-Yves Rochon's design at the Shangri-La is an ode to French imperialism, with lavish colonial-style paintings, knick-knacks and light fittings, artfully mixed with century-old marble floors, stained-glass windows and thick velveteen fabrics. Half of the

The W-factor

The luxury hotel chain's new Paris outpost is a stunner.

'Wacky', 'wild' and 'wonderful' – the 'w' in the upmarket **Hôtel W Paris-Opéra** (see p171) could stand for any of those words. This spanking new joint, overlooking the Opéra Garnier, is the Starwood hotel group's latest venture. It took two and a half years to finish, but it was worth the wait, with 91 rooms (designed by architecture firm Rockwell) that ooze NYC style from every nook and cranny; a clubbing theme that is taken to the extreme with a stream of DJ nights by La Clique (aka André and Lionel from the Baron); a DJ booth; and black corridors with sparkling lights that make you feel like you're walking through the reverse side of a disco ball. David Guetta eat your heart out.

In the guest rooms, nightclub touches prevail in the light fittings (which replicate the corridor walls) but, otherwise, the vibe is relaxing, with thick velvet and satin fabrics, marshmallowy pillows and dreamy views over the Opéra Garnier. For an all-out treat, the 'Extreme Wow' suite will set you back a whopping €2,300 (don't worry, standard doubles start at the more affordable €340), but you'll get 88sq m of smart modern design all to yourself, and the feeling that you've walked onto the set of a James Bond movie, with a hidden shower, a circular bed and proper Belle Epoque mouldings (a nod to the building's Haussmannian past).

Back on the ground floor, the bar is an airy space for a cocktail, with a giant mirror decorated with black cartoon characters and a list of tempting drinks – the hotel brought in a specialist from Washington DC to create the menu. But it's in the restaurant where things get really interesting, with such delights as white asparagus on a bed of almonds and olives, and Barcelona-style *canellones*, all concocted by Michelin-starred Catalonian chef Sergi Arola.

Dear Mary,

I followed your advice and checked the ParisAddress website to look for an apartment. This place we booked is just amazing, it has everything we were expecting and even more !

> Instant availability
> Instant booking
> Easy process
> Prices all included, no hidden fees !
> Personal greeting
> Assistance 7/7

WWW.PARISADDRESS.COM

You wish to live like a true Parisian ?
Saint-Germain-Des-Prés, the Latin Quarter, St Louis Island, the Marais, Eiffel Tower and so many other great areas for you to discover !
To make your next trip in Paris an unique and unforgettable experience, rent an apartment and discover Paris from 'within'.
ParisAddress invites you to discover picturesque and fully furnished apartments !

www.parisaddress.com - booking@parisaddress.com - +33 1 43 20 91 57

81 rooms and suites look out on to Eiffel's filigree tower, and the top-floor Suite Panoramique provides what could easily be Paris's best panorama over the Left Bank. Shangri-La may be a Chinese company, but it has gone out of its way to ensure that the building's 'French' architectural heritage remains intact: the mansion, built in 1896 by botanist Roland Bonaparte (Napoleon Bonaparte's great-nephew), drips in Napoleonic carvings and gilding; and there's a Louis XIV-style salon whose splendour rivals Versailles. Dining-wise, expect the best of France and Asia, including Shang Palace, Paris's first gourmet Cantonese restaurant.

Opéra to Les Halles

Hôtel Brighton
218 rue de Rivoli, 1st (01.47.03. 61.61, www.esprit-de-france.com). M° Tuileries. €€.
With several of the bedrooms looking out over the Tuileries gardens, the Brighton is great value, so ask for a room with a view. Recently restored, it has a classical atmosphere, from the high ceilings in the rooms to the faux-marble and mosaic decor downstairs.

Hôtel Chopin
10 bd Montmartre or 46 passage Jouffroy, 9th (01.47.70.58.10, www.hotel-chopin.com). M° Grands Boulevards. €.
Handsomely set in a historic, glass-roofed arcade next door to the Grévin musuem, the Chopin's original 1846 façade adds to its old-fashioned appeal. The 36 rooms are quiet and functional, done out in salmon and green or blue.

Hôtel Concorde Opéra Paris
108 rue St-Lazare, 8th (01.40.08. 44.44, www.concordestlazare-paris.com). M° St-Lazare. €€€.
Guests here are cocooned in sound-proofed luxury. The 19th-century lobby

with jewel-encrusted granite columns is a historic landmark: the high ceilings, walls and sculptures look much as they have for over a century. Rooms are spacious, with double entrance doors and exclusive Annick Goutal toiletries; the belle époque brasserie, Café Terminus, and sexy Golden Black Bar were designed by Sonia Rykiel. Guests have access to a nearby fitness centre and there's free Wi-Fi.

Hôtel Ritz
15 pl Vendôme, 1st (01.43.16.30.30, www.ritzparis.com). M° Concorde or Opéra. €€€€.
Chic hasn't lost its cool at the grande dame of Paris hotels, where each of the 162 bedrooms, from the romantic Frédéric Chopin to the glitzy Impérial, ooze sumptuousness. But then what else can one expect from a hotel that has proffered hospitality to the likes of Coco Chanel, the Duke of Windsor, Proust, and Dodi and Di? There are plenty of corners to strike a pose or quench a thirst, from Hemingway's cigar bar to the poolside hangout.

Hôtel W Paris-Opéra
4 rue Meyerbeer, 9th (01.77.48.94.94, www.wparisopera.fr). M° Opéra/RER Auber. €€€€.
See box p169.

Hôtel Westminster
13 rue de la Paix, 2nd (01.42.61.57.46, www.warwickwestminsteropera.com). M° Opéra/RER Auber. €€€€.
This luxury hotel near place Vendôme has more than a touch of British warmth about it, no doubt owing to the influence of its favourite 19th-century guest, the Duke of Westminster (after whom the hotel was named; the current Duke reportedly stays here as well). The hotel fitness centre has an enviable top-floor location, with a beautiful tiled steam room and views over the city, and the cosy bar features deep leather chairs, a fireplace and live jazz at weekends.

ESSENTIALS

InterContinental Paris Le Grand

2 rue Scribe, 9th (01.40.07.32.32, www.paris.intercontinental.com). M° Opéra. €€€€.

This 1862 hotel is the chain's European flagship – the landmark establishment occupies the entire block (three wings, almost 500 rooms) next to the opera house; some 80 of the honey-coloured rooms overlook the Palais Garnier. The space under the vast *verrière* is one of the best oases in town, and the hotel's restaurant and elegant coffeehouse, the Café de la Paix, poached its chef, Laurent Delarbre, from the Ritz. For a relaxing daytime break, head to I-Spa for one of its seawater treatments.

Le Meurice

228 rue de Rivoli, 1st (01.44.58.10.10, www.lemeurice.com). M° Tuileries. €€€€.

With its extravagant Louis XVI decor, intricate mosaic tiled floors and clever, modish restyling by Philippe Starck, Le Meurice is looking grander than ever. All 160 rooms (kitted out with iPod-ready radio alarms) are done up in distinct historical styles; the Belle Etoile suite on the seventh floor provides stunning 360-degree panoramic views of Paris from its terrace. You can relax in the Winter Garden to the strains of jazz performances; for some more intensive intervention, head over to the lavish spa complex.

Montmartre & Pigalle

Hôtel Amour

8 rue Navarin, 9th (01.48.78.31.80, www.hotelamourparis.fr). M° St-Georges. €€.

This boutique hotel is a real hit with the in crowd. Each of the 20 rooms (with free Wi-Fi) is unique, decorated on the theme of love or eroticism by a coterie of contemporary artists and designers such as Marc Newson and Sophie Calle. Seven of the rooms contain artists' installations, and two others have their own private bar and a large terrace on which to hold your own party. The late-night brasserie has a coveted outdoor garden.

Hôtel Banke

20 rue La Fayette, 9th (01.55.33. 22.22, www.derbyhotels.com). M° Le Peletier. €€€.

The Banke may well have the most eye-popping lobby in the city, a huge two-storey space done in outrageous belle époque style, all crimson, black pillars and gold leaf beneath a whopping glass roof. After such opulence, the rooms are perhaps something of a let-down; but they are stylish and comfortably equipped. The mezzanine bar partakes of the lobby's *luxe*, and the Josefin restaurant serves nouvelle Med cuisine.

Hôtel Particulier Montmartre

23 av Junot, 18th (01.53.41.81.40, www.hotel-particulier-montmartre.com). M° Lamarck Caulaincourt. €€€€.

Visitors lucky (and wealthy) enough to manage to book a suite at the Hôtel Particulier Montmartre will find themselves in one of the city's hidden gems. Nestled in a quiet passage off rue Lepic, this sumptuous *Directoire*-style house is dedicated to art, with each of the five luxurious suites personalised by an avant-garde artist. Free Wi-Fi.

Hôtel Royal Fromentin

11 rue Fromentin, 9th (01.48.74. 85.93, www.hotelroyalfromentin.com). M° Blanche or Pigalle. €€.

Wood panelling, art deco windows and a vintage glass lift echo the hotel's origins as a 1930s cabaret hall; its theatrical feel attracted Blondie and Nirvana. Many of its 47 rooms have views of Sacré-Coeur. Rooms have been renovated in French style, with bright fabrics and an old-fashioned feel.

Kube Hotel

1-5 passage Ruelle, 18th (01.42.05. 20.00, www.kubehotel.com). M° La Chapelle. €€€.

The younger sister of the Murano Urban Resort, Kube is a more hip and affordable design hotel. Like the Murano, it sits behind an unremarkable façade in an unlikely neighbourhood, the ethnically diverse Goutte d'Or. The Ice Kube bar serves vodka in glasses that, like the bar itself, are carved from ice. Also on the menu are 'apérifood' and 'snackubes' by Pierre Auge. Access to the 41 rooms is by fingerprint identification technology and there's free Wi-Fi access.

North-east Paris

Hôtel Garden Saint-Martin

35 rue Yves Toudic, 10th (01.42.40. 17.72, www.hotelgardensaintmartin-paris.com). M° Jacques Bonsergent. €.
The shops, cafés and bars along the Canal St-Martin draw visitors to this hotel, where creature comforts are guaranteed at an excellent rate. No prizes will be won for the ordinary decor, but there is a very pleasant patio garden, and the staff are helpful.

Mama Shelter

109 rue de Bagnolet, 20th (01.43.48. 49.49, www.mamashelter.com). M° Alexandre Dumas, Maraîchers or Porte de Bagnolet. €.

Philippe Starck's design commission is set a stone's throw east of Père Lachaise, and its decor appeals to the young-at-heart with Batman and Incredible Hulk light fittings, dark walls, polished wood and splashes of bright fabrics. Every room comes with an iMac computer, TV, free internet access and a CD and DVD player; and when hunger strikes, there's a brasserie with a romantic terrace. If you're sure of your dates, book online and take advantage of the saver's rate.

St Christopher's Inn

159 rue de Crimée, 19th (01.40.34. 34.40, www.st-christophers.co.uk/paris-hostels). M° Crimée, Jaurès, Laumière or Stalingrad. €.
If you don't mind bunking up with others, you could try this Paris branch of the English youth hostel chain. The decor in the bedrooms has a sailor's cabin feel, with round, colourful mirrors, bubble-pattern wallpaper and 1950s-inspired cabin furniture. The hostel really comes into its own in its bar, Belushi's, where the usual backpack brigade are joined by Parisians bent on taking advantage of the canalside setting, satellite sports, lunchtime brasserie and some of the cheapest drinks in the capital.

Hôtel Amour p172

105 rue de Vaugirard
F - 75006 Paris

Saint Germain-des-Prés

depuis 1856

★ ★ ★

A·VI·A·TIC

H O T E L

Tel: +33(0)153632550
welcome@aviatichotel.com

Special offers on
our website
www.aviatichotel.com

Le 20 Prieuré Hôtel

20 rue du Grand Prieuré, 11th (01.47. 00.74.14, www.hotel20prieure.com). Mº République. €.

This young, funky and affordable place benefits from particularly welcoming staff. Each room features a huge blow-up of a Paris landmark covering the entire wall behind the bed, giving you the illusion that you are sleeping halfway up the Eiffel Tower, or on Bir-Hakeim bridge as the métro speeds by. Bath-rooms are mundane in comparison, but things brighten up again in the light-flooded breakfast room, with pop art portraits and a reworked 1970s look.

Grand Hôtel Jeanne d'Arc

3 rue de Jarente, 4th (01.48.87. 62.11, www.hoteljeannedarc.com). Mº Chemin Vert. €.

The Jeanne d'Arc's strong point is its lovely location on a quiet road close to pretty place du Marché-Ste-Catherine. Refurbishment has made the reception area striking. The bedrooms are simple but comfortable.

Hôtel Bourg Tibourg

19 rue du Bourg-Tibourg, 4th (01.42.78.47.39, www.hotelbourg tibourg.com). Mº Hôtel de Ville. €€€.

The Bourg Tibourg has the same owners as Hôtel Costes and the same interior decorator – but don't expect this jewel box of a boutique hotel to look like a miniature replica. Aside from its enviable location in the heart of the Marais and its fashion-pack fans, here it's all about Jacques Garcia's neo-Gothic-cum-Byzantine decor – impressive and imaginative. Exotic, scented candles, mosaic-tiled bathrooms and luxurious fabrics in rich colours create the perfect escape from the outside world. There's no restaurant or lounge – posing is done in the neighbourhood bars. Free Wi-Fi.

Hôtel de la Bretonnerie

22 rue Ste-Croix-de-la-Bretonnerie, 4th (01.48.87.77.63, www.bretonnerie. com). Mº Hôtel de Ville. €€.

With its combination of wrought iron-work, exposed stone and wooden beams, the labyrinth of corridors and passages in this 17th-century *hôtel particulier* are full of atmosphere. Tapestries, rich colours and the occasional four-poster bed give the 29 suites and bedrooms individuality. Location is convenient too. Free Wi-Fi.

Hôtel Gabriel

25 rue du Grand Prieuré, 11th (01.47.00.13.38, www.gabrielparis marais.com). Mº République. €€.

Paris's first 'detox hotel' is a shrine to quality kip. The air-conditioned, pure white rooms are not short on techno wizardry: there's an iPod station; free Wi-Fi, of course; and the sine qua non of sleep aids, the NightCove device. This white box is easily programmed to emit sounds and light that stimulate melatonin: choose between sleep, nap or wake-up programmes. If you're still feeling rundown, then head downstairs for a detox massage. A partner gym, suggested jogging routes and green taxis complete the healthy vibe.

Hôtel Jules & Jim

11 rue des Gravilliers, 4th (01.44.54. 13.13, www.hoteljulesetjim.com). Mº Arts et Métiers. €€€.

Located in the heart of the Marais, this modern hotel is surrounded by two paved courtyards and has lovely rooftop views. Guest rooms are comfortable, with all mod cons, while a Continental buffet breakfast is served in the chic dining area. Guests can enjoy cocktails at the bar or on the terrace.

Hôtel du Petit Moulin

29-31 rue de Poitou, 3rd (01.42.74. 10.10, www.hoteldupetitmoulin.com). Mº St-Sébastien Froissart. €€.

Within striking distance of the hip shops on rue Charlot, this listed, turn-

ESSENTIALS

Artus Hotel p179

of-the-century façade masks what was once the oldest *boulangerie* in Paris, lovingly restored as a boutique hotel by Nadia Murano and Denis Nourry. The couple recruited Christian Lacroix for the decor, and the result is a riot of colour, trompe l'oeil effects and a savvy mix of old and new. Each of its 17 exquisitely appointed rooms is unique, and the walls in rooms 202, 204 and 205 feature swirling, extravagant drawings and scribbles taken from Lacroix's sketchbook. Free parking.

Murano Urban Resort

13 bd du Temple, 3rd (01.42.71.20.00, www.muranoresort.com). M° Filles du Calvaire or Oberkampf. €€€€.
Behind this unremarkable façade is a super cool and supremely luxurious hotel, popular with the fashion set for its slick lounge-style design, excellent restaurant and high-tech flourishes – including coloured light co-ordinators that enable you to change the mood of your room at the touch of a button. The handsome bar has a mind-boggling 140 varieties of vodka to sample, which can bring the op art fabrics in the lift to life and make the fingerprint access to the hotel's 43 rooms and nine suites (two of which feature private pools) a late-night godsend. Free Wi-Fi.

Le Quartier Bastille, Le Faubourg

9 rue de Reuilly, 12th (01.43.70.04.04, www.lequartierhotelbf.com). M° Faidherbe Chaligny or Reuilly-Diderot. €€.
Within walking distance of Bastille, the Quartier Bastille (a branch of Franck Altruie's chain of budget design hotels) flashes funky, neo-1970s furniture and just the right amount of colour. Rooms are minimalist but very comfortable.

The Seine & Islands

Hôtel des Deux-Îles

59 rue St-Louis-en-l'Île, 4th (01.43.26.13.35, www.deuxiles-paris-hotel.com). M° Pont Marie. €€.
This peaceful 17th-century townhouse offers 17 soundproofed, air-conditioned rooms kitted out in toned-down stripes, *toile de Jouy* fabrics and neo colonial-style furniture. Its star features are a tiny courtyard off the lobby and a vaulted stone breakfast area. All the rooms and bathrooms were freshened up in recent years. There's free Wi-Fi available too.

Hôtel du Jeu de Paume

54 rue St-Louis-en-l'Île, 4th (01.43.26.14.18, www.jeudepaumehotel.com). M° Pont Marie. €€€.

With a discreet courtyard entrance, 17th-century beams, private garden and a unique timbered breakfast room that was once a real tennis court built under Louis XIII, this is a charming and romantic hotel. These days, it is filled with an attractive array of modern and classical art, and has a coveted billiards table. A dramatic glass lift and catwalks lead to the rooms and two self-catering apartments, which are simple and tasteful.

The 7th & Western Paris

Le Bellechasse

8 rue de Bellechasse, 7th (01.45.50. 22.31, www.lebellechasse.com). M° Assemblée Nationale or Solférino/ RER Musée d'Orsay. €€€€.
This former *hôtel particulier* was transformed by Christian Lacroix into a trendy boutique hotel. Only a few steps away from the Musée d'Orsay, it offers 34 splendid – though small – rooms, in seven decorative styles. Book early, as the Bellechasse is very popular.

Hôtel Duc de Saint-Simon

14 rue de St-Simon, 7th (01.44.39. 20.20, www.hotelducdesaintsimon.com). M° Rue du Bac. €€€.
A lovely courtyard leads the way into this popular hotel on the edge of St-Germain-des-Prés. Of the 34 bedrooms, four have terraces over a closed-off, leafy garden. It's perfect for lovers, though if you can do without a four-poster bed there are more spacious rooms than the Honeymoon Suite.

Hôtel Eiffel Rive Gauche

6 rue du Gros-Caillou, 7th (01.45.51. 51.51, www.hotel-eiffel.com). M° Ecole Militaire. €.
The Provençal decor and warm welcome make this a nice retreat. All 29 rooms feature Empire-style bedheads and modern bathrooms. Outside, there's a tiny, tiled courtyard with a

bridge. If this is fully booked, try sister hotel Eiffel Villa Garibaldi (48 bd Garibaldi, 15th, 01.56.58.56.58).

Hôtel Lenox

9 rue de l'Université, 7th (01.42.96. 10.95, www.lenoxsaintgermain.com). M° St-Germain-des-Prés. €€.
Its location may be in the seventh arrondissement, but this venerable literary and artistic haunt is unmistakeably part of St-Germain-des-Prés. The art deco-style Lenox Club Bar, open to the public, features comfortable leather club chairs and jazz instruments on the walls. Bedrooms, which are reached by an astonishing glass lift, have traditional decor and city views.

Le Montalembert

3 rue Montalembert, 7th (01.45.49. 68.68, www.montalembert.com). M° Rue du Bac. €€€.
Grace Leo-Andrieu's impeccable boutique hotel is a benchmark of quality and service. It has everything that *mode* maniacs could want: bathrooms stuffed with Molton Brown toiletries, a set of digital scales and plenty of mirrors with which to keep an eye on their figure. Decorated in pale lilac, cinnamon and olive tones, the entire hotel has Wi-Fi access, and each room is equipped with a flat-screen TV. Clattery two-person stairwell lifts are a nice nod to old-fashioned ways.

Sublim Eiffel

94 bd Garibaldi, 15th (01.40.65.95.95, www.sublimeiffel.com). M° Sèvres-Lecourbe. €€.
Some Barry White on your iPod is essential for this luuurve hotel not far from the Eiffel Tower. Carpets printed with paving stones and manhole covers lead to the rooms, where everything has been put in place for steamy nights. It's all to do with the lighting effects, which include a starry Eiffel Tower or street-scene lights above the bed and sparkling LEDs in the showers, filtered by coloured glass doors. All guests get

ESSENTIALS

ATELIER **103**
RIVE GAUCHE

A stylish aparthotel in the heart of Paris

www.atelier103.fr

Tel: +33 (0)1 53 63 25 50
welcome@atelier103.fr

Saint Germain-des-Prés

the use of the mini-gym and hammam, and there is a massage room too. The bar adds a bit of jazz.

St-Germain-des-Prés & Odéon

Artus Hotel

34 rue de Buci, 6th (01.43.29.07.20, www.artushotel.com). M° Mabillon. €€.
The renovated Artus Hotel is the ideal spot for a classic taste of Paris – you couldn't be any closer to the heart of the Left Bank action if you tried. Inside the look is chic boutique, with 27 individually designed rooms and suites, ranging from cosy to capacious. Staff are eager to help and full of local tips.

Le Clos Médicis

56 rue Monsieur-le-Prince, 6th (01.43.29.10.80, www.closmedicis.com). M° Odéon/RER Luxembourg. €€.
Designed more like a stylish, private townhouse than a hotel, Le Clos Médicis is located by the Luxembourg gardens. The hotel's decor is refreshingly modern, with rooms done out with taffeta curtains and chenille bedcovers, and antique floor tiles in the bathrooms. The cosy lounge has a working fireplace.

Grand Hôtel de l'Univers

6 rue Grégoire-de-Tours, 6th (01.43.29.37.00, www.hotel-paris-univers.com). M° Odéon. €€.
Making the most of its 15th-century origins, this hotel features exposed wooden beams, high ceilings, antique furnishings and toile-covered walls. Manuel Canovas fabrics lend a posh touch, but there are also useful services such as a laptop for hire. The same team runs the Hôtel St-Germain-des-Prés (36 rue Bonaparte, 6th, 01.43.26.00.19).

L'Hôtel

13 rue des Beaux-Arts, 6th (01.44.41. 99.00, www.l-hotel.com). M° Mabillon or St-Germain-des-Prés. €€€.
Guests at the sumptuously decorated L'Hôtel are more likely to be models and film stars than the starving writers who frequented it during Oscar Wilde's last days (the playwright died in a room on the ground floor in November 1900). Under Jacques Garcia's restoration, each room has a theme: Mistinguett's *chambre* retains its art deco mirror bed, and Wilde's tribute room is appropriately clad in green peacock murals. In the basement is a small pool, which is wonderfully private – only two people are allowed down here at a time.

Hôtel de l'Abbaye Saint-Germain

10 rue Cassette, 6th (01.45.44.38.11, www.hotelabbayeparis.com). M° Rennes or St-Sulpice. €€€.
A monumental entrance opens the way through a courtyard into this tranquil hotel, originally part of a convent. Wood panelling, well-stuffed sofas and an open fireplace in the drawing room make for a relaxed atmosphere but, best of all, there's a surprisingly large garden where breakfast is served in the warmer months. The 43 rooms and duplex apartment are tasteful and luxurious.

Hôtel La Belle Juliette

92 rue du Cherche-Midi, 6th (01.42.22.97.40, www.hotel-belle-juliette-paris.com). M° Vaneau. €€€.
Juliette Récamier was the great society beauty of the Napoleonic era, and is the inspiration for this four-star hotel. Designer Anne Gelbard has filled the 34 rooms with the distinctive colours of the Napoleonic era and of Juliette's famous portrait by Gérard – pale yellow, eau-de-nil, duck-egg blue, slate and Augustan red. It's classical without being constricting, as there are also contemporary furniture and lighting, high-tech communications and luxury bathrooms. The Talma bar is named after a romantic actor of the time and offers organic breakfasts, lunches and Italian tapas at night inspired by Juliette's exile in Italy.

Hôtel du Globe

*15 rue des Quatre-Vents, 6th
(01.43.26.35.50, www.hotel-du-globe.fr). Mº Odéon.* €€.

The Hôtel du Globe has managed to retain much of its 17th-century character – and very pleasant it is too. Gothic wrought-iron doors open into the florid corridors, and an unexplained suit of armour supervises guests from the tiny salon. The bedrooms with baths are somewhat larger than those with showers, and if you're an early booker you might even strike it lucky and get the room with the four-poster bed.

Hôtel des Saints-Pères

*65 rue des Sts-Pères, 6th (01.45.
44.50.00, www.espritfrance.com).
Mº St-Germain-des-Prés.* €€.

Built in 1658 by one of Louis XIV's architects, this hotel has an enviable location near St-Germain-des-Prés' boutiques. It boasts a charming garden and a sophisticated, if small, bar. The most coveted room is no.100, with its fine 17th-century ceiling by painters from the Versailles School; it also has an open bathroom, so you can gaze at scenes from the myth of Leda and the Swan while you scrub.

Hôtel Villa Madame

*44 rue Madame, 6th (01.45.48.02.81,
www.hotelvillamadameparis.com).
Mº St-Sulpice.* €€€.

This revamped hotel (formerly called the Regents), located in a quiet street, is a lovely surprise, with its courtyard garden used for breakfast in the summer months. Honey- and chocolate-coloured woods mix with warm-toned velvets to make the rooms (which all feature plasma screens) feel cosy and inviting; some even have small balconies with loungers.

Relais Saint-Germain

*9 carrefour de l'Odéon, 6th (01.43.29.
12.05, www.hotel-paris-relais-saint-germain.com). Mº Odéon.* €€€.

The wood-beamed ceilings remain intact at the Relais Saint-Germain, a 17th-century hotel renovated by acclaimed chef Yves Camdeborde (originator of the *bistronomique* dining trend) and his wife Claudine. Each of the 22 rooms has a different take on eclectic Provençal charm, and the marble bathrooms are huge by Paris standards. Guests get first dibs on highly sought-after seats in the 15-table Le Comptoir restaurant next door.

Familia Hôtel

*11 rue des Ecoles, 5th (01.43.54.55.27,
www.hotel-paris-familia.com). Mº
Cardinal Lemoine or Jussieu.* €.

This old-fashioned Latin Quarter hotel has balconies hung with tumbling plants and walls draped with replica French tapestries. Owner Eric Gaucheron extends a warm welcome, and the 30 rooms have personalised touches such as sepia murals, cherry-wood furniture and stone walls. The Gaucherons also own the Minerve next door – book in advance for both.

Five Hôtel

*3 rue Flatters, 5th (01.43.31.74.21,
www.thefivehotel.com). Mº Les Gobelins
or Port Royal.* €€€.

The rooms in this stunning boutique hotel may be small, but they're all exquisitely designed, with Chinese lacquer and velvety fabrics. Fibre optics built into the walls create the illusion of sleeping under a starry sky, and you can choose from four fragrances to subtly perfume your room. Guests staying in the suite have access to a private garden with a jacuzzi.

Hôtel les Degrés de Notre-Dame

*10 rue des Grands-Degrés, 5th (01.55.
42.88.88, www.lesdegreshotel.com). Mº
Maubert-Mutualité or St-Michel.* €€.

On a tiny street across the river from Notre-Dame, this vintage hotel is an absolute gem. Its ten rooms are full of character, with original paintings, antique furniture and exposed wooden beams (nos.47 and 501 have views of the cathedral). It has an adorable restaurant and, a few streets away, two studio apartments that the owner rents to preferred customers only.

Hôtel du Panthéon

19 pl du Panthéon, 5th (01.43.54. 32.95, www.hoteldupantheon.com). Mº Cluny La Sorbonne or Maubert Mutualité/RER Luxembourg. €€.
The 36 rooms of this elegant hotel are beautifully decorated with classic French *toile de Jouy* fabrics, antique furniture and painted woodwork. Some enjoy impressive views of the Panthéon; others squint out on to a hardly less romantic courtyard, complete with chestnut tree.

Hôtel Résidence Henri IV

50 rue des Bernardins, 5th (01.44.41. 31.81, www.residencehenri4.com). Mº Cardinal Lemoine. €€.
This belle époque-style hotel has a mere eight rooms and five apartments, so guests are assured of the staff's full attention. Peacefully situated next to leafy square Paul-Langevin, it's just minutes away from Notre-Dame. The four-person apartments come with a mini-kitchen featuring a hob, fridge and microwave. Free Wi-Fi available.

Hôtel de la Sorbonne

6 rue Victor-Cousin, 5th (01.43. 54.58.08, www.hotelsorbonne.com). Mº Cluny La Sorbonne/RER Luxembourg. €€.
It's out with the old at this charming, freshly renovated hotel, whose new look is very much a modern take on art nouveau, with bold wallpapers, floral prints, lush fabrics and quotes from French literature woven into the carpets. Rooms are all equipped with iMac computers.

Le Petit Paris

NEW *214 rue St-Jacques, 5th (01.53.10. 29.29, www.hotelpetitparis.com). Mº Maubert Mutualité/RER Luxembourg.* €€€.
This new venture is a dynamic exercise in taste and colour. The 20 rooms, designed by Sybille de Margerie, are arranged by era, running from the puce and purple of the medieval rooms to the wildly decadent orange, yellow and pink of the swinging '60s rooms. Luxury abounds with finest silks, velvets and taffetas. Some of the rooms have small terraces, and those with baths have a TV you can watch while soaking. An honesty bar in the lounge and jukebox encourage conviviality.

Montparnasse

Hôtel Aviatic

105 rue de Vaugirard, 6th (01.53.63.25.50, www.aviatic.fr). Mº Duroc, Montparnasse Bienvenüe or St-Placide. €€.
This historic hotel has masses of character, from the Empire-style lounge and garden atrium to the bistro-style breakfast room and marble floor in the lobby. New decoration throughout, in beautiful steely greys, warm reds, elegant, striped velvets and *toile de Jouy* fabrics, lends an impressive touch of glamour.

Solarhôtel

22 rue Boulard, 14th (01.43.21.08.20, www.solarhotel.fr). Mº Denfert Rochereau. €.
This hotel has managed to strike a great balance between price and sustainability. The simple ensuite bedrooms, which cost just €59 a night, are all equipped with low-energy lamps, and corridors are fitted with sensor-operated lights. Clients and staff are encouraged to recycle, with separate bins for plastics, paper, glass and batteries, and biodegradable waste from the organic breakfast gets turned into compost in a barrel in the garden.

ESSENTIALS

Getting Around

Airports

Roissy-Charles-de-Gaulle

01.70.36.39.50, www.adp.fr. 30km (19 miles) north-east of Paris.
For most international flights. The three main terminals are some way apart; check which one you need for your flight back. The terminals are linked by the CDGVAL free driverless train. The **RER B** line (36.58, www.transilien.com) is the quickest way to central Paris (40mins to Gare du Nord; 45mins to RER Châtelet-Les Halles; €9.10 single). RER trains run every 10-15mins, 4.58am-11.58pm daily.

Air France buses (08.92.35.08.20, www.cars-airfrance.com; €15 single, €24 return) leave every 20-30mins, 6am-11pm daily, and stop at Porte Maillot and place Charles-de-Gaulle (35-50min trip). Buses also run to Gare Montparnasse and Gare de Lyon (€16.50 single, €27 return) every 30mins (45-60min trip), 6am-10pm daily; a bus between Roissy and Orly (€19) runs every 30mins, 5.55am-10.30pm daily from Roissy.

RATP Roissybus (32.46, www.ratp.fr; €10) runs every 15-20mins, 5.45am-11pm daily, between the airport and the corner of rue Scribe/rue Auber (at least 45mins); buy your tickets on the bus.

Paris Airports Service is a 24-hour door-to-door minibus service between airports and hotels, seven days a week. Roissy prices go from €26 for one person to €99 for eight people, 6am-8pm (minimum €42, 4-6am, 8-10pm); you can reserve a place on 01.55.98.10.80, www.paris airportservice.com. A **taxi** into central Paris from Roissy-Charles-de-Gaulle airport should take 30-60mins and costs €40-€50, plus €1 per luggage item.

Orly

01.70.36.39.50, www.adp.fr. About 18km (11 miles) south of Paris.
Orly-Sud terminal is mainly international and Orly-Ouest is mainly domestic.

Air France buses (08.92.35.08.20, www.cars-airfrance.com; €11.50 single, €18.50 return) leave both terminals every 30mins, 6am-11.30pm daily, and stop at Invalides and Montparnasse (30-45mins).

The **RATP Orlybus** (32.46, www.ratp.fr) runs to Denfert-Rochereau every 15mins, 5.35am-11.30pm (30mins); buy tickets (€6.90) on the bus. High-speed **Orlyval** shuttle trains (www.orlyval.fr) run every 4-7mins (6am-11pm daily) to RER B station Antony (€10.75 to Châtelet-les-Halles); allow about 35mins for central Paris.

Orly prices for the Paris Airports Service (*see left*) are €25 for one and €5-€12 per passenger depending on the number. A **taxi** takes 20-40mins and costs €16-€26.

Paris Beauvais

08.92.68.20.66, www.aeroport beauvais.com. 70km (43 miles) north of Paris.
This is Paris's budget hub. **Buses** (€15) to/from Porte Maillot leave 15-30mins after each arrival and 3hrs 15mins before each departure. Tickets from Arrivals or buy tickets on the bus.

Arriving by car

Options for crossing the Channel with a car include: **Eurotunnel** (08.10.63.03.04, www.eurotunnel.com); **Brittany Ferries** (08.25.82.88.28, www.brittanyferries.com), **P&O Ferries** (08.25.12.01.56,

www.poferries.com) and
SeaFrance (0044.8454.580.666,
www.seafrance.com).

Arriving by coach

International coaches arrive at
**Gare Routière Internationale
Paris-Galliéni** at Porte de
Bagnolet, 20th. For tickets
(in English) call Eurolines on
08.92.89.90.91 or (UK) 01582 404
511, or visit www.eurolines.fr.

Arriving by rail

Eurostar from London St Pancras
International (0044.8432.186186,
www.eurostar.com) to Paris Gare
du Nord (08.92.35.35.35) takes
2hrs 15mins direct. You must
check in at least 30mins before
departure. Fares start at £69 for
a return ticket.

    Cycles can be taken as hand
luggage if they are dismantled
and carried in a bike bag. You
can also check them in at the
EuroDespatch depot at St Pancras
(Esprit Parcel Service, 0844 822
5822) or Sernam depot at Gare du
Nord (01.48.74.14.80). Check-in
must be done 24hrs ahead; a
Eurostar ticket must be shown.
The service costs £20/€25.

Maps

Free maps of the métro, bus and
RER systems are available at
airports and métro stations.

Public transport

RATP (32.46, www.ratp.fr) runs
the bus, métro and suburban tram
routes, as well as lines A and B of
the RER express railway, which
connects with the métro inside
Paris. State rail **SNCF** (36.35,
www.sncf.com) runs RER lines C,
D and E for the suburbs.

Fares & tickets

Paris and its suburbs are divided
into six travel zones, with 1 and 2
covering the city centre. RATP
tickets and passes are valid on the
métro, bus and RER. Tickets and
carnets can be bought at métro
stations, tourist offices and
tobacconists; single tickets can be
bought on buses. Retain your ticket
in case of spot checks; you'll also
need it to exit from RER stations.

    A ticket is €1.70, a carnet of ten
€12.50. A Mobilis day pass is €6.30
for zones 1 and 2 and €14 for zones
1-5 (not including airports).

Métro & RER

The Paris **métro** is the fastest way
of getting around. Trains run daily
5.30am-12.40am Mon-Thur, 5.30am-
1.30am Fri-Sun. Numbered lines
have their direction named after
the last stop. Follow the orange
Correspondance signs to change
lines. The five **RER** lines run
5.30am-1am daily across Paris
and into commuterland. Métro
tickets are valid for RER journeys
within zones 1 and 2.

Buses

Buses run 6.30am-8.30pm, with
some routes continuing until
12.30am, Mon-Sat; limited services
operate on selected lines Sun and
public holidays. You can use a
métro ticket, a ticket bought from
the driver (€1.90) or a travel pass.
Tickets should be punched in the
machine next to the driver; passes
should be shown to the driver.

Night buses

The 47 **Noctilien** lines run from
place du Châtelet to the suburbs
(hourly 12.30am-5.30am Mon-Thur;
half-hourly 1am-5.35am Fri, Sat);

look out for the Noctilien logo or the N in front of the route number. A ticket costs €1.70 (€1.90 from the driver); travel passes are valid.

River transport

Batobus

08.25.05.01.01, www.batobus.com. Nov, Dec, Feb-mid Mar 10.30am-4.30pm; mid Mar-May, Sept, Oct 10am-7pm; June-Aug 10am-9.30pm. One-day pass €14 (€7, €9 reductions).
River buses stop every 15-30mins at the Eiffel Tower, Musée d'Orsay, St-Germain-des-Prés (quai Malaquais), Notre-Dame, Jardin des Plantes, Hôtel de Ville, the Louvre, Champs-Elysées (Pont Alexandre III). Tickets are available from Batobus stops, RATP and tourist offices.

Rail travel

Versailles and Disneyland Paris are served by the RER. Most locations out of the city are served by the SNCF railway; the TGV high-speed train is steadily being extended to all the main regions. Tickets can be bought at any SNCF station, SNCF shops and travel agents. If you reserve online or by phone, you can pay and pick up your tickets from the station or have them sent to your home. SNCF automatic machines (*billeterie automatique*) only work with French credit/debit cards. Buy tickets in advance to secure the cheaper fare. Before you board any train, stamp your ticket in the orange *composteur* machines on the platforms, or you might have to pay a hefty fine.

SNCF

36.35, www.sncf.com.
Open 7am-10pm daily.
The line can also be reached (inside France) by dialling 3635 and saying '*billet*' at the prompt.

Taxis

Taxis are hard to find at rush hour or early in the morning. Ranks are indicated with a blue sign. A white light on a taxi's roof means it's free; an orange one means it's busy. You also pay for the time it takes your radioed taxi to arrive. Payment by credit card – mention this when you book – is usually €15 minimum.

Alpha

01.45.85.85.85, www.alphataxis.fr.
G7
36.07, www.taxis-g7.fr.
Taxis Bleus
08.91.70.10.10, www.taxis-bleus.com.

Driving

If you're planning to bring your car to France, you must bring its registration and insurance documents with you.

Bison Futé

08.00.10.02.00, www.bison-fute.equipement.gouv.fr.
Infotrafic
08.92.70.77.66 (€0.34/min), www.infotrafic.fr.

Breakdown services

The AA and RAC do not have reciprocal arrangements with an equivalent motoring organisation in France, so it's advisable to take out additional breakdown insurance cover before travelling there, for example with Europ Assistance (UK: 0844 338 5533, www.europ-assistance.co.uk). If you don't have insurance, you can use its service (08.10.00.50.50), but it will charge you the full cost. Other 24-hour breakdown services in Paris include Dan Dépann Auto (08.00.25.10.00, www.dandepann.fr).

Parking

There are still a few free on-street parking areas in Paris, but they're often full. If you park illegally, your car may be clamped or towed away. Don't park in zones marked for deliveries (*livraisons*) or taxis. *Horodateurs*, pay-and-display machines, take a special card (*carte de stationnement* at €15 or €40, from tobacconists). Parking is often free at weekends, after 7pm and in August. Underground car parks cost around €2.50 per hour. Some have lower rates after 6pm. See www.parkingsdeparis.com.

Vehicle removal

If your car is impounded, contact the nearest police station. There are eight car pounds (*préfourrières*) in Paris; to find out where your car might be, visit www.prefecture-police-paris.interieur.gouv.fr.

Car hire

To hire a car you must be 25 or over and have held a licence for at least a year. Some agencies accept drivers aged 21-24, but a day fee of €20-€25 is usual. Take your licence and passport. Bargain firms may have a high charge for damage: read the small print before signing.

Ada
www.ada.fr.
Avis
08.21.23.07.60, www.avis.fr.
Budget
08.25.00.35.64, www.budget.fr.
EasyCar
www.easycar.com.
Europcar
08.25.35.83.58, www.europcar.fr.
Hertz
01.55.31.93.21, www.hertz.fr.
Rent-a-Car
08.91.70.02.00, www.rentacar.fr.

Cycling

In 2007, the mayor launched a municipal bike hire scheme – Vélib (www.velib.paris.fr). There are now over 20,000 bicycles available 24 hours a day, at nearly 1,500 'stations' across the city. Just swipe your travel card to release the bikes from their stands. The *mairie* actively promotes cycling in the city and the Vélib scheme is complemented by the 400km (250 miles) of bike lanes snaking their way around Paris.

A free *Paris à Vélo* map can be picked up at any *mairie* or from bike shops. Cycle lanes (*pistes cyclables*) run mostly N–S and E–W. N–S routes include rue de Rennes, av d'Italie, bd Sébastopol and av Marceau. E–W routes take in the rue de Rivoli, bd St-Germain, bd St-Jacques and av Daumesnil. You could be fined (€22) if you don't use them, which is a bit rich considering the lanes are often blocked by delivery vans. Cyclists are also entitled to use certain bus lanes (especially the new ones set off by a strip of kerb stones).

Cycle hire

Note that bike insurance may not cover theft: check before you sign.

Freescoot
63 quai de la Tournelle, 5th (01.44.07.06.72, www.freescoot.fr). M° Maubert Mutualité or St-Michel. **Open** 9am-1pm, 2-9pm daily; closed Sun Oct-mid Apr.
Bicycles and scooters for hire.

Left Bank Scooters
(06.82.70.13.82, www.leftbank scooters.com).
This company hires out vintage-style Vespas (from €70 per day), with delivery and collection from your apartment or hotel. Tours available.

Resources A-Z

For information on travelling to France from within the European Union, including details of visa regulations and healthcare provision, see the EU's travel website: http://europa.eu/travel.

Accident & emergency

In a medical emergency, you should call the Sapeurs-Pompiers, who have trained paramedics.

Ambulance (SAMU)	**15**
Police	**17**
Fire (Sapeurs-Pompiers)	**18**
Emergency	
(from a mobile phone)	**112**

Credit card loss

Call one of these 24hr services.

American Express *01.44.77.72.00*
Diners Club *08.20.82.05.36*
MasterCard *08.00.90.13.87*
Visa *08.92.70.57.05*

Customs

Non-EU residents can claim a tax refund or *détaxe* (around 12%) on VAT if they spend over €175 in one purchase and if they live outside the EU for more than six months in the year. At the shop ask for a *bordereau de vente à l'exportation*.

Dental emergencies

Look in the *Pages Jaunes* (www. pagesjaunes.fr) under *Dentistes*. For emergencies contact:

Hôpital de la Pitié-Salpêtrière
47-83 bd de l'Hôpital, 13th (01.42. 16.00.00). Mº Gare d'Austerlitz.
Open 24hrs.

SOS Dentaire
87 bd Port-Royal, 13th (01.43.37.51.00). Mº Les Gobelins/RER Port-Royal.
Open by phone 9am-midnight.

Disabled

General information (in French) is available on the Secrétaire d'Etat aux Personnes Handicapées website: www.handicap.gouv.fr.

Electricity

France uses the standard 220-240V, 50-cycle AC system. Visitors with 240V British appliances need an adapter (*adaptateur*). US 110V appliances need an adapter and a transformer (*transformateur*).

Embassies & consulates

Australian Embassy
4 rue Jean-Rey, 15th (01.40.59.33.00, www.france.embassy.gov.au). Mº Bir-Hakeim. **Open** *Consular services 9am-noon, 2-4pm Mon-Fri. Visas 10am-noon Mon-Fri.*

British Embassy
35 rue du Fbg-St-Honoré, 8th (01.44. 51.31.00, www.ukinfrance.fco.gov.uk). Mº Concorde. Consular services 18bis rue d'Anjou, 8th. Mº Concorde. **Open** 9.30am-12.30pm, 2.30-4.30pm Mon-Fri. *Visas 16 rue d'Anjou, 8th (01.44.51. 31.01).* **Open** 9.30am-1pm, 2.30-6pm Mon-Fri.
British citizens wanting consular services (such as new passports) should ignore the queue at 16 rue d'Anjou and walk in at no.18bis.

Canadian Embassy
35 av Montaigne, 8th (01.44.43. 29.00, www.amb-canada.fr). Mº Franklin D Roosevelt. Consular

services (01.44.43.29.02). **Open** 9am-noon, 2-5pm Mon-Fri. *Visas 37 av Montaigne, 8th (01.44.43.29.16).* **Open** 8.30-10.30am Mon-Fri.

Irish Embassy
12 av Foch, 16th. Consulate 4 rue Rude, 16th (01.44.17.67.00, www.embassyofireland.fr). M° Charles de Gaulle Etoile. **Open** *Consular/visas* 9.30am-noon Mon-Fri. *By phone* 9.30am-1pm, 2.30-5.30pm Mon-Fri.

New Zealand Embassy
7ter rue Léonard-de-Vinci, 16th (01.45.01.43.43, www.nzembassy.com/france). M° Victor Hugo. **Open** 9am-1pm, 2-5.30pm Mon-Thur; 9am-1pm, 2-4pm Fri. *July, Aug* 9am-1pm, 2-4.30pm Mon-Thur; 9am-2pm Fri. *Visas* 9am-12.30pm Mon-Fri. Visas for travel to New Zealand can be applied for on the website www.immigration.govt.nz.

South African Embassy
59 quai d'Orsay, 7th (01.53.59.23.23, www.afriquesud.net). M° Invalides. **Open** 8.30am-5.15pm Mon-Fri. *Consulate/visas* 9am-noon Mon-Fri.

US Embassy
2 av Gabriel, 8th (01.43.12.22.22, http://france.usembassy.gov). M° Concorde. Consulate/visas 4 av Gabriel, 8th (08.10.26.46.26). M° Concorde. **Open** *Consular services* 9am-12.30pm, 1-3pm Mon-Fri. *Visas* 08.92.23.84.72.

Internet

Milk
31 bd de Sébastopol, 1st (01.40.13.06.51, www.milklub.com). M° Châtelet or Rambuteau/RER Châtelet Les Halles. **Open** 24hrs daily.

Opening hours

Standard opening hours for shops are generally 9am/10am-7pm/8pm Mon-Sat. Some close on Mondays, some for lunch (usually 12.30-2pm) and some in August.

Pharmacies

All *pharmacies* sport a green neon cross. If closed, a pharmacy will have a sign indicating the nearest one open. Staff can provide basic medical services like disinfecting and bandaging wounds (for a small fee) and will indicate the nearest doctor on duty. The following are all open late:

Matignon
1 av Matignon, 8th (01.43.59.86.55). M° Franklin D Roosevelt. **Open** 24hrs daily.

Pharmacie des Champs-Elysées
84 av des Champs-Elysées, 8th (01.45.62.02.41). M° George V. **Open** 24hrs daily.

Pharmacie Européenne de la Place de Clichy
6 pl de Clichy, 9th (01.48.74.65.18). M° Place de Clichy. **Open** 24hrs daily.

Pharmacie des Halles
10 bd de Sébastopol, 4th (01.42.72.03.23). M° Châtelet. **Open** 9am-midnight Mon-Sat; 9am-10pm Sun.

Police

The French equivalent of 999/911 is **17** (**112** from a mobile), but don't expect a speedy response. If you're assaulted or robbed, report the incident as soon as possible. Make a statement (*procès verbal*) at the *point d'accueil* closest to the crime. To find it, contact the Préfecture Centrale (08.91.01.22.22) or go to www.prefecture-police-paris.interieur.gouv.fr. You'll need to obtain a statement for insurance purposes.

Post

Post offices (*bureaux de poste*) are open 8am-7pm Mon-Fri; 8am-noon Sat, apart from the 24hr one listed below. All are listed in the phone book: under *Administration*

ESSENTIALS

des PTT in the *Pages Jaunes*; under *Poste* in the *Pages Blanches*. Most post offices have machines that weigh your letter, print out a stamp and give change, saving you from queuing. You can also buy stamps at a tobacconist.

Main Post Office
52 rue du Louvre, 1st (36.31). Mº Les Halles or Louvre Rivoli. **Open** 24hrs daily.

Smoking

Smoking is prohibited in all enclosed public spaces. Hotels can still offer smoking rooms.

Telephones

All French phone numbers have ten digits. Paris and Ile-de-France numbers begin with 01; the rest of France is divided into four zones, 02 to 05. Mobile phone numbers start with 06. Numbers beginning with 08 can only be reached from inside France. The France country code is 33; leave off the first 0 at the start of the ten-digit number. Most public phones use *télécartes* (phonecards). These are sold at post offices and tobacconists, and they cost €7.50 for 50 units or €15 for 120 units.

Time

France is one hour ahead of GMT and uses the 24hr system (for example, 18h means 6pm).

Tipping

A service charge of ten to 15% is legally included in your bill at all restaurants, cafés and bars. However, it's polite to round up the final amount for drinks, or to leave a cash tip of €1-€2 or more for a meal, depending on service.

Toilets

The city's automatic street toilets are not as terrifying as they first appear. Each loo is washed down and disinfected after use. If a space age-style experience doesn't appeal, you can nip into the toilets of a café; although theoretically reserved for customers, a polite request should win sympathy with the waiter.

Tourist information

Office de Tourisme et des Congrès de Paris
25 rue des Pyramides (08.92.68.30.00, www.parisinfo.com). Mº Pyramides. **Open** *Summer* 9am-7pm daily. *Winter* 10am-7pm daily. Info on Paris and the suburbs; tickets. **Other locations** *Anvers, 72 bd Rochechouart, 9th. Gare de Lyon, 20 bd Diderot, 12th. Gare du Nord, 18 rue de Dunkerque, 10th. Gare de l'Est, Place du 11 Novembre 1918, 10th. Montmartre, 21 pl du Tertre, 18th. Porte de Versailles, 1 place de la Porte de Versailles, 15th.*

Visas

European Union nationals do not need a visa to enter France, nor do US, Canadian, Australian, New Zealand or South African citizens for stays of up to three months. Nationals of other countries should enquire at the nearest French Consulate before leaving home. If you are travelling to France from one of the countries included in the Schengen agreement (most of the EU, but not Britain or Ireland), the visa from that country should be sufficient.

What's on

There are two listings magazines: *L'Officiel des Spectacles* (€0.35) and *Pariscope* (€0.40).

Vocabulary

General expressions

good morning/hello *bonjour*; good evening *bonsoir*; goodbye *au revoir*; hi *salut*; OK *d'accord*; yes *oui*; no *non*; how are you? *comment allez-vous?*; how's it going? *comment ça va?/ça va?*; sir/Mr *monsieur* (M); madam/Mrs *madame* (Mme); miss *mademoiselle* (Mlle); please *s'il vous plaît*; thank you *merci*; thank you very much *merci beaucoup*; sorry *pardon*; excuse me *excusez-moi*; do you speak English? *parlez-vous anglais?*; I don't speak French *je ne parle pas français*; I don't understand *je ne comprends pas*; speak more slowly, please *parlez plus lentement, s'il vous plaît*; good *bon/bonne*; bad *mauvais/mauvaise*; small *petit/petite*; big *grand/grande*; beautiful *beau/belle*; well *bien*; badly *mal*; a bit *un peu*; a lot *beaucoup*; very *très*; with *avec*; without *sans*; and *et*; or *ou*; because *parce que*; who? *qui?*; when? *quand?*; what? *quoi?*; which? *quel?*; where? *où?*; why? *pourquoi?*; how? *comment?*; at what time? *à quelle heure?*; forbidden *interdit/défendu*; out of order *hors service* (HS)/*en panne*; daily *tous les jours* (tlj)

Getting around

where is the (nearest) métro? *où est le métro (le plus proche)?*; when is the next train for... ? *c'est quand le prochain train pour..?*; ticket *un billet*; station *la gare*; platform *le quai*; entrance *entrée*; exit *sortie*; left *gauche*; right *droite*; straight on *tout droit*; far *loin*; near *pas loin/près d'ici*; street map *le plan*; bank *la banque*; is there a bank near here? *est-ce qu'il y a une banque près d'ici?*

Accommodation

do you have a room (for this evening/for two people)? *avez-vous une chambre (pour ce soir/pour deux personnes)?*; full *complet*; room *une chambre*; bed *un lit*; double bed *un grand lit*; (a room with) twin beds *(une chambre à) deux lits*; with bath(room)/shower *avec (salle de) bain/douche*; breakfast *le petit déjeuner*; included *compris*

At the restaurant

I'd like to book a table (for three/at 8pm) *je voudrais réserver une table (pour trois personnes/à vingt heures)*; lunch *le déjeuner*; dinner *le dîner*; coffee (espresso) *un café*; white coffee *un café au lait/café crème*; tea *du thé*; wine *du vin*; beer *la bière*; mineral water *eau minérale*; fizzy *gazeuse*; still *plate*; tap water *eau du robinet/une carafe d'eau*; the bill, please *l'addition, s'il vous plaît*

Numbers

0 *zéro*; 1 *un, une*; 2 *deux*; 3 *trois*; 4 *quatre*; 5 *cinq*; 6 *six*; 7 *sept*; 8 *huit*; 9 *neuf*; 10 *dix*; 11 *onze*; 12 *douze*; 13 *treize*; 14 *quatorze*; 15 *quinze*; 16 *seize*; 17 *dix-sept*; 18 *dix-huit*; 19 *dix-neuf*; 20 *vingt*; 21 *vingt-et-un*; 22 *vingt-deux*; 30 *trente*; 40 *quarante*; 50 *cinquante*; 60 *soixante*; 70 *soixante-dix*; 80 *quatre-vingts*; 90 *quatre-vingt-dix*; 100 *cent*; 1000 *mille*; 1,000,000 *un million*

Index

Sights & Areas

ESSENTIALS

ESSENTIALS

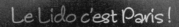